I LOVE, THEREFORE I AM

The Theological Legacy of Archimandrite Sophrony

Archimandrite Sophrony

I LOVE,

therefore

I AM

The Theological Legacy of
Archimandrite Sophrony

Nicholas V. Sakharov

ST VLADIMIR'S SEMINARY PRESS
CRESTWOOD, NEW YORK 10707
2002

Library of Congress Cataloging-in-Publication Data

Sakharov, Nicholas V.
    I love, therefore I am : the theological legacy of Archimandrite Sophrony /
Nicholas V. Sakharov.
      p.   cm.
    Rev. ed. of: Amo ergo sum.
    Includes bibliographical references (p.) and index.
    ISBN 0-88141-236-8 (alk. paper)
     1. Sofroniæ, Archimandrite, 1896-   2. Orthodox Eastern Church—Russia
(Federation)—Doctrines.   I. Sakharov, Nicholas V. Amo ergo sum.   II. Title.

BX597.S62 S24 2002
230'.19'092—dc21

2002068263

COPYRIGHT © 2002
ST VLADIMIR'S SEMINARY PRESS
575 Scarsdale Rd, Crestwood, NY 10707
1-800-204-2665

ISBN 0-88141-236-8

PRINTED IN THE UNITED STATES OF AMERICA

Acknowledgments

First and foremost, I should like to express my deep gratitude to the Right Reverend Dr Kallistos Ware, Bishop of Diokleia, for his wholehearted involvement and encouraging support throughout my studies at Oxford for the BA degree and then as a D.Phil. student.

A special debt of gratitude is owed to the Monastic Community of St John the Baptist, whose indispensable help and support I have enjoyed at every stage of my work.

I am pleased to extend my gratitude and acknowledge the assistance of various people—the Right Reverend Dr Hilarion Alfeyev, Bishop of Kerch; Dr R. Swinburne, Oriel College, Oxford; Professor Andrew Louth, University of Durham; Dr R. Papadopoulos, University of Essex; Dr S. Thomas, University of Kent; Reverend Canon D. Allchin; and Professor G. Mantzaridis, University of Thessaloniki, Greece—whose advice and recommendations contributed to the present study.

Contents

Foreword

Archimandrite Sophrony Sakharov (1896-1993) is an outstanding Christian ascetic, monk and mystic of the twentieth century. His teaching has rarely as yet been approached in such a way as to unveil his true dimension as a theologian within the history of Christianity. Yet already his books, such as *St Silouan the Athonite*, have become an indispensable part of the church tradition. Inasmuch as he is our contemporary, his theological kerygma has become an event to many people in the modern world. Through his own ascetic experience he lived the eternal truths of Christian faith in their profundity. His message is a mighty testimony that Christianity is not just an academic discipline but very reality, life itself. This reality imprints a mark of indisputable authenticity upon each of Fr Sophrony's writings. Strange to abstract scholasticism, his words breathe the inspiration of the living tradition, where Christ is the divine absolute, "the same yesterday, today and forever" (Heb 13:8).

The universal nature of his word is determined by the all-embracing character of his living experience. Because Fr Sophrony traversed the major religious and intellectual movements of our time, his spiritual makeup is enriched by various currents of thought. Notwithstanding this diversity, never does his theology transcend the boundaries set out by the Orthodox tradition. The patristic heritage has for him indubitable authority. He absorbed the legacy of the fathers in its living depth. This came not by way of academic research, but through his ascetic strivings on Mount Athos. His wide spiritual and intellectual background elevates the Orthodox tradition to an authentic level where it opens up to universal dimensions. In order to deliver Orthodoxy to the mind of modern man, Fr Sophrony enriches his theological language with ideas that go beyond the traditional means of expression of "classical" theology. He absorbs the riches of world philosophy, literature, poetry, art. Through his own mystical experience he integrates these different layers of thought into one single vision. This latter makes up what we may call the "teaching of Archimandrite Sophrony."

The present work is a first attempt to present to the western academic world a critical study of Fr Sophrony as a theologian. It aims to bring his ideas into a dialogue with a wider range of academic issues. This study aspires to situate his "whereabouts" within the vast scope of contemporary and traditional theology. As well as indicating the most significant areas of Fr Sophrony's background—Russian religious thought, the eastern patristic tradition, the contemporary Athonite tradition and his own ascetic experience—our aim is to present the overall framework of his theology. Through an analysis of various themes it will emerge that Fr Sophrony's distinctive teaching revolves around the concept of hypostasis, both in God and in man.

CHAPTER ONE

Fr Sophrony's Theological Formation

Reflecting on Fr Sophrony as a theological event, one might be astonished at the universality of his appeal. His books have already been translated into more than twenty languages, covering all the continents of the world. His writings seem to inspire a response from the widest range of readership: from theologically illiterate readers to an audience with the highest level of academic interests, from a simple Russian babushka to a renowned scholar of a western university. To explain the mystery of this universal appeal, one may recall the words of the apostle Paul, who confessed to the Corinthians: "I have become all things to all men" (1 Cor 9:22). To preach Christ, Paul addressed his audience in their own cultural language, born from within their respective backgrounds. In this way his good tidings were proclaimed throughout the whole Roman empire.

In a similar way, the mere facts of Fr Sophrony's biography allude to the all-embracing universality of his figure. His lifespan covers almost the entire twentieth century. Born in Russia, he later lived in the west. Coming from a bourgeois family, he started his career as an artist. Brought up as a Christian, he also experienced oriental mysticism. Plunged into the cultural crucible of the Russian intelligentsia and having experienced the glamor of a successful artist in Paris, he abandoned the world and lived as a simple monk in a monastery, then as a hermit in utter poverty. As a priest he continued to serve thousands of people, opening up thereby to their individual worlds.

Fr Sophrony himself was reluctant to convey bare facts of his outward history. In his own words, "usually people prefer to focus on outward events, while the history of each and all depends on their inner predisposition." It is to this inner development that we confine our interest, highlighting only the key factors that influenced his mystical-spiritual and intellectual pilgrimage. Its outline will provide a necessary insight into the formation of the multifaceted background of his theological makeup.

Russia (1896–1922)

Childhood and Student Years

Sergei Symeonovich Sakharov (as Fr Sophrony was called in the world) was born in Moscow on September 22, 1896, into a bourgeois family, who were practicing Orthodox Christians. The experience of being reared in the Orthodox Christian tradition, with its stress on daily prayer, left a lifelong impression on him. Sergei became accustomed to this practice so much so that even as a child he "could pray easily for three quarters of an hour."[1] It undoubtedly deepened his "mystical sensitivity": it is no coincidence that Fr Sophrony ascribes his first experience of uncreated light to his childhood days.

From a young age Fr Sophrony became acquainted the rich heritage of the Russian culture of the eighteenth and nineteenth centuries, whose main focus was Christianity. He read with great enthusiasm the works of Gogol, Turgenev, Tolstoy, Dostoyevsky, and Pushkin. He deeply absorbed the "kenotic" perception of Christianity intrinsic to Russian thought.[2]

His characteristic intensity continued to be prominent throughout his student years. His spiritual makeup during this time was affected by two factors: his painting and oriental mysticism.

As a child, Fr Sophrony revealed an outstanding artistic talent, and for that reason he went to study from 1915 to 1917 at the Academy of Arts, and in 1920–1921 at the Moscow School of Painting, Sculpture, and Architecture. The whole atmosphere of Russian art then was marked by a profound search for new forms of artistic expression. J.-L. Daval envisages the Russian artistic world at the beginning of the twentieth century in the following terms:

> All systems of thought seemed in decay; the artist found no other truth than the authenticity of his own intellectual or spiritual experience, faithfulness to his own intuition. Artists, discerning new realities deep down within themselves, had to destroy the habitual working of the mind in order to make these realities apparent. At the same time as they aspired to a new way of presenting things they had to lay the foundations of a new language. . . . Consequently the artist appeared as a prophet—he no longer merely illustrated: he *revealed*.[3]

---

[1] *Letters to Russia*, ed. Nicholas Sakharov (Moscow, 1997) 18.
[2] See N. Gorodetzky, *The Humiliated Christ in Modern Russian Thought* (London, 1938).
[3] J.-L. Daval, *Journal de l'art moderne 1884-1914. Les années décisives* (Geneva, 1979) 12; see M.

In his painting, Fr Sophrony attempted to discover eternal beauty, the *mystery* of each visible object. For him, art was a powerful means of breaking through present reality, through time, into new horizons of being. These artistic experiences bore a quasi-mystical character. He recalls several experiences of "falling out" of time,[4] and of contemplation of the "light of artistic inspiration." This would later allow him to draw a clear distinction between the natural light of the human intellect and the uncreated light of God.

Fr Sophrony and Contemporary Russia

Fr Sophrony's philosophical and spiritual pilgrimage, as he recalls, was marked by an intensive inner search for the basis of reality. Fr Sophrony's total dedication to creative work led to an artistic isolation that limited the scope of his outward involvement in the prevailing intellectual tendencies in contemporary Russia. Yet the whole intellectual climate of pre- and postrevolutionary Russia, with its upheavals and instability, undoubtedly created a fertile matrix for new directions of thinking.

From the mid-nineteenth century, Russia experienced an unprecedented philosophical awakening. Russian religious philosophy of that period takes up the philosophical calling of the west, where philosophy operated with the subject-versus-object categories, as well as with analytic detachment of reason in the process of cognition, and had reached a dead end. In an intensive search for their own philosophical identity, Russians, notably Ivan Kirievsky, developed a philosophy of *the knowing heart,* as a counterpart to the philosophy of the self-aware thinking mind in Hegel. True knowledge is achieved not through "objective" detachment (as in the west) but through "subjective" *participation, communion.* This is finally articulated by Bulgakov and Florensky, who do away with "conceptual algebra" in cognition. It is on this model of knowledge that Fr Sophrony would later postulate his ideas of cognition of God.

Naturally, with the rejection of a logic of opposition and the cultivation of a logic of personal participation, the theme of *person* comes to the forefront of Russian thought. This theme also challenged Fr Sophrony's thought. The idea of communion allows Russians to work out the distinction between the person, as "communal being," from the individual, as a self-enclosed unit. As such,

---

Egger, "Archimandrite Sophrony, Moine pour le Monde," *Buisson Ardent. Cahiers Saint-Silouane l'Athonite* 1 (1996) 34.
[4]*Letters to Russia,* 21.

the person is a mysterious, indefinable, godlike center, which realizes itself in communion and above all in love: *amo ergo sum*—"I love, therefore I am." As a result, Russian philosophy comes up with a distinctive "communal," "interpersonal" concept like *sobornost* (conciliarity). From the dialectics of society and person, Russian philosophy grew to the awareness that man is infinite in his potential and value. Man's dignity is such that he reaches out to the divine: man is *microtheos* (micro-god).

From this concern for communal and unifying aspects of humanity in Russian thought emerges an exigency to work out a philosophical system that would see all that is as one integral whole. Thus the theme of *vse-edinstvo* (pan-unity) preoccupies such philosophers as Vladimir Soloviev. Unity, as a principle, becomes a controlling feature of his philosophical system. His concern was to disclose this principle of unity behind existing reality—the principle that would lead creation to God and thereby to its integrity and realization. Soloviev and his followers bring forward the teaching on divine Wisdom—*Sophia*. The divine Wisdom is seen as the basis of communion between the human and divine worlds. It opens up the possibilities for the transfiguration of the material world. Divine Wisdom is that principle in the universe that moves toward God, toward integration, toward beauty, toward harmony.

All these ideas were widely discussed in Fr Sophrony's times. The emergence of religious-philosophical societies between 1901 and 1903 is a notable reflection of this intensive intellectual search. The Russian intelligentsia, in its move away from the radicalism, positivism, and "nihilism" of the preceding epoch and toward idealism, sought rapprochement with Christianity and with the church heritage in general. However, in their return to Christianity, Russian thinkers evaluated the Orthodox tradition in different ways. For example, as a repercussion of Tolstoy's evangelical radicalism, with its nihilistic tendencies, people of the so-called "new religious consciousness"—like Dmitry Merezhkovsky (1865-1941), Nicholas Berdyaev (1874-1948), and Vasily Rozanov (1856-1919)—attempted to rejuvenate Christianity by stretching its bounds beyond the church and tradition.[5] On the other hand, Sergius Bulgakov (1871-1944) and Symeon Frank (1877-1950) found church tradition an adequate expression of the essence of Christianity.[6]

Though a Muscovite, Fr Sophrony remained alien to the intellectual tendencies of the "Muscovite ethos," marked by the romantic emphasis of the

[5]P. Bori and P. Bettiolo, *Movimenti religiosi in Russa prima della rivoluzione* (Brescia, 1978) 83ff.
[6]Ibid., 179ff.

Slavophiles on "Russianness" in their philosophical principles. If we would "situate" Fr Sophrony on the map of the contemporary intellectual scene, he would have belonged at this time to the first group of thinkers, those who looked beyond "ecclesiastical tradition" and advocated a wide-ranging intellectual freedom. This broad and *free* scope for religious thought provided a necessary background for Fr Sophrony's bold investigation of non-Christian religious cultures.

Oriental Mysticism

It was at this time that Fr Sophrony became acutely aware of the contrast between the finitude of our present reality and the infinity of divine eternal reality. As a result, his mystical life was marked by profound experiences of *mindfulness of death.* This contrast (finitude–infinity) aroused in him an urgent longing to penetrate to the heart of divine eternity—to achieve what he terms "breakthrough into eternity." He wondered how he, as a human being, related to eternity, to the divine absolute. In all this, he was convinced that the human spirit cannot accept the idea of death. His search for eternity led him to Indian non-Christian mysticism. Christianity, with its stress on personal love toward a personal absolute, seemed to him less profound than some strands of eastern mysticism, which spoke of a suprapersonal absolute. Christianity appeared to him as a merely psychological, moral doctrine that did not account for reality *ontologically.* Within the Christian framework of beliefs, built on faith in the personal-hypostatic Godhead, the concept of the divine absolute seemed inconceivable, since the concept of person, as he then understood it, implied *particularity* and, hence, *ontological limitation.* The absolute, he thought, must be beyond everything, beyond every concept or measure: it therefore transcends Christian categories.

Berdyaev seems to have faced the same dilemma, which demonstrates that such a problematic was familiar in the contemporary Russian thought-world. Berdyaev sees contradictions between the concept of the Christian God in the Bible and that of the divine absolute; he concludes that the Christian God is neither omnipotent nor omniscient. The divine *nothingness*—as he understood the absolute, because it is beyond concrete expression—cannot be the creator of the world.[7]

[7]See N. Berdyaev, *Destiny of Man*, tr. N. Duddington (London, 1937) 23–44.

Under the exigency of the Christian "scandal of particularity," which he envisaged as incompatible with the idea of the absolute, Berdyaev resorted to the concept of *real symbolism* in his philosophical system. He thus *adjusted* the Christian framework in the face of philosophical constraints. Fr Sophrony's solution was to abandon a Christian framework altogether as incompatible with the idea of the absolute. The catastrophic events of the First World War and the subsequent revolution in Russia only strengthened his striving toward the otherworldly. His God, the all-transcendent absolute, could be attained only through divesting the self of all visual and mental images.

Thus his art, his thinking, and his inner state combined to drive him insatiably toward the abstract, that is, the pan-transcendent.

Paris (1922-1925)

In the turmoil of postrevolutionary Russia, Lenin's government in 1922-1923 gave an opportunity for non-Marxist intellectuals, among whom were Berdyaev, Bulgakov, and Nicholas and Vladimir Lossky, to leave Russia. Fr Sophrony had left shortly before, in 1921, so as to continue his artistic career abroad. He spent a few months in Italy and then in Berlin. In 1922 he arrived in Paris. There his artistic career advanced so rapidly as to attract the attention of the French media. He exhibited at the Salon d'Automne and the even more elite Salon des Tuileries. At the same time his spiritual and ideological pilgrimage continued.

Return to Christianity

His predominant questions, then, were those of ontology and gnoseology. On the one hand, he was frustrated at the inability of art to express the pure other. On the other, he tried to comprehend how man can arrive at the ultimate knowledge of reality. Purely intellectual reasoning could not provide a sufficient answer to his question. As he saw it, purely rational knowledge is inherent to science. It was unable to serve the ultimate aim of Fr Sophrony's acquisition of knowledge: "surmounting the finitude of death." Science, as an intellectual discipline, is relevant only in the limited sphere of reality, where one event is determined by another. But his artistic experience suggested that there are phenomena that belong to "undetermined reality," where science is not applicable.

This quest culminated in his discovery that Christ's precept to love God with all one's heart, mind, and strength is not a moralistic *psychology* but a profound *ontology*. Love emerged as an authentic source of cognition. If God is to be known by love, then the divine absolute is a *personal* being.[8] Fr Sophrony understood that this personeity is implied in the formula of Exodus 3:14: "I AM THAT I AM." It was at this moment that Fr Sophrony's experience of uncreated light returned in a more powerful form than during his childhood. It began on Holy Saturday in 1924 and remained until the third day of Easter Week; the strength of this experience was never matched in his later visions of light.[9] These experiences and discoveries resulted in his return to Christianity, a volte-face so dramatic that he began to distance himself even from his art.

Orthodoxy in Paris

The life of the Russian community in Paris in those years was marked by dynamism within various spheres of activity. As Paul Anderson recalls, it was "a time of the most intensive creativity." The massive return of the intelligentsia to the Orthodox Church within the New Russia in the years 1917-1925 had its parallel among the Russian emigrants. Anderson observes: "The basic common feature of Russian refugee society was the Church."[10] The year 1922 was marked by the establishment of the Russian Christian Youth Movement, which brought to the forefront the question of theological education. As a result, in 1924 the Orthodox Theological Institute was founded in Paris. Fr Sophrony was among its first students. There he was surrounded by the elite of Russian theologians and philosophers. As Nicolas Zernov notes: "The Institute became the main intellectual centre of the Russian Church and an equally important point of contact between Eastern Orthodoxy and Western Christians."[11] In 1924 the teaching personnel consisted of Bishop Veniamin (Fedchenkov), Anton Kartashev, Kassian Bezobrazov, and Evgraph Kovalevsky, who in 1925 were joined by Bulgakov, Vasily Zenkovsky, Symeon Frank, Sergei Troitsky, Vladimir Ilyin and Georges Florovsky.

In this atmosphere his exposure to Russian religious ideas intensified. It came about largely though his personal contact with Bulgakov and Berdyaev.

---

[8] *Letters to Russia*, 22-23.

[9] Letters to David Balfour, in the Archive of the Gennadeios Library (Athens), unpublished, C16 (April 18, 1935) 4; ibid., 10 (December 3, 1932) 14.

[10] See P. Anderson, *No East or West* (Paris, 1985) 40, 44ff.

[11] N. Zernov, *Russian Religious Renaissance of the Twentieth Century* (London, 1963) 231.

Fr Sergius Bulgakov

The most profound influence on Fr Sophrony in the field of dogmatic theology came from Fr Sergius Bulgakov. At the institute Bulgakov taught dogmatics. Apart from being Fr Sophrony's teacher, Bulgakov was at the same time his spiritual father. It is no coincidence that his range of theological issues, his vocabulary, and his style of theologizing were determinative for Fr Sophrony's theological growth. Bulgakov had a rich background in patristic literature as well as in philosophy (notably Kant, Fichte, Feuerbach, Hegel, and Schelling, as well as Soloviev and Florensky). Bulgakov's theology evolved as a result of his philosophical transition from Marxism to idealism.[12] This synthesis of the fathers and modern philosophy constitutes the originality of his approach, which sometimes goes beyond the scope of patristic Orthodoxy, as, for example, in his sophiology. Soloviev's theme of *Bogochelovechestvo* (Godmanhood) made him more attentive to the anthropological implications of Chalcedonian christology and the trinitarian theology of the Cappadocians.[13]

Among Bulgakov's theological ideas that had the most direct impact on Fr Sophrony are trinitarian theology, kenoticism, and anthropology. Thus, Bulgakov precedes Fr Sophrony in elaborating on the relational character of divine *hypostases* in the Trinity and the antinomy of the absolute identity and absolute distinction of the divine *personae*. This absolute unity is ensured by the mode of the divine being, which is love: this unity therefore is not static but dynamic. This love is sacrificial, self-denying love.[14] Bulgakov works out the relational dynamic nature of hypostatic being and arrives at the self-denying character of love within the Trinity. Due to Schellingian influence (A. Nichols' view) and that of Russian christology (Gorodetzky's view),[15] Bulgakov works out the kenotic dimension in the very constitution of the Holy Trinity, as well as in the act of creation.[16] Also important for Fr Sophrony was Bulgakov's view of Christ's *kenosis* (self-emptying) on the level of the intratrinitarian being. Kenosis, furthermore, does not exhaust itself with the resurrection but also concerns the post-Easter glorified Christ, and this is largely related to the sacrament of the eucharist.[17] This kenotic element in the

---

[12]See Bori, 226–32.
[13]S. Bulgakov, *The Lamb of God* (Paris, 1937) 207.
[14]S. Bulgakov, *The Comforter* (Paris, 1936) 66–68, 79; *The Lamb of God*, 118.
[15]A. Nichols, *Light from the East* (London, 1995) 59; cf Gorodetzky, 156ff.
[16]*The Lamb of God*, 121–22; *The Comforter*, 253.
[17]*The Lamb of God*, 252, 348ff, 434ff.

eucharist marks Fr Sophrony's liturgical theology as well. It is noteworthy that Bulgakov works out the idea of the kenosis of the Spirit in his *operation*.[18] This allowed Fr Sophrony later to apply the idea of the *variable measure of operation and perceptibility* of the Holy Spirit to his ascetic theory of godforsakenness. Bulgakov's anthropology and that of Fr Sophrony are marked by similar maximalist categories. Bulgakov anticipates Fr Sophrony in his understanding of the biblical expression *dextera Patris*, related to Christ's ascension to "the right hand of God" (Mk 16:19), as the elevation-deification of humanity to the point of *tozhestvo* (equality-identity) with the divinity.[19] Bulgakov points to the relation between the divine and human modes of being and brings them to close relation in a quasi-platonic manner. Man as image is in fact *povtorenie* (repetition) of God; man is a micro-absolute, an express image of the divine absoluteness. Humankind is a divine "cryptogram," a mystery in its hypostasity. As such, man and his *hypostasis* are indefinable.[20] This allows Bulgakov to assert *identity* between man and God: *humana natura capax divini*.[21]

Later Fr Sophrony was cautious in making much overt use of Bulgakov. It seems that the extent of Bulgakov's influence on Fr Sophrony was obscured and limited by the controversy over Bulgakov's theology.

Nicholas Berdyaev

Fr Sophrony's personal contact with Berdyaev undoubtedly left traces on his theology. Berdyaev's "personalism" crowns the development of the maximalist trend within the Russian philosophy of *lichnost* (persona).[22] Thus, Berdyaev uses a theologically innovative term: man is *microtheos*, which was taken up by Fr Sophrony as a basis for his own anthropology. However, Berdyaev's influence should not be overestimated. Many of his concepts of persona, and of the freedom and creativity of man, went against the Orthodox ascetic tradition: "Man, who embarks on the path of Christian asceticism, is lost for creative work." This difference of wavelength became explicit even in Paris; when Fr Sophrony announced to Berdyaev his monastic vocation, he met with disapproval.

[18] *The Comforter*, 289; cf *The Lamb of God*, 345.

[19] *The Lamb of God*, 421ff.

[20] S. Bulgakov, *Unfading Light* (Moscow, 1917) 278-83; *The Lamb of God*, 114-17, 138, 158-61, 209, 258.

[21] *The Lamb of God*, 160, 215, 258, 279.

[22] See O. Clément, *Berdiaev. Un philosophe russe en France* (Paris, 1991) 39-62.

At this stage, though, however fruitful the contact with Bulgakov and Berdyaev may have been, formal theology did not fulfil Fr Sophrony's hope of being taught how to pray, how to have the right attitude toward God, how to overcome one's passions and attain *eternity*. So in 1925 he made his way to Mount Athos.

Mount Athos (1925-1947)

On Mount Athos Fr Sophrony joined the Russian Orthodox Monastery of St Panteleimon. During this period the main source of his theological inspiration was his own mystical experience. He states that he underwent profound repentance over his apostasy and the inadequacy of his spiritual condition, of his "incapability of living according to the precepts of the gospel."

Silouan the Athonite

The second determinative factor of Fr Sophrony's theological formation was his contact with an Athonite elder, Silouan, from 1930 until 1938. Elder Silouan's ascetic formula, "Keep your mind in hell, and despair not,"[23] was matched by Fr Sophrony's own spiritual motto: "Stay on the brink of despair, but when you feel you are falling over, step back." This parallel experience was the basis of their spiritual contact. Elder Silouan's concern for an existential, living dimension in the knowledge of God is reflected in Fr Sophrony's principle of theology: "It is one thing to believe in God and another thing to know God" in the Holy Spirit. B. Gooskens analyzes pertinently the implications of Silouan's stress on the pneumatological dimension in his ascetic theology.[24]

Though elder Silouan had no distinctive theological system,[25] his simply expressed theological and ascetic concepts formed an integral basis for Fr Sophrony's theological development. Among them the most significant are: *prayer for the whole world*, *Christ-like humility*, and *love toward one's enemies*.

[23] *St Silouan the Athonite*, tr. Rosemary Edmonds (New York, 1998) 42, 208ff. For the analysis of the formula, see J.-C. Larchet, "La formule 'Tiens ton esprit en enfer et ne désespère pas' à la lumière de la tradition patristique," *Buisson Ardent* 1 (1996) 51-68.

[24] B. Gooskens, *L'expérience de l'Esprit Saint chez le Staretz Silouane* (Paris, 1971).

[25] For the most significant studies of Silouan's spirituality, see ibid.; C. Cervera, "Silvano del Monte Athos, il monaco che amavo teneramente la Madre di Dio," *Mater Ecclesiae* 16 (1980) 45-54; L. Cremaschi, "La vergogna di stare ogli inferi secondo Silvano del Monte Athos," *Parola Spirito e Vita* 20 (1989) 285-303.

Elder Silouan pays particular attention to the type of prayer "for the whole creation": "Let *the whole world* come to know Thee." Elder Silouan precedes Fr Sophrony in using the expression *the whole Adam,* which indicates the ontological oneness of the human race. His chapter "Adam's Lament" expresses his universal application of the term "Adam": Adam is "the father of the universe" and, as such, he emerges as a collective personality.[26] Christ-like love is the bond that links the whole Adam.

The universality of this love is often expressed by elder Silouan as "love toward one's enemies," which was central to his thinking to an unprecedented extent. It became his criterion for the authenticity of any Christian message.[27] Christ's commandment (Mt 5:44) is a projection of the divine mode of being onto the level of human relationship, since it reflects the absolute character of divine love.

Silouan also precedes Fr Sophrony in the concept of Christ-like humility, which he distinguishes from ascetic humility. Silouan's experience of Christ-like humility reflects Christ's commandment—"Learn from me; for I am gentle and lowly in heart" (Mt 11:29).[28] Though elder Silouan does not expound on these words, Fr Sophrony would discern the ontological dimension of Christ's self-description: "lowliness of heart" signifies the transfer of the focus of existential concern from self to other(s), when *I* is disregarded for the sake of *Thou.* It manifests Christ's hypostasis in his eternal self-orientation within the Trinity. Thus it implicitly reflects the intratrinitarian mode of being, where the hypostasis kenotically assimilates the life of the other(s). This christological dimension is implicitly present in Silouan: he expresses this Christ-like re-orientation from self to the other in the following passage: "When the soul has given herself up to the will of God, the mind then contains nought save God."[29] It is a supernatural state of participation in the kenotic existential commitment of one hypostasis of the Trinity to the other.

The same christological model is behind Silouan's teaching on ascetic obedience: he compares the obedient ascetic to Christ in his commitment to the Father. The importance of obedience for Silouan receives its theological

[26] *St Silouan the Athonite,* 47. On the concept of "Adam our father" ("total Adam") in Silouan, see K. Ware, " 'We Must Pray For All': Salvation according to St Silouan," *Sobornost* 19:1 (1997) 44–50.

[27] *St Silouan the Athonite,* 231–32. See J.-C. Larchet, "L'amour des ennemis selon saint Silouan l'Athonite et dans la tradition patristique," *Buisson Ardent* 2 (1996) 66–95.

[28] *St Silouan the Athonite,* 278, 310, and so forth.

[29] Ibid., 310–11.

justification in Fr Sophrony when he further highlights the connection
between obedience and the trinitarian mode of being.

These concepts lay the foundation for Fr Sophrony's theological principle
of the commensurability and affinity of divine and human existence. In
embryo, Silouan's concepts presuppose a (not always explicit) christological
and consequently trinitarian perspective for understanding the ascetic life.
Though Silouan himself does not pursue this connection in his writings, he
provides for Fr Sophrony a starting point for an application of the christotrinitarian model to the level of human existence.

Correspondence with David Balfour (1932-1946)

On Athos, Fr Sophrony became well acquainted with the patristic ascetic her-
itage. Fr Sophrony's letters to Fr David Balfour, a Catholic who converted to
Orthodoxy, from this period reveal his acquaintance with the writings and
ideas of the holy fathers: Basil the Great, Macarius of Egypt, Hesychius of
Jerusalem, Diadochus of Photice, Dionysius the Areopagite, Barsanuphius and
John, John Climacus, Isaac the Syrian, Symeon the New Theologian,
Philotheus of Sinai, Gregory of Sinai, Ignaty Bryanchaninov, Seraphim of
Sarov, Paisy Velichkovsky, Theophan the Recluse, and John of Krondstadt. Fr
Sophrony knew quite well the *Philokalia*. At a later stage, when Fr Sophrony
had learned Greek, so that he was able to read the patristic sources in the orig-
inal, he read Gregory Palamas. Among other books, Fr Sophrony mentions
The Ancient Paterikon and *The Way of a Pilgrim*.

The correspondence with Fr David Balfour (1932-1946) provides a valuable insight into Fr Sophrony's own spiritual development. As well as being
full of references to and quotations from the patristic writers, the letters also
touch on the difference between eastern Orthodox and western thought, in
both Christian and philosophical writings. Thus, Fr Sophrony mentions
Schleiermacher, Spinoza, Kant, and John of the Cross (*The Dark Night of the
Soul*). He dedicates a few pages to the concepts of the *heart* and *prayer*. In eastern Christianity, he argues, the spiritual heart is not an abstract notion but is
linked with our biological heart and has its physical location. In opposition to
the western search for some visionary mystical experience, Fr Sophrony advocates the prayer of repentance, which is the basis of all spiritual life.[30]

---

[30]See Letter to D. Balfour 11 (December 12, 1932), 1ff.

In these letters we find, in embryonic form, ideas determinative for Fr Sophrony's later theological development, particularly the concepts of god-forsakenness, maximalist anthropology, and the interdependence of asceticism and dogmatic vision.

Fr Sophrony works out a distinction between two types of godforsakenness. The first one is when "man deserts God": "To the extent that we live in this world, to that same extent we are dead in God." The second one is when God hides from man—a dreadful state of godforsakenness. When man has no more life in this world, that is, cannot live by this world, the memory of the divine world draws him "there," yet despite all this, darkness encompasses his soul. He explains: "these fluctuations of the presence and absence of grace are our destiny until the end of our earthly life."[31] Fr Sophrony saw suffering as a *necessary stage* in ascetic development: "Divine grace comes only in the soul that has undergone suffering."[32] Fr Sophrony thus parallels his own experience with that of the dark night in John of the Cross, whose writings assisted his comprehension of ascetic suffering. He calls him a "genius" and admits that the description of states, while being different in methods and terminology from the eastern fathers, in its main dogmatic statements is in accord and on a par with the greatest writers of eastern asceticism.

Fr Sophrony highlights other important points in John of the Cross, such as the determination to follow the hard path against the utmost resistance; the concern to preserve the mind pure of any image in his striving toward the divine; and the understanding of the spiritually perfect life as the unity of love. He points out that John's book does indeed excite the soul toward determination to follow patiently through the dry and dark wilderness toward the "promised land."

Despite their common traits, Fr Sophrony also points out differences between Eastern Orthodox spirituality and that of John. Fr Sophrony sees John's spiritual path as a *method*. In general he himself is not eager to promote any method or "artificial techniques" (not even the "mechanical" methods of hesychasm).[33] Further, the darkness of abandonment is not envisaged as a *positive* knowledge of and communion with God (as in John) but a *negative* stage on the way toward communion with God, who is light. The idea, Fr Sophrony writes, that immersion into darkness, divested of any concept or image, is of

[31]Ibid., CII (April 19, 1936), 12–13.
[32]Ibid., CI (August 10, 1934), 3.
[33]See *His Life Is Mine*, tr. Rosemary Edmonds (Oxford, 1977) 115.

itself a final stage in communion with God is alien to the Orthodox ascetic tradition.[34] Finally, John's prayer, according to Fr Sophrony, does not start with repentance, but he strives toward visionary imaginative experience, which disagrees with the eastern practice.[35]

Where Fr Sophrony raises the question of deification, the maximalism of his anthropology is manifest. He refers to Gregory Palamas, who applies the term *anarchos* (without beginning) to the ultimate condition of human deification: "We long for participation in eternal life. What actually happens is that man becomes not only immortal, but *beznachalny* [without beginning] as well."[36]

As a reply to Balfour's doubt over the importance of specifically eastern ascetic and dogmatic traditions, Fr Sophrony asserts the organic integrity and integrality of ascetic life, dogma, and the church. Criticizing Schleiermacher in connection with this issue, he writes: "There are three things I cannot take in: nondogmatic faith, nonecclesiological Christianity and nonascetic Christianity. These three—the church, dogma, and asceticism—constitute one single life for me."[37]

In reply to Balfour's doubt over the need for "negative asceticism," Fr Sophrony argues that positive asceticism (love) necessarily entails negative forms (limitations of oneself). The positive form is integral to the final goal, but in the initial stages of ascetic growth negative forms are necessary and fruitful. His main contention about dogma is that any religious culture has its own ascetic teaching, since asceticism is an ontological (living) expression of one's religious vision. He warns that any religious growth has stages and that it is dangerous to overturn the right order of these stages. Within the framework of Christian belief, pantheistic mysticism (search for a divine absolute above any conceptualization or particularity) is only a stage in religious development, and should not be seen as superior to the Christian personalistic concept of God. Fr Sophrony singles out Kant as an example of the confusion of the hierarchical order of these stages. Kant believed that the mind undergoes three stages, which accord with his idea of the development of the mind's perception of the world: theological, metaphysical, and positivist. Fr Sophrony, by contrast, implies that metaphysical and theological (which for Fr Sophrony implies *dogmatic*) perception should be seen as superior to positivist intellectualism.

[34]See *St Silouan the Athonite*, 178ff.
[35]See Letter to D. Balfour 11 (December 18, 1932) 6-7; 12 (December 14, 1932) 27-28.
[36]Ibid., C6 (May 26, 1935) 3.
[37]Ibid., D4 (August 21, 1945) 12.

Fr Sophrony diagnoses Balfour's concern about "confessional limitations" as only an initial stage of his spiritual growth. It was Schleiermacher's error to "dogmatize" this initial stage—the uncertainty of religious anguish (*Angst*)—as something ultimate. This came as a result of his rejection of the dogmatic foundations of religious experience. In Fr Sophrony's view, Schleiermacher is not far from pantheism: "His adogmatic Christianity and faith led him to define Spinoza's *pantheistic* perception of the world as the classic expression of the religious life." Also, in Kant's theological system the concepts of *personal* immortality and of the *personal* God do not play the fundamental role they have in traditional Christianity.

Responding to Balfour's question "How important are dogmas for Orthodoxy?" Fr Sophrony emphasizes the role of dogma in constituting the Orthodox tradition: "If one rejects the Orthodox creed and the eastern ascetic experience of life in Christ, which has been acquired throughout the centuries, then Orthodox culture would be left with nothing but the Greek minor [key] and Russian tetraphony."

Fr Sophrony also warns against attributing to intellectual reasoning the status of being the sole basis for religious search:

Historical experience has demonstrated that natural intellectual reasoning, left to its own devices, fatally arrives at pantheistic mysticism with its particular perception of reality. If this takes place in the soul of the Christian who does not want to reject Christ (as in the case of Leo Tolstoy), he arrives at Protestant rationalism or at spiritualism, which stands mystically close to *pantheism* . . . I am convinced that the rejection of the church will lead to the rejection of the apostolic message about "that which was from the beginning, which we have HEARD, which we have SEEN WITH OUR EYES . . . and our hands have HANDLED" (1 Jn 1:1).[38]

Thus, the correspondence with Balfour, by compelling Fr Sophrony to express himself theologically, became the first stage in Fr Sophrony's theological articulation. It is both significant and determinative, outlining as it does the range of theological interests and issues that came to be developed in his later writings.

[38]Ibid., 26.

Desert (1939-1947): Spiritual Fatherhood

After the death of Silouan (†September 24,1938), and following upon his advice, Fr Sophrony departed from the Monastery of St Panteleimon into the Athonite "desert." He resided first at Karoulia, and afterward in a cave near St Paul's Monastery.

Those years were marked by two significant happenings. First, in 1941, Fr Sophrony was ordained a priest. On becoming confessor and spiritual guide for many ascetics on Mount Athos, Fr Sophrony had unique access to the personal experiences of all those who confessed to him. This allowed him to observe and analyze certain regularly repeated patterns in monastic spiritual life. These observations became the basis for his ascetic teaching. The idea came to him of writing a book about the Athonite ascetic tradition, to record its principles and describe living examples that would help others to find their bearings.

Secondly, the Second World War was a time of prayer for the world so intense that Fr Sophrony's health was affected. Through such prayer he came to discover directly the interdependence of his own being and that of the whole of mankind, whose ontological unity became a central feature of his anthropology.[39] In prayer for the whole world Fr Sophrony understood the principles of what he later wrote about as *hypostatic being*. He came to realize that *persona* is the opposite of *individuum*: it does not exclude that which is *not-I* but, on the contrary, takes everything *not-I* into *I*.

Return to Paris (1947-1959)

In the postwar years Fr Sophrony resumed contact with Balfour. The latter helped Fr Sophrony to obtain a visa to go to France. It is difficult to establish any single cause for Fr Sophrony's departure from Mount Athos in 1947. On the one hand, Fr Sophrony had been entrusted by Silouan with the task of publishing his writings, if, as Silouan had put it, "you think they could be useful." Paris, as the cultural heart of the Russian emigration, would be the best place for this, and could provide resources unavailable on Athos. On the other hand he wished to complete his theological studies at St Sergius. The institute agreed to allow him to sit the examinations of the whole four-year course,

[39]Letter to D. Balfour D5 (December 4, 1945) 1.

and to provide him with accommodation and food. Other possible reasons are Fr Sophrony's deteriorating health and the difficulties he faced as a non-Greek in postwar Greece: "the [political] situation is deteriorating as time goes by," he writes to Balfour.

Fr Sophrony and the Institute of St Sergius

On his arrival in Paris, the institute questioned Fr Sophrony about his attitude toward the Russian Orthodox Church. They had previously demanded "confirmation" from Fr Sophrony that he would not "undertake propaganda of the views of [the Moscow Patriarchate]," giving as a motive for their demand the explanation that "the church had entered a period of ecclesiastical instability" after the death of Metropolitan Evlogy (†August 8, 1946). Their fear of any sympathy on Fr Sophrony's part toward the Russian patriarchate was not unjustified. Metropolitan Sergius' ecclesiology was in accord with that of Fr Sophrony: Sergius disagreed with the tendency among Russian Slavophile emigrants to deny the legitimacy of the "Soviet" or "Red church" as an Orthodox church, and thus to propagate a distorted conception of the institution of the church. The Slavophiles saw the Russian Church as unbreakably bound to its *cultural* roots. Metropolitan Sergius saw the church as a *heavenly* as well as an earthly institution, which was not ultimately conditioned by earthly historical reality. This view is in line with Fr Sophrony's universalistic vision of Orthodoxy.

After Metropolitan Evlogy's excommunication from the Russian patriarchal church in 1930, he went under the jurisdiction of the ecumenical patriarchate in 1931. The following years were marked by intense controversy between the supporters of Metropolitan Evlogy (notably the Institute of St Sergius) and adherents of the Russian patriarchate (the Brotherhood of St Photius, including Vladimir Lossky). The controversy reached a pinnacle in 1935–1936 over the condemnation of Bulgakov's sophianic teaching.[40] In spite of Evlogy's attempt at reunion with Moscow in 1945, the appointment by Moscow in 1946 of Bishop Seraphim, a renowned collaborator with the Nazis, as successor of Evlogy only aggravated the situation. In this situation, Fr Sophrony not only recognized the Moscow patriarchate but considered its church as the church of the living martyrs. He was far from sharing slavophilic nostalgia and never "canonized" the Old Russia as a theological or

[40]See A. Nichols, "Bulgakov and Sophiology," *Sobornost* 13:2 (1992) 25.

ideological concept: such nationalism contradicts his concern with universal categories and personal asceticism. He gave preference to the patristic tradition, whereas many Slavophiles drew on Dostoyevsky as a *theological* source.

Naturally, Fr Sophrony's sympathies toward the Russian church became an obstacle for his acceptance at St Sergius. Yet he was not left without moral support: his new friends Vladimir Lossky and Fr Boris Stark wholeheartedly shared his sympathies. Two years later Fr Sophrony collaborated with Lossky on the magazine *Messager de l'Exarchat du Patriarche Russe en Europe Occidentale*. To assert his allegiance to the Russian patriarchate, in 1951 Fr Sophrony published an article in which he paid glowing tribute to the memory of Patriarch Sergius, calling him an "outstanding pastor" and comparing him to the greatest hierarchs of the eastern church—Basil the Great, Athanasius of Alexandria, and Photius of Constantinopole. In response to the attacks of the anti-Soviet "camp" against the "Red church" and its "Red leader," he vigorously argues in favor of Patriarch Sergius' approach, which recognizes the twofold structure of the church, comprising two levels: heavenly and earthly.

Having been rejected by the St Sergius Institute, Fr Sophrony never completed any formal theological training. He settled in the Russian House in the small suburb of St Geneviève-des-Bois, which had a Russian church. There he continued his ministry as a celebrating priest and father confessor. His health deteriorating, he underwent major surgery on a stomach ulcer.

Theological Development

His poor health did not, however, arrest his theological development. In Paris Fr Sophrony was plunged once again into the Russian theological milieu. By now, however, he had acquired distinction as someone who possessed a living knowledge of monasticism, gained through his own ascetic practice, his acquaintance with Silouan, and his experience as a spiritual guide. He continued widening his intellectual horizons by reading contemporary theological literature. He became more closely acquainted with the published works of Bulgakov, Kern, Florovsky, Berdyaev, Lossky, and Glubokovsky. Reading these writers, Fr Sophrony came to a deeper appreciation of his own living experience as a basis to counter the distorted conceptions of the monastic ascetic tradition that had begun to spread among Russian thinkers in Paris.[41]

[41]Berdyaev (*Dream and Reality*, tr. K. Lampert [London, 1950] 72-99) argues that monasticism "contradicts the spirit of Christ's commandments" (78) and "perverts the very idea of obedience" (85). See T. Špidlík, *L'idée russe: une autre vision de l'homme* (Rome, 1994) 252-53.

His thought underwent a process of theological synthesis, as he evaluated the heritage of Russian theology and philosophy through the prism of his own ascetic experience.

These years proved most productive in terms of theological writings. He thus wrote his first major book, *Staretz Silouan*, and produced a mimeographed edition in 1948; it came out as a "professional" edition in 1952 and brought about his fame. Later the book was translated into more than twenty-two languages. Its impact was worldwide: veneration of elder Silouan grew, and he was numbered among the saints by the ecumenical patriarchate in 1987. In this book Fr Sophrony outlines the principles of his theology, and explains many of the concepts fundamental to his thought: prayer for the whole world, godforsakenness, the principle of hypostatic being ("Love assimilates the life of the beloved"—the mutual coinherence of being).

Fr Sophrony and Vladimir Lossky

Fr Sophrony established contact with Vladimir Lossky, to whom he first showed the writings of Silouan. Despite common grounds in their position (their attitude to Russia, their deep roots in the patristic and "ecclesiastical" traditions), they had different points of view on various theological issues. Thus, although Lossky appreciated the piety demonstrated in Silouan's writings, he claimed they lacked theological value. The dismissive attitude of Lossky and others compelled Fr Sophrony to write a theological introduction to the writings of Silouan, to explain the principles underlying his simple language. Once more we see Fr Sophrony's theology as a bridge between thought-worlds.

There emerged two major points where Fr Sophrony's views diverged from those of Lossky.

Whereas Lossky made much of Dionysius the Areopagite's concept of "divine darkness,"[42] Fr Sophrony is reserved in using the term "darkness" and disagrees with a literal interpretation of the term, on the basis of his own ascetic experience of divine light: "To talk about the 'divine' vision is entirely a figure of speech, for God is Light in whom there is no darkness at all. He always appears as light."[43] He situates "darkness" on the verge *between* the entire

[42]V. Lossky, *The Mystical Theology of the Eastern Church*, tr. the Fellowship of St Albans and St Sergius (Cambridge, 1991) 23-43.
[43]*St Silouan the Athonite*, 180.

divestment of the mind (the pure mind) and the apparition of divine light, and warns that there is no God in that darkness. This *darkness* signifies divine *absence*, while divine *presence* implies *light*. As for the "darkness" language in Gregory of Nyssa and Dionysius the Areopagite, it is not an existential event, but a figure of speech, a theological image, used by the Cappadocians as a weapon against Eunomian claims to see God's essence. From the mystical/existential point of view Fr Sophrony would wholly agree with Dionysius and the Cappadocians, for whom divine darkness is an overwhelming light that "exceedingly illuminates."[44] It is to Parisian misconceptions of the term that he objects. Their literalism in interpretation of God primarily as darkness opens the door to confusion between the dereliction of the Carmelite dark night and the "darkness of theophany."

Moreover, by drawing this sharp distinction between darkness/absence and light/presence, Fr Sophrony, in contrast to Lossky, provides a clearer ground for a theological integration of the experience of godforsakenness. Lossky sees godforsakennessas as a western conception (*derelictio*). For him the loss of grace and Gethsemane-like experience result from dogmatic deviations (especially the *filioque*), as was the case, he believes, with John of the Cross in his "dark night of the soul." Fr Sophrony asserts that periods of the loss of grace are necessary stages in ascetic growth, and are in fact paradoxically a manifestation of divine love. The experience of godforsakenness contains life-generating divine power.[45]

In the years 1950-1957, as the main editor of *Messager*, Fr Sophrony worked side by side with Vladimir Lossky, and naturally the themes of Fr Sophrony's theology of that time show signs of exposure to Lossky's interests. Among other articles he published his famous texts on "Unity of the Church" (1950) and "Principles of Orthodox Asceticism" (1952).

The article "Unity of the Church" in particular reflects the influence of current theological debates: many themes are paralleled in contemporary theologians, notably Lossky. So significant was the article that it stirred theological debate.[46] The first part is particularly important for tracing the new theological perspectives in Fr Sophrony's development. (The other three parts of the article are dedicated to questions of contemporary church politics.) The

---

[44] Dionysius the Areopagite, *Myst. Theol.*, 142; cf *Epist.* 5, 162.

[45] *St Silouan the Athonite*, 205; *We Shall See Him as He Is*, tr, Rosemary Edmonds (Essex, 1988) 135.

[46] Cf G. Dejaifve, "Sobornost or Papacy," ECQ 10 (1953-1954) esp. 81ff; H.-J. Ruppert, "Das Prinzip der Sobornost' in der russischen Orthodoxie," *Kirche im Osten* 16 (Göttingen, 1973) 47ff.

first section is devoted to questions of trinitarian theology. It is from that time that the trinitarian model became ever-present as the background of Fr Sophrony's writings. For the first time this article presents in clearly developed form his perception of the Trinity as the model for the human being. The article uses the trinitarian model for human ontological principles to justify Fr Sophrony's view on the jurisdictional organization of the body of the church. Later, a new version of the article was published in French,[47] where the trinitarian model was applied not to the church alone but to the whole of mankind, and the context of intraecclesiastical polemics was completely removed.

Lossky remained important to Fr Sophrony; in later years he recommended his explanations of the hypostasis and his forthright accounts of the *filioque*. Comparison between them is still illuminating for Fr Sophrony's later writings. In his later books another difference emerges more explicitly: Fr Sophrony's maximalist view of human nature. In *His Life Is Mine* (1977) and *We Shall See Him as He Is* (1985), he asserts *tozhestvo*, the identity of the divine and deified human nature.[48] Lossky was not inclined to bridge the gulf between God and man in such a bold manner.

Great Britain (1959-1993)

While Fr Sophrony was living at the Church in St Geneviève-des-Bois in the late 1950s many people used to come to him for spiritual guidance. By 1958, Fr Sophrony had a permanent group of people living near him and seeking the monastic life. By that time Fr Sophrony had already been enjoying considerable popularity in the United Kingdom. His book *Staretz Silouan* had been partially translated into English and was published in 1958 under the title *The Undistorted Image: Staretz Silouan, 1866-1938*. It had a favorable reception by the British ecclesiastical press.[49] Fr Sophrony had already visited the United Kingdom and delivered a number of talks, papers, and homilies. For example, he gave a talk at Oxford on the occasion of the commemoration of Vladimir Lossky.

[47]See *La félicité de connaître la voie* (Geneva, 1988) 11-55.
[48]*We Shall See Him as He Is*, 108, 172.
[49]Notably N. Mosley ("Introduction to 'Adam's Lament,'" *Prism* 5:2 [London, 1958] 38) sees Silouan's writings as having not only theological but also artistic literary value. J.-R. Lewis ("Reviews," 61) writes that an anthology of Russian literature is "no longer conceivable without 'Adam's lament' by Silouan the Athonite."

Monastic Community

Thus Fr Sophrony, with the help of people in the United Kingdom, succeeded in buying a property in Essex (at Tolleshunt Knights), which he had first inspected in 1958. He moved there in 1959 to form a religious community with a group from France, which then numbered six people. That is how the present Community of St John the Baptist came into being. The Russian patriarchate gave a positive answer to Fr Sophrony's request to move under the jurisdiction of Metropolitan Anthony of Sourozh. In 1965 the monastery, with Patriarch Alexy's blessing, became subject to the authority of the ecumenical patriarchate, which later granted the monastery stavropighial status.

To this community Fr Sophrony dedicated himself until his death in 1993. In his monastery Fr Sophrony attempted to restore the deepest principles of monastic life, so as to avoid distorted conceptions of the cenobitic life and its purpose. His main concern was primarily *inner asceticism*: inner perfection is more valuable than perfect outward conformity. The monastery does not have a written code of monastic rules, regulating fasting and hours of sleep. His teaching was largely focused on cultivation of the mind and the heart. While he was far from indifferent to everyday details and mundane tasks, he tended to integrate them within the wider spectrum of his theological framework.

It is notable that circumstances were such that the community included both monks and nuns, since Fr Sophrony could not run two separate communities. The *typikon* (prayer rule) of the monastery is distinct from the traditional Eastern Orthodox monastery. Instead of the service books with their daily cycle, the monastery often uses the Jesus prayer in the form of common worship—invocation of the divine name, usually adding up to four hours each day. The liturgy is celebrated three or four times per week. On the one hand this pattern was more appropriate to a small multinational community: reading services in one particular language would have excluded some (members or visitors) from full participation in the service. On the other hand, this was Fr Sophrony's own practice during his life in the desert. When applying such a practice, Fr Sophrony found precedents for replacing daily offices by the Jesus Prayer (recited in the church in common) in the Athonite skete practice, notably in the *Vita* of Nicodemus of Mount Athos and in Paisy Velichkovsky's monastery.[50]

[50]Cf C. Karambelas, *Contemporary Ascetics of Mount Athos* (Platina, Calif., 1992) 467. On Nicodemus' similar practice, see I. Kotsonis, *Athonikon Gerontikon* (Thessaloniki, 1992) 332.

Theological Writings

During this period Fr Sophrony's written work moves onto another theological level. It reflects his effort to build a theological bridge between one's ascetic experience and dogmatic vision. Naturally, he subjected his own ascetic experience to further theological analysis. His theology was now ever more firmly controlled by christotrinitarian implications of the notion of *persona*.

This shift can be detected, for example, in his correspondence with various people. One of the longest-running series (1958-1986) in his "theological" correspondence is addressed to his sister in Moscow M. Kalashnikova: his letter to her of January 7, 1968, is one of his first attempts to formulate the principle of *persona*.

The further exigency for a firmer theological grounding of his message came as a result of his interactive dialogue with the western world. He delivered a number of papers on various occasions—meetings, assemblies, receptions—where he expounded to a non-Orthodox audience his viewpoint on numerous ecclesiastical questions of our time: feminism, the relationship between the east and the west, the concept of sanctity, iconography, and other subjects. In 1962 he took part in the Second Patristic Conference in Oxford, where he delivered a paper "On the Necessity of Three Renunciations according to Cassian of Rome and John the Climacus."

The slightly fuller translation of *Staretz Silouan* came out as *The Monk of Mount Athos* (1973), which comprised a selection from Fr Sophrony's explanation of Silouan's life and teaching, and *Wisdom from Mount Athos* (1975)—the writings of Silouan himself. His new introduction to this book reflects his growing attention to the concept of hypostasis.[51]

His second major work, *His Life Is Mine*, proved a watershed in his theological thought. This first "autobiographical" book is actually addressed to a wider circle in the spiritual situation of the 1970s. In it we see the quintessence of the theological ideas of his old age. He writes about such concepts as persona, the cognition of God, and anthropology, while developing further his earlier themes of prayer for the whole world (the prayer of Gethsemane), suffering, and the contemplation of the uncreated light. In this book Fr Sophrony asserts *commensurability* between the Creator and his creation, which

[51]See "Foreword," in *Wisdom from Mount Athos: The Writings of Staretz Silouan 1866-1938*, tr. Rosemary Edmonds (New York, 1974) 8ff.

constitutes the core of his anthropology.[52] This allowed him to develop even
further the application of the divine model (both the Trinity-model and
Christ-model) to human beings.

This book prepared the ground for his final work *We Shall See Him as He
Is*. It had a mixed reception. In the west the book was welcomed: some considered the book to be an event[53] and even a breakthrough in Christian ascetic theology.[54] On the Orthodox side, with a few exceptions,[55] the reception
was less than supportive, especially from Russian readers. The main points of
criticism were his ambitious frankness in putting on paper his personal experience of God, his "blatantly high opinion of himself," his "familiarity with
God," his mystical sensuality and descriptions of visions, and his allegedly
overexuberant language. Some criticism was so bitter that, together with his
declining strength, it discouraged Fr Sophrony from producing any other theological writing. *We Shall See Him* is marked by a deeper analysis of the dogmatic inheritance of the church. It marks the completion of Fr Sophrony's
theological formulation, and contains his boldest theological ideas. On the one
hand Fr Sophrony develops, especially by fuller self-description than previously, themes already touched upon in previous books: uncreated light, liturgical prayer, cognition of God. On the other hand, he undertakes a more
articulate theological presentation of other themes: kenosis and godforsakenness, the remembrance of death, persona, love to the point of self-hatred.

Last Years

In the years preceding his death Fr Sophrony delivered talks to his monastic
community on a regular basis. These talks provide valuable evidence of the
full merging of his dogmatic and ascetic ideas. His "Testament," issued in 1991,
sets the trinitarian model as a principle of life for the monastic community.

---

[52]*His Life Is Mine*, 77.

[53]Cf M. Gimenez, "*Voir Dieu tel qu'il est* by Archimandrite Sophrony," *Sobornost* 7:1 (1985)
72–73; H. Moore, "Radical Redemption," *Christian Missionary Society Newsletter* 484 (1988) 1–
2; A. de Halleux, "Archimandrite Sophrony *Voir Dieu tel qu'il est*," *Revue théologique de Louvain*
16:3 (1985) 361-63; J. de Miguel, "Archimandrite Sophrony, *Voir Dieu tel qu'il est*," *Comunidades*
48 (1985) 93.

[54]Cf A. Franquesa, "Archimandrite Sophrony, *Voir Dieu tel qu'il est*," *Questions de Vida Christiana* 124 (1984) 130-31; P. de Luis, "Archimandrite Sophrony, *Voir Dieu tel qu'il est*," *Estudio
Agustiniano* 3 (1984) 49.

[55]In "The Letter to Archimandrite Sophrony" (July 13, 1984), *Archive* (1984) 1, K. Ware
wrote that "it is a remarkable book."

This was his final written theological farewell before his death on July 11, 1993. Fr Sophrony entrusted to the community his considerable archive, which is yet to be published. His community continues his theological message through its pastoral and publishing activity. M. Egger thus describes its present situation:

> Today it numbers twenty-five monks and nuns of twelve different nationalities. It is a place where hundreds of pilgrims from all over the world are welcomed: it is not only one of the main centres from which Orthodoxy is radiated in the West, but also one of the strongest affirmations of the universality of Orthodoxy.[56]

Fr Sophrony's theological formation determined the originality of his theological method, marked by active dialogue between various thought-worlds, such as current religious philosophy, the patristic tradition, and reflection on his personal mystical experience. The synthetic character of his theology is controlled by an exigency to create a bridge between differing worlds: the modern western world, the Russian intellectual elite in Paris, with its intense intellectual search, and Athonite monasticism, with its ancient patristic tradition and concern for the existential (practical-ascetic) relevance of theology. Fr Sophrony's theology evolved as an integration of these various strands into an organic synthesis through the prism of his own mystical experience. This is reflected in the principles of his theology, to which we now turn.

---

[56]M. Egger, "Preface," in Archimandrite Sophrony, *Words of Life*, tr. Sr Magdalene (Essex, 1996) 5.

CHAPTER TWO

Principles of Theology in Fr Sophrony

Fr Sophrony's approach to theology marks him out from among contemporary Russian theologians, especially from "the speculative and intellectualist stream which has penetrated modern Orthodoxy."[1] His main writings are dedicated neither to a systematic exposition of patristic ideas (as we find in Lossky) nor to building an innovative, complete, and unified theological system (as in Bulgakov) but to an analytical *description* of ascetic experience. His first book—*St Silouan the Athonite* (1952)—is based upon Silouan's living experience. Fr Sophrony's other major book—*We Shall See Him as He Is* (1985)—is his spiritual autobiography, where he relates the "spiritual states" that he experienced. These are sometimes qualified with various dogmatic christotrinitarian or anthropological statements, but with no attempt at a logically systematic presentation. Throughout his books one cannot fail to notice the large amount of repetition: one and the same thought comes under different forms. The book *On Prayer* is also largely dedicated to his own experience of prayer and his pastoral ministry. It is the same "personal living experience" that determines the scope of the themes that he touches on. Can we therefore speak of any coherent "theological system" or "principles" or even "doctrinal teaching" of Fr Sophrony? Or should his books rather be classified as belonging to the genre of "memoirs," where his "theology" is built, using J. Lucas' definition of such "theology," "on just expressing [one's] emotional preferences"?

We shall attempt to show that not only are there theological principles in Fr Sophrony but also that they are his personal response to the modern quest for an adequate method of theologizing.

Among his writings, the articles "Unity of the Church in the Image of the Holy Trinity" (1950) and "The Ways of the Theological Ascesis" in the anthol-

---

[1]L. Gillet, *Orthodox Spirituality: An Outline of the Orthodox Ascetic and Mystical Tradition*, 2d ed. (London, 1978) 2.

ogy of his articles *Birth into the Kingdom Which Cannot Be Moved* (1999) stand
out as most explicitly theological. Here his theological principles receive clear
and articulate expression.

The Principles Outlined

The Anthropological Basis for Human Knowledge of God

Fr Sophrony's anthropology has Genesis 1:26 as its starting point: the creation
of man in the image and likeness of God. The concept in itself presupposes a
certain *affinity* and *commensurability* between the divine and human modes of
being: "To dismiss this idea of commensurability would make it totally impossible to interpret any form of cognition [of the divine] as truth."[2] There is thus
a direct link between theology and anthropology. Fr Sophrony notes:

> The created nature of man, made in the image and likeness of God the
> Creator, reveals not only the possibility of receiving the divine revela-
> tion, but also the faculty of conceiving in some way the divine being.[3]

Fr Sophrony echoes Justin Martyr when he asserts that every man is potentially capable of coming to partial knowledge of God[4] and communion with
him. This idea is based on John 1:9: "Christ enlightens *every* man." But this
does not mean that every man can aptly theologize about God on the basis of
his own rationality. Man's rationality is limited in its capacities, and as such it
is inadequate for assessing the reality of the infinite. That is why Fr Sophrony
concludes: "knowledge of God cannot be attained by rational thought." The
best achievement of human rationality in its effort to come to knowledge of
God is found by Fr Sophrony in Acts 17:23. In putting up the altar to the
"unknown god" the Greek philosophers "have attained the limits of knowledge." Finite human rationality is not an adequate conceptual apparatus to
operate with the categories of the infinite: "Human conceptions, however, do
not lead to the true knowledge of the divine mystery."[5] In contrast to the trend

[2]*His Life Is Mine*, 77.
[3]*La félicité de connaître la voie*, 11.
[4]Justin Martyr, *Apolog.* 2:10: 8, 210; ibid., 2:13:3, 217; see L. Bouyer, *La spiritualité orthodoxe et la spiritualité protestante et anglicane* (Paris, 1965) 216-19.
[5]*La félicité de connaître la voie*, 11.

of *naive religious realism*, which "assumes that the divine reality is just as spoken about in the language of some one tradition,"[6] Fr Sophrony advocates apophatic limitations in his assessment of the capacities of human language to express theological truths:

> Human language never allowed anyone to express adequately either spiritual experience, or the knowledge of God brought about by Christ . . . Men lived the [divine] reality in prayer . . . But all the words, which conveyed the new teaching and new life from generation to generation, to a greater or lesser extent led the mind astray from a real contemplation of God.[7]

According to Fr Sophrony, these limitations of human language are partly overcome by the very fact of recognizing its limitations. This justifies the apophatic method of theologizing.

Divine Revelation as the Basis of the Human Theological Response

Since a purely autonomous rationality cannot be a sufficient basis for theology, Fr Sophrony rejects the "from below" type of theology, which builds its framework drawing on the resources of the human intellect. How then can humans know God? A genuine theological process has revelation "from above" as its starting point: the intellect can only theologize on the basis of the given revelation. In church tradition the *datum* of revelation is encapsulated in the form of *dogma*: "The human spirit, confronted by dogma, will then look for its own ways to assimilate the gifts of divine revelation and to appropriate what they contain. At this point what is called *theological development* begins."[8]

This predominance of *revelation* in theology determines the task of theology: in fact, it is not a speculative building up of new theological systems with a more perfected logical framework, but an exposition of the datum "from above" and an integration of the divine revelation into the categories of human experience and expression. "Theological development fundamentally has no other function than that of rendering unchangeable dogmatic truths

[6]J. Hick, "Religious Realism and Non-Realism: Defining the Issue," in *Is God Real?* ed. J. Runzo, 7 (London, 1993).
[7]*Birth into the Kingdom Which Cannot Be Moved*, ed. N. Sakharov (Essex, 1999) 27-28.
[8]*La félicité de connaître la voie*, 24.

accessible to souls, by 'translating' them into a language suited to the men for whom they were intended."[9]

Systematization is not valuable as an aim in itself, and therefore the *structure of presentation* is not the determinative factor in the theological process. The scholastic *summa theologica* is alien to his understanding of the theological principles of the eastern tradition. He summarizes his idea of the theology of the church in the following passage:

> The dogmatic and ascetic teaching of the Orthodox Church is not an aggregation of human inventions . . . The form of presentation to an audience learning the results of living experience is not subject to systematization (Rom 10:14-15). In its main mass the teaching of the church is the account in human words about that which the apostles, the fathers, and the ascetics saw and came to know (cf 1 Jn 1:1-3, Gal 1:11-12). When we speak about personal communion between a free God and free humans, we face the task of expressing the ever-living streams of the infinite ocean of divine life by the poor means of our human language . . . By virtue of the action of the one God everything is characterized by an internal ontological wholeness, which is many-sided, inexhaustibly rich."[10]

Fr Sophrony's Gnoseology

The divine initiative through revelation presupposes a *personal* relationship between the recipient (man) and the source of the revelation (God). On this basis Fr Sophrony expounds his theory of *knowledge of God.*

He makes a distinction between "scientific knowledge" and "real knowledge" or, as he calls it, "spiritual knowledge."[11] This distinction between scientific and religious modes of knowledge, which are incompatible on many points, is sustained by other modern thinkers.[12] M. Cohen, for example, says that in scientific knowledge "the pursuit of truth is determined by *logical* considerations." He defines its main question as "what general conditions or

[9] Ibid., 25-26.
[10] *Birth into the Kingdom*, 32.
[11] *We Shall See Him as He Is*, 176, 231.
[12] See I. Barbour, *Issues in Science and Religion* (London, 1966) 121.

considerations determine this or that to be so?'[13] D. Stanesby demonstrates the profound impact of *empirical positivism* as a fundamental principle of modern science. As he writes: "The logical empiricist [as a representative of modern scientific knowledge] never allows argument for theism to get started. If, as he stipulates, the only thing that can count as knowledge is that which is in principle empirically verifiable, then knowledge of a non-sensory object, that is God, is ruled out by definition."[14] For Fr Sophrony also, scientific knowledge has a limited range of operation, which embraces the objects of empirical reality. Indeed, its criteria can hardly be applied to the nonempirical sphere of religious knowledge. This agrees with A. Louth's observation that "the lure of the scientific method" has been damaging to theology (and the humanities). Louth criticizes a subsequent one-sided understanding of truth, which he associates with a "dissociation of sensibility," in western culture.[15] Fr Sophrony summarizes the principle of science by saying that it deals with the deterministic concepts of being. Fr Sophrony also describes in other terms how spiritual knowledge differs from scientific knowledge. Spiritual knowledge is "living," "ontological" and *personal.* These points are so fundamental that we shall examine each in more detail.

LIVING KNOWLEDGE. As far as spiritual knowledge is concerned, it has a unique basis: "Our knowledge is a result of the revelation from above." Spiritual knowledge is understood as "con-joined existence," or "co-existence" (*sobytie*), as "uniting fusion" (*spaika*) of very being. In *Félicité,* Fr Sophrony writes: "Knowledge is conceived as communion in being."[16]

Scientific "knowledge" rests on the resources of human rational thinking, while "authentic" theological knowledge embraces *all* aspects of human being. Man who is striving to acquire knowledge of God has to abandon the categories of abstract intellectual knowledge as incapable of conveying the facts of divine reality:

> Such direct knowledge is not provable by logic. It is even impossible with the aid of the concept with which human reason operates to circumscribe this knowledge. And that, not only because the framework

[13]M. Cohen, *An Introduction to Logic and Scientific Method* (London, 1957) 192.
[14]D. Stanesby, *Science, Reason and Religion* (London and New York, 1985) 27.
[15]A. Louth, *Discerning the Mystery: An Essay on the Nature of Theology* (Oxford, 1989) 45–72.
[16]*La félicité de connaître la voie,* 30; cf *We Shall See Him as He Is,* 217.

of conceptual thought is too narrow and would not be able to contain divine realities, but above all because true knowledge of God is only granted at the existential level by an experience lived with all our being.[17]

Knowledge of the omnipresent God is accessible to all rational beings. But schools of theology and theological tomes are far from sufficient for its assimilation. In some inexplicable fashion true knowledge filters into our inmost being when he (God) is with us. The operative indwelling of God in us means that we are introduced into the very act of divine being. And this is precisely that way that our spirit is given living knowledge of him.[18]

Fr Sophrony's thought can be best summarized in the celebrated terminology of Martin Buber. The latter defines scientific knowledge in terms of the "I-it" detached analysis of things, but when the knowledge of the other person is involved, then *I-Thou* knowledge presupposes "total involvement and participation of the whole self."[19]

At the basis of Fr Sophrony's gnoseology lies the biblical idea of *gnosis*.[20] When applied to human relationship, the verb "to know" in the Bible implies the fullest and most intimate possible expression of knowledge. When applied to the relationship between God and man it implies *living communion*, and the element of "inner," intimate knowledge is understood in a spiritual sense. Fr Sophrony uses the biblical idea of knowledge to elucidate his idea of knowledge of God: "With the help of the biblical concept of knowledge we are going to clarify what has been said above of the unknowability of the essence: knowledge is conceived above all as a communion of being, a sharing of life."[21]

This communion of being is realized by the "indwelling" of God, of the Holy Spirit in man, by which man goes beyond the categories of empirical knowledge and is lifted up to the contemplation of the divine reality:

[17] *La félicité de connaître la voie*, 25.
[18] *We Shall See Him as He Is*, 44.
[19] See M. Buber, *I and Thou*, tr. R. Smith (Edinburgh, 1994) 15ff.
[20] On the biblical idea of knowledge, see I. Engnell, "'Knowledge' and 'Life' in the Creation Story," *Vetus Testamentum, Supplement* 3 (1955) 103-19; cf E. Baumann, "*Iadaa* und seine Derivate. Eine sprachlichexegetische Studie." In ZAW 28 (1908) 22-41, 110-43.
[21] *La félicité de connaître la voie*, 30.

How can one accomplish the transition from the canons of formal logic to the antinomies of real fact? The way out is mapped by Christ: Jesus said ..."He who loves me will keep my word and my Father shall love him and we will come and dwell in him" (Jn 14:23). This commandment is at the basis of our gnoseology. Only the dwelling in us of the Father, Son, and Holy Spirit will give us authentic knowledge of God.[22]

From this passage we see that knowledge is both a result of and equivalent to living communion. This communion is realized through *love*: love is thus the uniting principle. This "gnoseology" derives from trinitarian theology—absolute love between the divine hypostases ensures their absolute unity. This absolute unity/communion of the triune being results in the absolute mutual knowledge of each hypostasis. Great significance is attributed to the *perichoresis* (coinherence) between the divine persons—their absolute mutual coinherence. Fr Sophrony builds up a model of divine love within the trinitarian being:"The absolute perfection of love in the bosom of the Trinity reveals to us the perfect reciprocity of the 'interpenetration' of the three persons."[23]

This trinitarian model allows Fr Sophrony to make the connection between love and knowledge more explicit: "*God is love* (1 Jn 4:8) and He knows Himself and us absolutely; and everything in Him is one."[24] Fr Sophrony transfers the principle love=knowledge onto the human plane. The objects of knowledge here are both God and other humans. Fr Sophrony mentions knowledge of God in this context in his *Ascetic Discourses:* "The highest aim, according to Silouan is 'the more a person loves God, the more he knows Him' ... love unites the very being. When we have repulsion toward others, barriers and so on—this deprives us of life. When we have prayer, love and tears, this brings us closer to the highest 'science'—knowledge of the Father, Son, and Holy Spirit."

On the basis of his maximalist anthropology Fr Sophrony transfers the intratrinitarian principle of being to the level of multihypostatic human existence. As in the Trinity, in which the hypostases know each other through perichoretic love, so also humans come to know each other through love. This connection between *knowledge* and *love* on the human level is clearly expressed in *Letters to Russia:*"If I will love my brother and my neighbor as my own life,

---

[22] *Birth into the Kingdom*, 28.
[23] *La félicité de connaître la voie*, 21.
[24] *We Shall See Him as He Is*, 43.

and will not egoistically separate myself from him, then, clearly, I will come to know him more, and know him more deeply, in all his suffering, thoughts, and quests."[25]

Fr Sophrony inherits the idea of the *living* dimension of the knowledge of God from his elder Silouan. The golden thread of Silouan's ascetic theology is the idea that *living* knowledge of God is actualized in the communion of the Holy Spirit.[26] Fr Sophrony himself points out his dependence on Silouan in this respect.[27] In Silouan, the knowledge of God is always based on *revelatory experience* of some kind and therefore comes "from above." The faculty of the knowledge of God is placed not in man's rational faculty alone but in "the whole man": "The soul suddenly sees the Lord and knows that it is He . . . The Lord is made known in the Holy Spirit and the Holy Spirit pervades *the entire man—soul, mind and body*."[28]

KNOWLEDGE AND THE PERSONA. Fr Sophrony's idea of cognition is strongly related to his teaching on *persona*. In fact, real cognition is always *personal*. His starting point is that "ontological knowledge is a result of communion in being and not an intellectual hypothesis."[29] Therefore he asserts that all that cannot be communicated cannot be known. Here he has in mind above all the *essence* of God, which cannot be communicated to the created order of being. Thus knowledge of God is related above all to the hypostatic aspect of being—we come to knowledge of God as persona and not as essence. When speaking of the cognition of God, Fr Sophrony employs personal figurative language: man comes to know God "face to Face."[30]

Fr Sophrony draws a distinction between scientific knowledge, which is *impersonal* by virtue of objectification, and spiritual knowledge, which is *personal*. He notes that scientific knowledge approaches the question of divine being in a materialistic, impersonal perspective. He rephrases the Johannine prologue to show that for many modern scientists "in the beginning there was the hydrogen atom, and out of this atom everything that now exists came into

---

[25] *Letters to Russia*, 23.
[26] On Silouan's idea of knowledge of God, see T. Stylianopoulos, "Staretz Silouan: A Modern Orthodox Saint," in *God and Charity: Images of Eastern Orthodox Theology, Spirituality and Practice*, ed. T. Hopko, 40–43 (Brookline, Mass., 1979).
[27] *La félicité de connaître la voie*, 25.
[28] *St Silouan the Athonite*, 353; cf *Birth into the Kingdom*, 34.
[29] *Birth into the Kingdom*, 30.
[30] *We Shall See Him as He Is*, 123, 189; cf *Letters to Russia*, 127.

being." That is why science asks the question "*what* was in the beginning" and "*what* is being." Fr Sophrony concludes: "Studying the scientific cosmologies we find that there is no notion of person."[31]

He believes that if we apply the principles of scientific "impersonal" knowledge to theology, we arrive at the conclusion that primordial being is "impersonal" as well. Why is this so? According to the principles of human logic, the idea of man being the "image and likeness of God" tempts us to build up the prototype (God) according to the attributes of its image (man), that is, from below. In forming such an understanding of the prototype, human rationality, with its tendency to objectification and depersonalization, will inevitably, therefore, reflect its own attributes. In Buber's vocabulary, objectification would turn *Thou* into *It*. This objectification and consequent depersonalization are transferred to the divine prototype: "This tendency comes from the fact that the rational intellect is impersonal in the way it operates; abandoned to itself and acting according to its own laws, it forces itself to 'go beyond' the principal of the person in being, as much on the divine as on the human level, while for the Christian the person in the divine being is not a limiting principle but being-itself, the very Absolute." This "impersonality" of thinking affects human understanding of the divine being: "When man claims to attain the knowledge of eternal truth by his own thinking, he almost inevitably comes up against the concept of a 'metaphysical absolute,' a concept according to which the principle of the person is a limitation, a manifestation of an unmanifested God, of *Deus Absconditus*."[32]

This observation throws some light on the theological systems of some non-Christian religions, where the divine absolute is conceived in suprapersonal categories. Reaching such an absolute is linked not with building up a personal relationship with God but with divesting oneself of any limiting categories (including personal existence) by transcending them. This distinction is often referred to in Fr Sophrony's analysis of the Christian understanding of the divine absolute. Obviously, the focus on this distinction is also linked with Fr Sophrony's own experience of non-Christian eastern mysticism.

In contrast to the scientific de-personified approach, Fr Sophrony reformulates the basic quest: "We pose the question 'who is being?' and not 'what is being?'; 'who is truth?' and not 'what is truth?' "[33] The fact that the

[31] *Letters to Russia*, 30; cf ibid., 116.
[32] *La félicité de connaître la voie*, 13.
[33] *Letters to Russia*, 61.

For. Fr. Sophrony, the key to everything is that God is personal.

principal being—God—is personal determines the approach to the question of *true knowledge.* Persona is the vehicle for communication: "This Personal Being [God], unconditioned by anything or anyone, which determines itself in everything, is the Cause of our coming into the world. The revelation that this Being is personal makes it obvious that the knowledge about Him or (better to say) of Him can be achieved through His personal communion with us, as persons." Scientific objectification is alien to spiritual knowledge. In the cognition of God the process of objectification of the One who is perceived is eliminated: "God so fuses with man that man lives Him as his own life, and not in the least as an 'object' of cognition. The scientific, objectifying approach can in no way be applied to Him."[34]

That is why the hypostatic principle in the human being is the main recipient and vehicle of divine knowledge.

Forms of Knowledge

Empirical/scientific knowledge can be enclosed in the form of thoughts, objective ideas, and concepts, but these are insufficient for the perception of divine reality. Here we come to a crucial question: How and in what form then can nonconceptual and subjective knowledge of God be communicated to the human being?

To answer this question Fr Sophrony introduces a new concept: theology as a state of being. He writes that in the moment of divine revelation (as in contemplation of the divine light, for example) "profound knowledge descends on us, not as a thought, but as *sostoianie* [state] of our spirit."[35] These states usually occur during prayer. Fr Sophrony describes how in the moment of such prayer "our mind-spirit is included in the mind of God and receives an understanding of things which escapes any adequate expression in our daily language." He explains this communion in knowledge through the state of our spirit in the following example: "All things are created by His will, His thought. He conceives the world, and His creative thinking becomes created being. Not matter but the thinking of God the Creator is the initial factor. Thus we live this world not only through the prism of experiential knowledge, but in the Spirit also behold it in another fashion (cf Heb 11:1–3)."[36]

[34] *We Shall See Him as He Is,* 104; cf *His Life Is Mine,* 44.
[35] *We Shall See Him as He Is,* 223.
[36] Ibid., 227.

The problem with the term "state" is that it can be easily confused with the common use of the word, which has a very strong association with psychological conditions, or even with "feelings." The temptation to fall for this conclusion is strong indeed, especially when Fr Sophrony describes these states in terms of their psychological effect, as joy, or pain.[37] However, Fr Sophrony anticipates such misunderstanding and gives a clear definition of his technical term *state* in contrast to the usual use of the word in the context of psychology or human emotions:

> "*State*" is the fact of being, which prompts our thought, operating after its own fashion, to understand truth. Such understanding is not achieved by demonstrative reasoning but through an intuitive penetration or an establishment of fact as knowledge of Divine Being, descending on us from God.[38]

"State," as a fact of being, signifies the person's living participation in the divine reality. The term "state" assists Fr Sophrony to express the idea of existential involvement on every level of one's being. The word "feeling" cannot serve the same purpose, as it implies a merely empirical perception, rather than mystical participation.

Can this living knowledge, personal and beyond conceptualization, be communicated by one human being to another? H. Farmer believes that this knowledge is incommunicable to those who have no similar experience of God: "Who could describe light and colour to one who has known nothing but darkness?"[39] Fr Sophrony is also aware of the limitation of human communication, yet he adheres to the principles of the theological realists, that is, "those who while aware of the inability of any theological formulation to catch the Divine realities, nonetheless accept that there are Divine realities that theologians, however ham-fistedly, are trying to catch."[40] Within this perspective of theological realism, the "description of states" becomes an important theological medium for conveying the perception of divine reality. This reality is communicated as if through the "window" of one particular persona's perception. An attempt to communicate the perception of divine reality, encapsulated in the form of personal "states," is the main principle of Fr

[37]Ibid., 88, 92.
[38]Ibid., 229.
[39]H.H. Farmer, *Towards Belief in God* (London, 1942) 41.
[40]J. Soskice, "Theological Realism," in *The Rationality of Religious Belief*, 108 (Oxford, 1987).

Sophrony's theological language. This "descriptive" recollection, he claims, is the main theological principle of New Testament writers as well: the apostles "and the subsequent theologians of the Church relate *facts of being* that they came to know."[41]

This descriptive method of theologizing, with a prime stress on the description of the spiritual state as a medium for the communication of the perception of divine reality, brings about the introduction of new theological expressions. To emphasize the *living* dimension of the perception of the divine reality Fr Sophrony uses the verb "live" (*zhit'*) in a transitive sense instead of "experience" or "taste." Thus, he uses the expressions "to live God," "to live the liturgy," "to live the tragedy of the world."[42] Such a use allows him to convey vividly the idea of *living experience of* and *communion with* the "object": God, liturgy, and so forth.

Since spiritual knowledge is encapsulated in "spiritual states," the aim of theological language is to convey these states in an inspiring and accessible way. The efficacy of delivering the theological message is firmly linked with the efficacy of language. This determines the character of Fr Sophrony's language, which is marked by a boldness of expression. His strategy is to affect more powerfully the spiritual state of his readers by using striking vocabulary, formulas, and imagery.

We may summarize the main principles of Fr Sophrony's theology as follows. Theology is not based on the principles of "formal logic" but on divine revelation. The basis of the knowledge of God is a *personal* and *existential act of communion* with the divine reality. The words "personal and existential act" provide us with a key to the roots of Fr Sophrony's concept of knowledge.

The Roots of Fr Sophrony's Theological Principles

Existentialism and the Barthian School?

The subjectification, personalization, and abandonment of the categories of objectifying "scientific" thinking was inherent in the existentialist philosophy of the twentieth century, which widened the chasm between science and religion. I. Barbour defines the distinctive mark of existentialism as an awareness

---

[41] *We Shall See Him as He Is*, 180.
[42] Ibid., 104-6, 203; cf *Letters to Russia*.

of the dichotomy between *personal existence* and *impersonal objects*. The basic antithesis of existentialism (personal subjectivity as opposed to impersonal objectivity) seems to reflect well Fr Sophrony's perspective on knowledge. Projected on to theology, existentialism highlights the contrast between the "objects" of science and theology. The contrast of the modes of knowledge in science and religion is defined by existentialism as the difference between *subjective involvement* and *objective detachment*, or between the sphere of personal selfhood and the sphere of impersonal objects.[43]

We are thus justified in asking whether Fr Sophrony's theological principles are the result of the influence of existentialism. More specifically, we shall examine whether Fr Sophrony is an heir of the Russian form of existentialism of such as Berdyaev.

For the largest period of his life, Fr Sophrony lived in the west. In France particularly, with his excellent command of French, he might have absorbed the influence of French existentialists. But this hypothesis does not have much supportive evidence; Fr Sophrony nowhere mentions either existentialism or any existentialist writer.

A second possibility is to see the influence of existentialism via Russian thought. Already in the nineteenth century Russian philosophy was marked by the awareness of the potential for the knowledge of God inherent in every human being. There was a shift toward anthropocentrism and "subjectivity": whoever a person may be, his/her subjective experience of the divine reality becomes a sufficient basis for theologizing. From the 1830s Russian philosophers felt free to tackle dogmatic questions outside the authorized ecclesiastical institution. For example, such concepts as *godmanhood* and *sobornost* have their prehistory in "lay" philosophy, that is, outside the formal church. After exposure to the influence of western thought in general, and French existentialism of the twentieth century in particular, this *subjectification* of theological issues found its most articulate synthesis in the writings of Nicholas Berdyaev.

Berdyaev was well acquainted with contemporary philosophical and theological developments in the west. He maintains a *theocentric* dimension in his approach to theology—thus, he was certainly aware of and in agreement with the attack made by the resurgent neo-orthodoxy on the possibility of a natural (i.e., purely philosophical) theology. Kierkegaard was the first in a line of "anti-philosophists," who criticized the attempt to sustain self-sufficient metaphysical rational thinking, and instead asserted that knowledge of transcendent

[43]Barbour, 116-20.

reality is given through *revelation*, however paradoxical it may be for the reason. Christ, as the absolute paradox of faith, cannot be understood but can only
be believed in. The Christian revelation is "mediated to us . . . by the God-
man," says Kierkegaard, "in whom we can only have faith *in virtue of the
absurd*."[44] As for reason, its task is to recognize its limitation, constraining
thereby the sphere of its operation.[45] D. Emmet summarizes Kierkegaard's
existentialist critique of rational knowledge thus: "Each existence has its own
inner subjectivity opaque to objective thought, which cannot be mediated by
any direct communication. It can only be responded to in passionate 'inward-
ness' by another existing being from his own subjectivity."[46] As such, Kierkegaard has been traditionally labeled as existentialist, irrationalist, subjectivist,
and relativist.

Kierkegaard differs from Berdyaev on the anthropological dimension in
the knowledge of God. Kierkegaard stresses the *incommensurability* between
man and God: "the infinite qualitative distinction between God and man,"
which is summed up in the principle *finitum non capax infiniti*. This principle
excludes the fulness of the knowledge of God. The same direction was taken
up by the Barthian school: man is a *limited* being, a creaturely counterpart of
God, so there is an ontological "abyss" between God and man. On the basis
of incommensurability Barth limits the task of theology to the "passive" exposition of revelation. Revelation is something sui generis. Thus, Barth is the
advocate par excellence of theology "from above." Barth finds the scientific
standard of rationality irrelevant and refuses to take issue with the logical positivists on their own grounds. Instead he proposes the "logical economy" of
divine revelation in Christ. Christ, as God and man, alone has the fullest
knowledge of God and we participate in his knowledge through faith—
knowledge is thus confined to faith.[47] As for direct knowledge, man cannot
be united to God, who is "wholly other" (*der ganz Andere*) and belongs to a
different existential order.

The Barthian principles of theology—"from above" and nonobjecti-
vism—fit well within the epistemological framework of Berdyaev and Fr
Sophrony. Thus, though critical of Barth's anthropology, Berdyaev and Fr
Sophrony (indirectly) support Barth's and Kierkegaard's attack on the objective

[44]I quote from D. Emmet, *The Nature of Metaphysical Thinking* (1945) 125.
[45]S. Kierkegaard, *Concluding Unscientific Postscript*, tr. H. and E. Hong (Princeton, N.J., 1982)
504.
[46]Emmet, *The Nature of Metaphysical Thinking*, 123.
[47]K. Barth, *Church Dogmatics* 2:1 (Edinburgh, 1957) 12.

dimension in the knowledge of God. In Berdyaev's own words, existential philosophy, which he defends, on the whole "marks the transition from the interpretation of knowledge as objectification, to understanding it as *participation*,
union with the subject matter and entering into co-operation with it."[48]

Fr Sophrony and Berdyaev?

As we saw, echoes of Fr Sophrony's theological principles (personalism and
theology "from above") are found in Berdyaev, who shared much with existentialists and Barth.

We ought here to enlarge upon Berdyaev's epistemology since there are
many common points between Berdyaev and Fr Sophrony. Berdyaev points
out the difference between science and religion—they have their own worlds,
which makes it difficult to apply the principles of scientific knowledge to religion. He is aware of a "de-personalization" of knowledge in humanism, largely
linked with the tendency toward objectification. From the days of Kant, he
believes, German philosophy has always taken the relation between subject
and object as its starting point. Objectivity has been almost identified with
general validity. "Objectification is rationalization, the ejection of man into the
external, it is an exteriorization of him . . . [it] includes alienation."[49]

Berdyaev is also aware of the limitation of human language. For him, the
expression of inner experience inevitably leads to distortion of and alienation
from that experience.[50]

Like Fr Sophrony, he sees that the rational human mind is not the ultimate
recipient of truth. "It is a mistake to think that truth is revealed to the generic
mind. Truth is revealed to spiritual awareness, which lies on the borderline of
the supra-conscious; spirit is freedom . . . it is personality and love." Berdyaev
adheres to the existential dimension in cognition, which comes through being
rather than through objects. Thus, true knowledge ("philosophical apprehen-
sion" in Berdyaev) comes not through rationalized information but through
"a primary act, an act which precedes all rationalisation, an existential act, and
the measure of it is gauged by the depth and breadth of that act." This does
not imply that spiritual knowledge is pre-logical. It is, rather, "supra-logical,"
and as such it surpasses both the pre-logical and the logical.[51]

[48]N. Berdyaev, *The Beginning and the End*, tr. R. French (London, 1952) 61.
[49]Ibid., 60; cf 40, 87.
[50]Ibid., 73. See also Berdyaev, *Dream and Reality*, 171.
[51]Berdyaev, *The Beginning and the End*, 68, 72.

Thus, Fr Sophrony and Berdyaev agree on the limitation of reason and language, the personal dimension of knowledge, and that knowledge is not information but union and participation (in love).

Existentialism or Tradition?

Shall we therefore see Fr Sophrony as an heir of the Russian philosophical tradition, especially of its existentialist trend with its "subjectification" of theology? His style fits well E. Ilyenkov's observation about the existentialists' language: "[existentialists] . . . prefer to write [about the human person], not in scientific language, but in essayist, belle-lettres genre, or even in novels." Within such an "existentialist" perspective Fr Sophrony's memoir-like style can be indeed welcomed as an expression of his theological principles. By speaking about *states*, he deals with existential acts themselves, and presents them in their supralogical, unrationalized reality.

However, the basis of Fr Sophrony's supralogic is different from that of western thinkers on the one hand and of Berdyaev on the other.

As for the Kierkegaardian trend of thought, the central principle that determine man's knowledge of God is *finitum non capax infiniti*. Here emerges the fundamental difference between the theological basis of Fr Sophrony and that of the western thinkers influenced by Kierkegaard: Fr Sophrony follows Bulgakov and Berdyaev in saying that man, as persona, is infinite, hence— *humana natura capax divini*. Both Kierkegaard and Barth are reserved about the possibility of the *actual immediate* experience of the infinite transcended by the finite: their basis of theologizing is *faith* in the *scriptural revelation*.

The concern of Kierkegaard and Barth—to maintain the qualitative difference, the ontological incompatibility between God and man—proved to have a long-lasting impact on Christian ideas of the knowledge of God in the west. Western Christian theology was largely suspicious of the so-called "Palamite heresy"[52] and maintained the unknowability of God: it could not accept the idea of immediate participation and communion with the transcendent God. The western Christian existentialists are heirs of this approach. Thus, G. Griffith observes that for Kierkegaard "there was never any immediacy of contact with the Absolute through the senses, even for the first disciples."[53] Barth takes this so-called "flight from experience" [of God] to its

---

[52]See K. Ware, "The Debate about Palamism," ECR 9:1–2 (1977) 45f.
[53]G. Griffith, *Interpreters of Man: A Review of Secular and Religious Thought from Hegel to Barth* (London, 1943) 38.

extremes, so much so that the *experience* becomes "almost theologically illegitimate"[54] and the *proprium* of theology.

There are western Christian theologians who oppose the Barthian idea of Christ's revelation as the *only* mediation of the knowledge of God, and assert the possibility of encounter and conversing with God, but even these hesitate to go beyond the idea of "a *mediated* immediacy." God does confront and *converse* with us *now* but through the mediation of recorded biblical history. Behind this "mediated immediacy" lies Kierkegaard's doctrine of the "existential moment": that man can have a "valid" existential response to some divine action in the past, recorded in the Bible.[55] This line of theological epistemology has been recently subjected to criticism, and the criticism is shared by Fr Sophrony. He would agree that the denial of existential immediate communion with God reduces "the possibility of theology to its impossibility," thereby establishing intellectualism as the controlling feature in human knowledge of God. As for the "real" knowledge of God, it becomes problematic for Barth. God becomes no more than "an event in vocabulary," so much so that K. Bockmuehl suspects in the Barthian theological framework a fraud: a potential for a hidden atheism in theology.[56]

While being an advocate of the Barthian principle of theology "from above," Fr Sophrony follows Silouan in stressing that the true knowledge of God involves, along with faith, an existential, or living, *encounter, communion, and participation* in God.[57] His idea of knowledge of God incorporates both the revelation of scripture and the living mystical experience of divine reality, both in patristic tradition and in one's personal life.[58] Thus, for example, man knows of the Holy Spirit not only from scripture, but from his personal existential *experience* of communion with him, so much so that Silouan speaks even of empirical effects of this communion: the Spirit gives "sweetness to the heart," he fills even the body.[59] We have seen that to support the possibility of this "empirical" dimension of his theology Fr Sophrony refers to 1 John 1:1.

Why does Fr Sophrony consider the personal, immediate experience of God to be an indispensable part of his epistemology? We believe that this

[54]K. Bockmuehl, *The Unreal God of Modern Theology: Bultmann, Barth and the Theology of Atheism: A Call to Rediscovering the Truth of God's Reality* (Colorado Springs, 1988) 110, 112; cf Griffith, 221.

[55]Cf S. Kierkegaard., *Der Augenblick* (1855), 138.

[56]Bockmuehl, 117.

[57]See Stylianopoulos, 40–41.

[58]*We Shall See Him as He Is*, 80, 122.

[59]Ibid., 66, 89, 172; *St Silouan the Athonite*, 120, 320.

epistemological stance is determined by Fr Sophrony's strong patristic roots, which guide him in expressing his own experience of encounter with God. The immediacy of encounter is determined by the "immediate mediation" of the uncreated energies, through which man participates in God in his fulness. These strong Palamite roots also determine Fr Sophrony's use of the terms *microtheos* and *commensurability* between God and man, shared with Berdyaev. Berdyaev arrives at the conclusion that man is microtheos as a result of philosophical consideration: he traces the dead ends of various philosophical currents and leaves the door open mainly to subjective supralogic and to extreme anthropocentrism.[60] Berdyaev's point of departure for "microtheosity" and "commensurability" is the fact of man's freedom, which finds its ultimate expression in man's capacity for creativity, whereas for Fr Sophrony microtheos means that man participates fully in God through the uncreated energies and inherits the fulness of the divine mode of being. Fr Sophrony believes that this idea of existential participation in God is the basic principle of patristic theology, to which we now turn.

Fr Sophrony and Theologia in the Fathers

Multiple similarities between Fr Sophrony and patristic tradition justify our proposition that Fr Sophrony's "existentialism" has its source in the fathers.

As D. Emmet and K. Scouteris demonstrate, in Greek philosophy and early Christianity we may speak, if not of existentialism, then at least of the *existential dimension* of dogmatic teaching.[61] Thus, Emmet claims "the catchphrase of the Marxists, 'the unity of theory and practice,' might have been taken by some of the founders of philosophical theology in Greek and early Christian times to express its condition as they saw it."[62] Thus, in one way or another, *theologia* in the fathers presupposes the experience of God. For example, speaking of the Cappadocian fathers, A. Louth summarizes: "*theologia* ... means not just the *doctrine* of the Trinity, but *contemplation* of the Trinity."[63] P. Hadot and F. Kattenbusch admirably demonstrate that the existential dimension of Christian gnoseology continues the tradition of Greek philosophy, namely its stress on the ascetic side.[64]

---

[60]See Berdyaev's arguments in *The Beginning and the End*, 3–88.
[61]D. Emmet, "Theoria and the Way of Life," JTS 17 (1966) 38–52.
[62]Ibid., 38.
[63]Louth, *Discerning the Mystery*, 3–4.
[64]P. Hadot, *Exercices spirituels et philosophie antique* (Paris, 1987) 59–74; F. Kattenbusch, *Die*

One of the first to work out the idea of Christian knowledge in detail was Clement of Alexandria, whose thought has echoes in Fr Sophrony. Thus Clement, like Fr Sophrony, makes use of 1 Corinthians 13:12, "face to face," which highlights a personal dimension in knowledge.[65] For him, theology is rooted in contemplation, and therefore requires ascetic preparation. Moral and intellectual purification are needed if man is to attain to the likeness of God. Clement anticipates Fr Sophrony in relating knowledge to *love*, by which one assimilates the object of *gnosis* and comes to a "perfect knowledge."[66]

St Clement's ideas are taken up by later writers. Thus, Augustine emphasizes the experiential dimension in the knowledge of God. Emmet notes that in Cappadocian thought the idea of knowledge implies the demand for ascetic training in *arete* (virtue), moral excellence, rather than for rigorous thinking on a high level of abstraction. The notion of *teleiosis* (perfection) has the connotation of a process leading toward integral wholeness rather than just moral impeccability: within such a context *theoria* evolves as a kind of contemplation with an existential involvement, knowledge which is union with God.[67]

For the Cappadocians the process of Christian education (*paideia*) involves "existential" *metamorphosis*—which they express in terms of becoming *God-like*. Training in *theologia* involved asceticism in order to attain the state of *apatheia* (dispassion) and union with God—the fundamental requirements for theologizing.[68] For example, Diadochus of Photice writes:"nothing is poorer than a mind that philosophizes about the things of God while outside God."[69] The theologian, for him, is a person who is able to penetrate into the open spaces of *apatheia*.[70] No wonder that, as an experimental tradition, *theoria* had its first laboratory among the solitaries in the Egyptian desert and their cenobitic communities. This concern for the existential involvement in *gnosis* determines the style and principles of theology: in the Greeks, as well as in the fathers, *theologia* was associated not so much with an academic discipline as with "talking about divine things." Thus, a theologian is more a (prayerful)

Entstehung einer christlichen Theologie zur Geschichte der Ausdrücke theologia, theologein, theologos (Darmstadt, 1962).

[65] Cf *Strom.* 6.12.102, 483.

[66] *Strom.* 2.6.31, 129; 2.9.45, 136; on love as perfect knowledge, see *Strom.* 6.9.78, 470.

[67] Emmet, "Theoria and the Way of Life," 42.

[68] Gregory of Nazianzus, *Or.* 28.1, 100; *Or.* 2.39, 140; *Or.* 27.3.1–13, 76.

[69] *Chapt.* 7, 87; cf Symeon the New Theologian, *Hymn.* 21.161–78, 142–44.

[70] *Chapt.* 72, 131.

poet than a professor.[71] Within such a perspective knowledge of God is a naturally personal, inner matter.

As we saw in chapter one, Fr Sophrony was well versed in patristic literature and lived within the tradition of Orthodoxy, which makes the similarities between the fathers and Fr Sophrony quite understandable. It is the patristic tradition, and not Berdyaev's influence, that determines Fr Sophrony's insistence on existential personal involvement in the field of theology, the "descriptive" character of his theology, and his theological style.

This latter point is reinforced if we examine two further aspects. First, Fr Sophrony makes an explicit appeal to the eastern tradition when he refers to methods of theologizing found in scripture and in the fathers. Second, Berdyaev and Fr Sophrony differ concerning the extent to which human nature is distorted by the fall: Berdyaev optimistically rejects the significance of the fallen state and, thereby, the need for asceticism as a means to reach *apatheia*.

THE APPEAL TO SCRIPTURE. Fr Sophrony points to the authority of scripture (and not of philosophical existentialism) for saying that knowledge of God is achieved through the agency of divine revelation "from above." First, Fr Sophrony points out that in Matthew 16:17, by the testimony of Christ himself, Peter's crucial confession of Christ's divinity was brought about by divine action and not by Peter's human efforts or intellectual search. The source of knowledge was "not flesh and blood but my Father who is in heaven." *Flesh and blood* is a hebraism that generalizes the idea of humanity as opposed to the order of "heaven." Second, in Galatians 1:11-12 the apostle Paul claims for his message divine origins and not his own intellectual resources: his gospel is "not according to man," "it came *through revelation*." In this passage once again human reality and resources are contrasted with those of divine reality. The same source is claimed by apostle Paul in 1 Corinthains 2:10: The message was "revealed by the Holy Spirit." Third, Fr Sophrony appeals to John 16:23—"In that day you will ask nothing of me"—to support his opinion that at the moment of divine revelation and *living* communion with God, any sort of intellectual quest or inquiry is out of place. The passage confirms that the reasoning faculty of man is not the only (or even main) recipient of the message: "all discursive thinking subsides as soon as man has an immediate vision of God (Jn 16:23)."[72]

---

[71]Emmet, "Theoria and the Way of Life," 45; cf Kattenbusch, 44.
[72]*La félicité de connaître la voie*, 24-26.

THE APPEAL TO PATRISTIC METHODS OF THEOLOGIZING. First, Fr Sophrony defines the style of patristic writings. The mode of their theologizing is marked not by logical consistency, but by "wholeness of vision." Thus, admitting the lack of literary coherence in his *Letters to Russia*, he justifies himself by appealing to the style of the fathers: "Even in the works of the great fathers there is no 'scholastic system,' if 'system' means a certain 'order' of exposition or presentation of material, and not an inner profound 'wholeness of vision.' "[73]

Second, Fr Sophrony points out that in the patristic dogmatic formulas there is always a paradoxical statement, which makes them incomprehensible for human reason per se. He notes:

> Dogmas are syntheses of the faith; they are expressed by extremely dense and concise formulas that have a quite unique character: their core contains a fundamental paradox, the joining of two seemingly incompatible affirmations or negations that present themselves to "pure reason" as a contradiction bordering on the absurd.[74]

Fr Sophrony discusses the paradoxes inherent in the two basic church dogmas: the trinitarian dogma and the christological formula of Chalcedon. Both of them contain *antinomy*. These dogmas allowed Fr Sophrony to work out the method of theologizing that lies behind them. The human intellect is not the main source of the theological method in the fathers; it is, rather, only a receptacle: "Far from being the fruit of intellectual research or the result of theological thought, dogma is essentially the verbal expression of 'evidence.' A true understanding of the dogmas of the church is only possible if we cease to apply the way of thinking that belongs to human reason." It is because of this nature of church dogmas that Fr Sophrony asserts that the main source of dogmatic theology is "from above": "When the spirit of man, through faith (cf Heb 11:1), thanks to inspiration from on high, is confronted by evidence of the *Supreme Fact*, then such surpassing of limits is natural to it; it is precisely an experience of this kind that is at the foundation of dogmatic synthesis." Thus, at the root of the dogmas there is a revelation, prior to their intellectual assimilation. They are a verbal expression, or rather description, of evidence of the divine reality: "Dogma places us before the *fact* of divine being without giving us rational explanations."[75]

[73]*Letters to Russia*, 54.
[74]*La félicité de connaître la voie*, 27.
[75]Ibid., 24.

Apophatic negatives "fence" a permissible domain for human logical analysis. For Fr Sophrony, the negatives of the trinitarian and christological dogmas confine our reason as if in a vice, "which does not let it turn to either side. In such a manner, we are called to surpass formal logic and to live God in the reality of [his] being, as it is revealed to us."[76] The function of dogmas is precisely to limit the supremacy of the intellect in theological thinking and to shift theology from the intellectual to the living, that is, ontological, level.

> The church, insofar as it is the guardian of the fulness of the revelation, by its dogmas forbids the surpassing of certain limits. It encloses human intelligence as in a vice from which it is not easy to break free. In order to do this, it must cease to move on the level of thought, and ascend vertically, into another sphere.[77]

BERDYAEV AND THE FALL. Berdyaev accepts the fact of man's fallen state with a certain reservation. It would be only a slight exaggeration to assert that for Berdyaev almost every man, as *persona-microtheos*, can "claim his right" for theologizing. Thus he rejects the idea that the fall could have drastically limited capacity for concepts about God.

For Fr Sophrony, the fact of the distortion of human nature in the fall serves as an obstacle to the human ability to theologize. Fr Sophrony's anthropological perspective is largely based on scriptural passages, where the element of "not yet" in the process of human development is emphasized. In passages such as John 16:12; 1 John 3:2, and 1 Corinthians 13:12, the future tense is used when the fullest communion with God is mentioned. If we make a distinction between the stage of *eschatological* realization and his *present* stage, we may even say that man in his present stage of actualization is a distorted and incomplete image of God. Though anthropological models proceed from theological ones and are very closely related to them, they should not determine a vice-versa "modeling." God is not to be conceived in the categories of the humanity-model because in fallen man God's image is not faithfully reflected:

> It must always be remembered, when thinking of God, that we should not fall into the error of anthropomorphism. Though man is created

---

[76] *Birth into the Kingdom*, 28.
[77] *La félicité de connaître la voie*, 25.

in the image of God, he overturns the hierarchy of existence as soon
as he begins to apply to God his own gifts of knowledge, and thus to
"create" God in his own image and likeness.[78]

THE NEED FOR ASCETICISM. Berdyaev's disregard for the distortion of human
nature leads him to underestimate the need for ascetic preparation for theologizing. Indeed, Berdyaev is highly critical of traditional ascetic practice (especially of its negative side understood as "abstinence from").[79] In contrast to
Berdyaev, Fr Sophrony believes that in order to cross over into the *living*
dimension of thinking, one must pass through ascetic discipline. For him,
monastic ascetic practices are designed to lead to living communion with
God. For example, to prepare one's mind for the comprehension of the dogmas of the church, one has to purify it, so as not to cloud the perception of
the divine reality with elements of human imagination:

> We need ascetic purification of our mind in order that our dogmatic
> teaching of the church about God, based on the revelation about the
> mode of divine being, should not be distorted by the elements of imag-
> ination coming from below. No human guess or postulate has a place
> in the dogma about the Holy Trinity.[80]

Speaking of the ascetic purification of one's mind, Fr Sophrony presupposes divesting the mind of all thoughts and imaginations (i.e., stillness of the
mind). Pure prayer is the safe way to cognition of God. The praying person
divests himself of all his external knowledge and of all the images that possess
him: "After experience of 'hypostatic' prayer we abandon the categories of
formal logic and move to those of existence itself. Truth is not the product
of human philosophy. Truth is HE WHO IS verily before all ages."[81]

Fr Sophrony asserts that in order to contemplate divine reality, one has to
abide in a state at least close to, if not the same as, that of the contemplated
reality. The approach to that condition is linked with "purification" from all
elements that are alien to divine reality. This process of conforming is expressed particularly in prayer of repentance. He writes that through our introduction into the very act of divine being our spirit receives living knowledge

[78]Ibid., 19.
[79]See Berdyaev, *Spirit and Reality*, tr. George Reavey (London, 1939) 79ff.
[80]*Birth into the Kingdom*, 29.
[81]*We Shall See Him as He Is*, 216.

of God. He continues: "The surest means to this good end is prayer of repentance as granted to us through faith in Christ."[82]

Thus, the context of the ascetic "preparation" of the theologian is an important idea within the framework of Fr Sophrony's theological system. Ascetic practice means a living, practical effort to conform to the divine reality. Thus we may define ascetic practice as a living preparation for receiving the divine knowledge, which has theology as its goal and purpose.

Difficulties

Reintroducing eastern patristic methods of theologizing in the twentieth century is a risky enterprise: can it withstand the critical evaluation of modern theology? To answer this question we will concentrate on the main points where Fr Sophrony's thought appears to be most vulnerable.

Historical Idealism?

Fr Sophrony seems to have a rather idealistic, "iconographically transfigured" conception of historical reality concerning the origins of church dogmas. If their origin is "from above," the dogmas ought to be given to a divinely inspired people who have achieved a high level of contemplation. He does not really account for the fact that each ecclesiastical dogma has a long history of controversial development. For example, the trinitarian dogma, as various scholars observe, was made up of a number of separate propositions, each of which, when given preference, leading to the exclusion of the rest, is a heresy.

The actual history of church doctrine shows that sometimes important theological formulas were coined in conditions that were not determined merely by theological and divinely inspired consensus within the church. Thus, concerning the first ecumenical council, Alexander Schmemann notes that "Emperor and empire were becoming providential instruments for the Kingdom." Thus, though "Constantine himself could not, of course, understand the essence of the theological dispute"(!), it was through him that the term *homoousios* (consubstantial) was "thrust upon" the council.[83] This story of the origin of the term does not fit Fr Sophrony's model of the divinely

---

[82]Ibid., 41.
[83]Schmemann, *The Historical Road of Eastern Orthodoxy* (London, 1963) 76, 78.

inspired council—he praises in one of his homilies the divinely inspired Athanasius as the author and person through whom the term was introduced.

The struggle between the Alexandrians and Antiochians at the fourth ecumenical council proves to be even more embarrassing for Fr Sophrony's theological scheme. Thus, the Chalcedonian definition is "an agreement to disagree" (Jaroslav Pelikan), an "external compromise, a mechanical joining of two conceptions which are incompatible and mutually conflicting" (Bulgakov). Bulgakov does take into account this lack of inspirational consensus among the fathers in general and among the delegates of the fourth ecumenical council in particular. He admits that "[the Chalcedonian dogma] was forcibly imposed on the council from outside." But it is precisely in this course of events that he discerns the hand of God working to reveal theological dogmas. Bulgakov's conclusion is that "The Spirit (the supreme Author of the Church teaching) blows wherever it wills"—even through historical and political events and not only through divinely inspired persons.

However, Fr Sophrony's idealism can partly be justified. On the whole, within the historical events, which Fr Sophrony passes over in silence, the original formulations came indeed from those who possessed living knowledge of God in the majority of cases. The most influential "dogmatic" writers are usually canonized saints: in their life they achieved a high level of divine contemplation. For example, it cannot be denied that the trinitarian dogma received its most articulate and perfected expression in the teaching of the Cappadocian fathers. It is on examples such as the Cappadocians that Fr Sophrony relies in his presentation of the church method of theology.

Irrationality?

Many scholars would agree with Kierkegaard and Barth about the inadequacy of reason in establishing belief: "Any claim of being able to offer a reasonable account of Christian belief ought in any case always to be received with sceptical suspicion." But it may appear that Fr Sophrony excludes reason from theological process to an even further degree. He states the "givenness" of the divine dogmas and seems to have no "theological" space to account for the "intellectual" rational struggle at the ecumenical councils. In reality it was, partly at least, *rationality* that determined the strength or weakness of any particular argument. Thus, for example the deductive method was used to derive the dogma of the two wills in Christ from the doctrine of the two natures.

However, Fr Sophrony is far from refusing the value of reason in a Hume-like manner. He counts theological awareness as an integral element of Christian experience:

> Those in whom the tendency to know God intellectually (through theological science) prevails do not receive the living experience of eternity. Neither do those satisfied with prayer alone reach perfection, though at the time they are more intensely close to God than the first ones . . . Neither theology without prayer of repentance, nor prayer, even fervent prayer, but without reasonable theological vision, are perfection. Only knowledge that includes both of the above-mentioned aspects in one whole life approaches fulness.[84]

Furthermore, Fr Sophrony does not exclude all theological intellectual reflection from within the scope defined by dogma: "Provided that our mind accepts the limits appointed in theological thinking, then human speculations are admissible." One example of such a type of theological intellectual reflection is the trinitarian analogies worked out by the fathers: they discovered the reflection of triunity in the created order of being on different levels.

Also, Fr Sophrony admits that in the course of the spiritual history of the Old Testament it was *natural theology* and *human rationality* (i.e., from below) that recognized the incomplete character of the divine revelation that had been so far granted. Though the revelation "I AM THAT I AM" was a turning point in Israelite history, yet Moses "of his own resources" was aware of the incompleteness of this revelation and therefore predicted the coming of the other great prophet, who would complete it.[85]

Thus, for Fr Sophrony reason is not opposed to revelation but requires it to complete our knowledge of a rational but personal God in whom we are led by reason to believe.

Mystical Experience—a Basis for Epistemology?

Fr Sophrony claims that the experience of God transcends all categories of human rational analysis. He refers to Silouan's idea that when the Holy Spirit testifies to the soul about eternal salvation, there is no need for any other

[84]*Birth into the Kingdom*, 27.
[85]*Letters to Russia*, 32; cf *His Life Is Mine*, 18–19.

witness[86]—"He who believes in the Son of God has the testimony in himself (1 Jn 5:10)." In another passage Fr Sophrony refers to the theological language of Silouan, which demonstrates with undoubted assurance his authenticity: "*Such* light, *such* love, *such* life-giving force of Life and Wisdom can proceed only from the true source of all that exists . . . perception of divine eternity is so keen that no logic or psychoanalysis can shake the obvious."[87]

If "existential" knowledge of God is subjective, unverifiable, and beyond rationality, what *objective* criterion of authenticity can be claimed for it? It lacks the criteria of authenticity that are accepted in empirical/scientific knowledge: these are precisely *objectivity* and *verification*, and hence the reliability of such knowledge. How can we claim objectivity for divine reality if it is perceived on the personal level, through personal living communion?

On this basis many have come to deny the objectivity of and hence the authenticity of knowledge built on personal experience. They are critical of the so-called "convincingness of unreasoned experience," whereby people commonly take their (private) revelation as authoritative without any critical evaluation of this experience. They assert an "almost total absence of independent testability of the statements about the divine." Some go as far as to assert that on the grounds of the irreconcilable diversity of religious experience it is impossible to claim to be in contact with one of God's ultimate faces. Thus we ought to reject mystical experience as a basis for knowledge altogether. Psychology undermines even further the claims of religious existential statements. They are reduced to a psychological phenomenon, such as, for example, "objectification of human nature" by man's consciousness (Feuerbach), or "projection of the parental complex, i.e., of the father figure" (Freud). This line of argument leads to a denial of the existence of God altogether.

From the late 1950s western thought has found it more and more difficult to maintain this "atheistic" line of argument, which is linked with the revival of Hume's agnostic argument: "the truth or falsity of statements which 'go beyond experience' can never be determined." In response to the criticism of subjectivity in religious knowledge, others highlight the weakness of the criteria of objectivity when applied to religious experience: even though a phenomenon cannot be tested or checked through procedures, it does not mean that it does not have an objective existence. Therefore there is *nothing contrary*

---

[86] *St Silouan the Athonite*, 225; cf *His Life Is Mine*, 23.
[87] *We Shall See Him as He Is*, 179.

to reason in taking faith as a basis of rationality. After all, it may be asked, is truth necessarily fully *rational*?

A further step out of the agnostic deadlock was offered by R. Swinburne's theories of *credulity* and *probability*—these *logically* allow us to justify trust in mystical experiences: "apparent perceptions ought to be taken at their face value in the absence of positive reason for challenge."[88] Swinburne's argument furthers the developments in epistemology that go under the title of *internalism*. The main argument of this trend of thought is that man can be internally justified in his belief to be objective.

How and where does Fr Sophrony fit into these intellectual polemics? In a Barthian way, he does not engage in polemics with positivists about "authenticity" on their own *rational* ground—the experiences are beyond rationality. Nonetheless, he does claim the *objectivity* of the divine reality on a *subjective* basis. He writes: "I am aware that my knowledge is not absolute but that does not mean that there is some other truth. I believe that I came in contact with Truth unoriginate ... But where is the criterion that would confirm our trust in what is granted to us of God Who is Truth?"[89]

In his writings we may find the answer to his own question. In *His Life is Mine*, Fr Sophrony employs an argument similar to the principle of verification of scientific knowledge. He writes that though the vision of God is personal, "yet the knowledge it offers has an objective *sui generis* character which we repeatedly observe down the centuries in the lives of many individuals largely identical in their experience and self-determining."[90] For example, he claims that his experience confirms the data of the revelation of the New Testament (1 Jn 1:5, 4:13,16): "God manifests himself to us as *God of love* and we live him within us as an absolute harmony."[91]

The same experience is repeated in the lives of the saints. A particular experience of God is not revelatory as an isolated occurrence but as part of a pattern, a revelatory *Gestalt*. It is not just personal experience that constitutes the basis of theology for Fr Sophrony, but an organic synthesis of scripture, patristic tradition—which incorporates the common experience of the saints—and personal experience.

The weakness of this argument has already been highlighted by the critics who appeal to the diversity of religious experience not only between world

[88]R. Swinburne, *The Existence of God* (Oxford, 1979) 275.
[89]*We Shall See Him as He Is*, 226.
[90]*His Life Is Mine*, 45.
[91]*We Shall See Him as He Is*, 227; cf ibid., 234.

religions but even within one particular framework of beliefs. The pluralism of experience is a stronghold of those who object to reliability of spiritual knowledge. Thus, in their analysis of "private illuminations" they highlight the dilemma caused by the divergent descriptions of God in various religions, which undermines the objectivity of any particular personal experience of God: "How could . . . the presence [of such an omnipotent personal God] be made accessible to man except by means of a powerful numinous experience which most men are only capable of receiving through the myths and images of their particular belief?"[92]

Fr Sophrony does not settle for a syncretist attempt to justify the diversity of experience of God in Christianity and non-Christian religions. He had a living mystical experience of both the major religions with their own "myths and images"—Christianity and the non-Christian east. Yet he speaks of his experiences in non-Christian mysticism in terms of *aberration* and *sin* against "God of love." It is only within Christianity that he claims to have been touched by the eternal truth.

Fr Sophrony further argues that, though personal, the experiences of divine reality are not the product of one's own imagination, pathology, or psychology (*pace* Feuerbach and Freud). He argues for the transcendental origins of these phenomena, which testify that they come from a source *other* than self, on the basis that they *surpass* our self: "It is not the product of our imagination, since this event of encounter with God *surpasses* our capacities of imagination (cf 1 Cor 2:9)." This partly answers the Freudian argument that God is "the projected father figure," which does not surpass our imagination, but in fact derives from it.

Fr Sophrony's further claim for objectivity is based on the fact that man is created in God's *image and likeness*: there is a certain affinity and kinship between God and man. Thus, man is capable of discerning the One who is akin to him. Fr Sophrony states that there is an element of *recognition*: "when Almighty God enters into communion with his spirit man can 'recognise' Him, since He is kin to him."[93]

The problem is that Fr Sophrony's kind of theological assertion will always have an unprovable character when considered objectively, "from outside." Fr Sophrony meets this objection simply by maintaining his certainty and by

---

[92] J. Gaskin, *The Quest for Eternity: An Outline of the Philosophy of Religion* (New York, 1984) 103.

[93] *We Shall See Him as He Is*, 226.

inviting his critics to "experience" this or that statement through their own existential involvement, especially through prayer. Thus, concerning the truth of the gospel, Fr Sophrony argues thus: "Those people who no longer read the gospel may say when they hear [what I say]: 'Let me try as well. Here [this] man decided and tried and look what has been given to him!'"[94] Appeal to a personal existential involvement proves to be a stronghold of Fr Sophrony's position. He refuses to tackle the issue outside the domain of personal experience.

We have seen that there *are* theological principles in the theology of Fr Sophrony, which determine his style and the scope of his ideas. These principles prove to be vulnerable to criticism if one applies the criteria of objectivist epistemology, yet they emerge with a stronger rational basis if one accepts Fr Sophrony's premises: that the knowledge of the divine reality can only be *given* as a gift from above; that it surpasses the limits of human rationality; and that reality is not to be equated with what rationality can demonstrate.

This makes it possible to define Fr Sophrony's style of theologizing as "neo-patristic." His revival of the patristic method comes as an adequate response to the quest for solid principles in contemporary theology, after the failure of the application of logical positivism to theology, on the one hand, and the dead end (i.e., hidden atheism) of the theology of the "flight from experience" on the other.

Once Fr Sophrony's principles are understood, we should abandon the task of demonstrating any systematic, logical, or rational "invulnerability" in his theology and limit ourselves to discovering the underlying theological "vision" (*theoria*) behind his "biographical" writings. The determinative concept of this vision is that of *persona*, to which we turn in our next chapter.

---

[94] *Letters to Russia*, 38.

CHAPTER THREE

The Person – Divine and Human

"What does it mean to be a person?"—this question lies at the heart of Fr Sophrony's theology. It comes to the forefront of his theological attention particularly in his later years—so much so, that the notion of *person* became the axis of his last book, *We Shall See Him as He Is*.

The centrality of the theme in Fr Sophrony is partly determined by the amount of attention the topic had recently been given by modern thinkers, not least by Russian theologians and philosophers. The Russian philosophy of personhood culminates in Berdyaev's thought. In the theological milieu it was largely Florensky, Bulgakov, and Lossky who brought the theme to the forefront of debate. Their trinitarian perspective of personhood contributed significantly to a revival of interest in trinitarian theology both in the east and in the west. In the preceding years, as Kallistos Ware rightly observes (along with K. Rahner), the relevance of trinitarian teaching in Christian theology was largely overlooked.[1]

A significant reestimation of the issue of personal identity in theology is also due to the impact of research in psychology. Freud and Jung enhanced the interest in the inner processes of self-awareness.

Fr Sophrony's personal experience allowed him to build up his own understanding of the concept. In this chapter we do not aim at presenting an exhaustive exposition of Fr Sophrony's approach to person. Rather we attempt to highlight those aspects of the theme that are not enlarged upon in his books. Our analysis is also aimed at mapping the way for our subsequent chapters, which will cover further aspects of the theme of the hypostatic commensurability between God and man.

---

[1]K. Ware, "The Human Person as an Icon of the Trinity," *Sobornost* 8:2 (1986) 6-23.

Defining the Persona

One cannot easily discover a clear definition within the eastern patristic tradition of hypostasis that would serve as a determinative background for Fr
Sophrony's understanding of the concept of a person. Indeed, there is no
clearly definable consensus among the fathers. As Ware observes: "There is in
the Greek Fathers no single, systematic theory of personhood, or even agreed
terminology, but only a series of overlapping approaches." Neither the dogmatic legacy of the ecumenical councils nor the Palamite councils and synods
offer any sufficiently full definition of hypostasis.[2] Concerning the church
teaching on the constitution of man, John Meyendorff observes: "There is no
dogma in physiology."[3]

In Fr Sophrony also, though the hypostatic principle determines his theology to the largest extent, there is, nevertheless, no full description of the
hypostatic principle and its meaning, not even in the chapter dedicated to that
theme. However, we may usefully examine some of Fr Sophrony's allusions to
his understanding of *person*. He uses the Latin term *persona* as the equivalent
and synonym of the Greek patristic term *hypostasis*. In his writings he seems
to overlook the difference between the Greek term *hypostasis* and the Latin
persona, which is based on an important difference between *objective* and *subjective* overtones.

He admits how vast is the scope of interpretation of the term hypostasis,
even in scripture: "[it] conveys actuality . . . In many instances it was used as
synonym for *essence* . . . In the Second Epistle to the Corinthians (2 Cor 11:17)
hypostasis denotes sober reality and is translated into English as *confidence* or
assurance." It also denotes the person of the Father (Heb 1:3), substance (Heb
2:1) and very being (Heb 1:3). All these various aspects stress, as Fr Sophrony
observes "the cardinal importance of the personal dimension in being."[4]

Besides scripture, Fr Sophrony's approach also reflects his traditional heritage. In tradition hypostasis emerges out of the distinction between *two different aspects of being* (the general and the particular): these were expressed in
Aristotelian terms as *prote ousia* (prime substance) and *deutera ousia* (secondary
substance). In the Cappadocians, who articulated the distinction between

---

[2]K. Ware, "The Unity of the Human Person according to the Greek Fathers," in *Person and
Personality*, eds. A. Peacocke and G. Gillett, 199 (Oxford, 1987).
[3]J. Meyendorff, *St Gregory Palamas and Orthodox Spirituality* (New York, 1974) 148.
[4]*His Life Is Mine*, 23.

hypostasis and *essence* in the Godhead, hypostasis corresponds to *prote ousia*. Fr Sophrony expresses the classical patristic "dualism" in his own vocabulary: "The hypostasis is a 'pole,' a 'moment' of the One and Simple Being, where essence is another 'moment.'"[5] However, this dualism is enriched and qualified by the Palamite conception of the divine being, which elaborates a clear distinction between *hypostasis, essence,* and *energies.* Fr Sophrony, however, prefers to focus on personeity in the Godhead and asserts the hypostatic principle as the basis of divine being:

> The principle of the Persona in God is not an abstract conception but essential reality possessing its own Nature and Energy of life. The Essence is not of primary or even pre-eminent importance in defining the Persons-Hypostases in their reciprocal relations. Divine Being contains nothing that could be extraneous to the hypostatic principle.[6]

Thus, in the Trinity, hypostasis subsumes other aspects of being under its principle: it determines divine being. The revelation I AM THAT I AM (I am Being) shows that the hypostatic dimension in the Godhead has a *prime significance.* John Zizioulas continues Fr Sophrony's argument on the basis of cosmological considerations. He rightly observes that creation was brought into being *ex nihilo* by *someone*—a particular (personal) being—*O on.* The biblical revelation does not focus on divine essence, placing primary stress on personeity in God, while in other cosmogonies, be they "Phoenician" (where cosmogony is identical with theogony) or "Greek" (with its dualism of *Demiourgos-hyle,* Creator-matter), "the particular [personal] is never the ontologically primary cause of being."[7] Hence, Fr Sophrony defines *persona* as "the one, who really lives." It is a pivot, an axis of all being: outside this living principle there can be nothing.

Fr Sophrony, having established the prime significance of persona in being, does not proceed to further definitions. As the principle, determinative to all other aspects of being, persona is not subject to any determination nor, hence, to any other definition. Even the human persona escapes definition, and remains "hidden": "In man, the image of the hypostatic God, the principle of

---

[5]*La félicité de connaître la voie,* 28.

[6]*We Shall See Him as He Is,* 193.

[7]J. Zizioulas, "On Being a Person: Towards an Ontology of Personhood," in *Persons, Divine and Human,* eds. C. Gunton and C. Schwöbel, 38 (Edinburgh, 1991).

persona is the very 'hidden man of the heart' (1 Pet 3:4) . . . It is also beyond definition." Neither is it subject to any rational explanation: "Scientific and philosophical cognition can be expressed in concepts and definitions: but person is being, not subject to philosophical or scientific forms of cognition. Like God, the *persona*-hypostasis cannot be throughly known from outside unless he reveals himself to another person."[8]

Fr Sophrony therefore abandons any attempt to give a direct definition of the concept. His form of expression, being controlled by practical ascetic concerns, does not demand such a direct definition. It is more important for his ascetic theology to establish *how* persona exists. Thus he is more concerned with descriptions of its attributes. We may call such approach "dynamic definition": persona can be, if not defined, at least characterized, dynamically and existentially, in its *active manifestation*. Thus persona in man is "manifested in his capacity for self-knowledge and self-determination; in his possession of creative energy; in his talent for cognition not only of the created world but also of the divine world."[9] Also persona manifests itself *in interrelation*: when it reveals itself to another persona. On this point, however, it is important not to lose the distinction between persona itself and its relational manifestations— a distinction that, according to Lossky, is partly erased in the Thomistic theological framework.

Persona as Revealed in God

Persona and the Divine Absolute

Fr Sophrony often repeats that within the Semitic-Christian theological framework the absolute is a *personal* being. If God is personal, then personal is an absolute transcendent category. As such persona-hypostasis in divine being cannot be a limiting principle. In the Christian perspective, as Fr Sophrony sees it, "*Persona-hypostasis* is the inmost principle of Absolute Being—its first and last dimension. 'I am Alpha and Omega, the beginning and the ending, saith the Lord, which is, and which was, and which is to come, the Almighty' (Rev 1:8)."[10]

---

[8] *We Shall See Him as He Is*, 192.
[9] *His Life Is Mine*, 44.
[10] *We Shall See Him as He Is*, 190, 192.

Our rational thinking conceives the divine absolute as transcending all limitation, all causality and other determinative elements. If so, can the divine absolute be hypostatic? If hypostasis-persona signifies something *particular* by singling out one subject from others, does it not introduce limitation, incompatible with the notion of absolute? One would indeed be introducing such limitation if one did not distinguish between the concepts of *individuum* and *persona* on the human level; one would risk projecting the human individuum onto the divine being. Such an "individualistic" perception of human personhood is due to the great influence of thinkers like Leibniz. In *Monadology* he emphasizes the idea of *isolation*, or "individuation," in the relation of persona to the whole universe, so much so that his framework is labeled as *ontological individualism*. Such personae-individuums, as "the true atoms of the nature," can be defined as the "self-oriented ego," *limited* to self, and, as K. Ware summarizes, each one is "shut off from others, self-centered, isolated, a unit recorded in a census." In Christian theology persona is closer to *prosopon*, face: while retaining this element of "atomic ego" as a basis of being, it is "outward looking, in relationship, involved with others. Where *atomon* signifies separation, *prosopon* signifies communion."[11] There are no bounds to this communion: a person may embrace all that is, even the infinite God. Similarly, for Fr Sophrony, persona is not a self-enclosed principle. He writes: "The *persona*, by contrast [to the individual], is inconceivable without all-embracing love either in the divine being or in the human being."[12]

An "individualistic" interpretation of personhood marked Fr Sophrony's understanding before his return to Christianity, and explains his rejection of the Christian faith: the separation of *individuum* was seen as limitation, incompatible with the divine absolute. He recalls with regret: "The very word *persona* was identical in my understanding with the conception of individual. Would it not be absurd to apply this dimension to Absolute Being?"[13]

That is why Fr Sophrony, having in mind eastern non-Christian mystics, as well as Greek philosophy, writes that "it is characteristic of the former to think of the First-Absolute as trans-personal. For them personeity at its best is the initial stage of the degradation, the self-restriction of the Absolute. For the others [i.e., Christians] it is precisely the *Persona* that lies at the root of all that

---

[11]Ware, "The Human Person as an Icon of the Trinity," 17; cf K. Ware, "The Mystery of the Human Person," *Sobornost* 3:1 (1981) 64.

[12]*His Life Is Mine*, 40.

[13]*We Shall See Him as He Is*, 195.

exists (cf Jn 1:3)."[14] In the Christian absolute, the God of love, persona possesses the infinite capacity to take all that is into itself. Such a persona therefore transcends all limitations and is infinite and immeasurable in its dimension. As such, persona is an absolute category.

Persona and the Trinity

Fr Sophrony explores the traditional trinitarian teaching, for the concise summary of which he cites the "Pseudo-Athanasian creed." Behind his triadology one can also discern some elements of the Cappadocians' teaching. These fathers spoke of the unity of the divine hypostases through unity of will, essence, energy and action, which manifests itself in their mutual communion (*koinonia*).[15]

The trinitarian teaching contains various rational tensions, which in Eastern Orthodox theology came to be accepted as antinomies. At the basis of these antinomies are the following paradoxes.

SIMPLICITY AND COMPLEXITY. From the fact that divine being is absolutely simple, or single, while there are also various "moments" of divine being (hypostasis, essence, energies), Fr Sophrony concludes that persona and essence are identical as well as essence and energy. Yet their identity and singleness do not exclude their absolute difference. This difference is ensured by the dogma that asserts the irreducibility of hypostasis to essence by maintaining a definite multiple number of hypostases—three. Here is the first antinomy of the trinitarian model: the absolute identity alongside the absolute difference of essence and hypostasis. Fr Sophrony points out that in the Old Testament and Islam— theologies of henotheism with a monohypostatic God—this difference is absent, and hence their concept of divine persona is different. In henotheism there is always a danger of reducing the notion of persona to that of essence by virtue of their identity. The multiplicity of the hypostases in the Christian monotheistic divine model prevents this reduction, showing that essence and hypostasis are different "moments" of the divine being:

> In the henotheistic and monohypostatic perspective of Islam and even in the Old Testament, this identity of person and essence can perhaps

[14]Ibid., 191.
[15]For example, see Basil the Great, *Spir.* 8.45, 406; *Epist.* 38.4, 84-7.

be thought of as total, even indistinguishable. But in trinitarian monotheism this identity is presented as an extreme antinomy, for the principal of the persona by virtue of the triunity cannot be reduced to the essence.[16]

That is why Fr Sophrony insists that it is only in Christianity, where God is revealed in three personae (Mt 28:19), that we find the completion of the revelation about divine persona.

Since the personae in their threeness cannot be reduced to their essence it follows that their relationship is determined by their personeity and not by their essence. Their self-determination in eternity is the eternal fact. In divine being, which is utterly personal, self-determination of the divine hypostases derives from the hypostases themselves and is in no way predetermined or imposed by the essence. Hence the first implication: in its self-determination in relations, persona is *absolutely free*. No factor necessitates its determination: "Where there is no liberty, there is no *persona*; and vice versa—without *persona* there is no liberty. This kind of eternal being uniquely concerns the *persona*, in no way the individual (cf 1 Cor 15:47-50)."[17]

ONE AND THREE. The fact that the three hypostases constitute one single being of the Trinity determines the chief attribute of the hypostatic being: "each hypostasis is fully identical with the other two hypostases of the Holy Trinity." Threeness also ensures that these hypostases are unique and irreducible each to the other, maintaining their absolute difference. Hence we arrive at the other antinomy—"the absolute identity alongside the absolute difference" between the hypostases. Fr Sophrony refers to John 14:9 as scriptural confirmation of the absolute identity and equally absolute difference of the hypostases. From this antinomy the following characteristics of the hypostatic principle are deduced.

First, by asserting the equality (as opposed to subordination) and identity of the hypostases the dogma implies that each hypostasis dynamically carries in itself the *fulness* of the divine being and possesses it in absolute measure. Each is "dynamically" equal to Trinity. Thus persona carries other persona(e) within itself. Hence the person's being is *absolutely dynamic* in its interpersonal dimension.

---

[16]*La félicité de connaître la voie*, 28.
[17]*We Shall See Him as He Is,* 110; cf *His Life Is Mine*, 66.

Second, this antinomy ($1=3$) rules out any arithmetical category being applied to hypostasis: *it cannot be numbered*. It is not an *atomon*, a unit: hypostasis both belongs to and transcends this category. Why then do we speak of the "three" and not of any other number? Fr Sophrony answers that it is not only a "pure fact" revealed from above. The number "three" contains an element of *mystery*: it avoids the *self-enclosedness* of the number "one," and the *opposition* of the number "two" (where one is set against the other). By the coming of a "third," it transcends both these limitations and becomes equal to infinity.[18]

SOVEREIGNTY AND INTERDEPENDENCY. The oneness determines the way the persons relate to each other. As we have already noted, for Fr Sophrony, persona realizes itself only in relation to other personae. Thus there is another antinomy: while persona is the principle of being and is "self-sufficient" and sovereign, it *requires* the other persona in order to be such. This antinomy can be summarized as sovereignty-with-dependence. Here is yet another fundamental distinction in the understanding of persona in henotheistic theological systems and Christian monotheism. The tension of the antinomy of sovereignty-with-interdependency is resolved by the character of the relationship between the hypostases. Their relations are constituted by love: love accounts for both dependency (since love itself presupposes the dynamics of relations, exchange, and communion) and sovereignty (since self-determination in the subject who loves is free). That is how Fr Sophrony understands 1 John 4:8: "The fundamental content of this life is love … The personal being realizes himself through loving contact with another person or persons."[19] Thus, persona presupposes other personae in order to realize itself. Love emerges as the inmost content and best expression of persona's essence. This implication may be summarized in a quasi-Cartesian formula: *amo, ergo sum*. It is reflected on the interpersonal level in the Trinity in the following way:

> Love transfers the existence of the person who loves into the beloved, and thus it assimilates the life of the loved one. So the person is permeated with love. The absolute perfection of love in the bosom of the Trinity reveals to us the perfect reciprocity of the "compenetration" of the three persons, to the degree that they only have within themselves one will, one energy, one power.[20]

[18]*La félicité de connaître la voie*, 28–29.
[19]*We Shall See Him as He Is*, 194.
[20]*La félicité de connaître la voie*, 21.

In the trinitarian model the *personae* live in each other by love: " 'The Father loves the Son' (Jn 3:35). He lives in the Son and in the Holy Spirit. The Son 'abides in the love of the Father' (Jn 15:10), and in the Holy Spirit. And the Holy Spirit . . . lives in him [the Father] and abides in the Son. This love makes the sum total of divine being a single eternal Act."[21] This idea is traditionally expressed in the notion of *perichoresis*—the mutual coinherence of the divine hypostases. The principle of perichoresis, developed later to express the Cappadocians' idea of communion (*koinonia*), provides a useful tool for the idea of dynamic unity. Fr Sophrony uses the concept in John of Damascus' sense (i.e., primarily within the trinitarian context rather than in Maximus' christological sense). It is the dynamic sense of perichoresis that Fr Sophrony makes use of: the dynamic *Ineinandergehen* (Latin: *circumincessio*), rather than static *Ineinandersein* (Latin: *circuminsessio*). The event of such absolute divine perichoresis determines a further attribute of the hypostatic being: the capacity of the hypostasis for the *total dynamic transference of being*. Persona, in order to live in another persona through love, empties itself and receives another persona into its own being. We may denote this two-way transference of being by the terms *modus agens* (active mode) and *modus patiendi* (receptive mode). In *modus agens*, the hypostasis ultimately empties itself in kenotic love toward another hypostasis, giving to the latter the fulness of its being. Thus, in the eternal generation of the Son, the Father gives all of himself, in the whole plenitude of his eternal being, to the Son. In *modus patiendi*, hypostasis can receive and contain the ultimate fulness of being of another hypostasis. By virtue of receiving the absolute fulness of the Father's eternal being the Son is equal to the Father.[22] To receive the other into the self, the self has to abase itself and become "transparent." In the context of the trinitarian model, transparency implies the absence of any sort of self-reservation. The capacity of the absolute "giving" and "receiving" constitutes the *absolute* unity in the Godhead. Thus this unity of personae in the divine being is not static but eternally dynamic:

> [in the Trinity] each Hypostasis is totally unveiled to the others; where kenotic love is manifest as the basic trait of Divine Life, because of which the Unity of the Trinity is complete and absolute.[23]

---

[21] *His Life Is Mine*, 29.
[22] *We Shall See Him as He Is*, 139.
[23] Ibid., 216.

Hence, persona, characterized by the capacity for the ultimate transference of being through love (i.e., ultimate kenosis in *modus agens* and ultimate receiving in *modus patiendi*), emerges as a unifying principle that constitutes the dynamic oneness in the multihypostatic being. These dynamics of love form the most profound reality in the fact of the eternal self-determination of the persons of the Trinity. The Tri-Unity of the Godhead is the being that is dynamic to the utmost extent.

The reflection of this kenotic trinitarian love is seen by Fr Sophrony in Christ's sayings, where he reveals his total commitment to the Father, as we see for example in John 3:35, 10:30, 15:10, 17:21, and above all on Calvary. Christ's absolute kenosis on the cross reflects the divine eternal kenotic love. Christ accomplished his kenosis on the cross with the cry: "It is finished" (Jn 19:30). It is then that the revelation about the kenotic character of divine love, which is characteristic of the hypostatic principle, was completed.

The Sovereignty of the Human Hypostasis

For Fr Sophrony, traditional christology demonstrates how the trinitarian hypostatic attributes are maintained within the confines of human nature. The divine persona in Christ retains its sovereignty in relation to his human nature. As Fr Sophrony points out, we confess the two perfect natures in Christ with all their respective attributes.[24] The fact that Christ's hypostasis is divine does not alter the equal truth that in ordinary man, just as in Jesus the man, the persona is not an element of the human nature, neither does it correspond to any of its parts, as for example *nous* or *pneuma*. His "I" lives, as it were, in control of nature. For Lossky and Berdyaev too, persona is "someone," who goes "beyond" his/her nature and who is not determined by it. Fr Sophrony expresses a similar idea in terms of the "immateriality" of the human hypostasis: "God is Spirit and man-hypostasis is spirit."[25] This christocentric approach to persona diverges from the direction taken by some contemporary western thinkers, for whom "the concept of a person is derivative, in the sense that it is capable of being analyzed into simpler elements." It is thus sometimes seen as a natural product of physical processes. These attempts revive the principles laid down by psychology. Freud seems to have emphasized the *biological dimension* (i.e., instincts and drives) as it interacts with the intrapsychic and

---

[24] *La félicité de connaître la voie*, 30.
[25] *We Shall See Him as He Is*, 196.

interpersonal realms. Jung's approach is more complex insofar as he introduced the *archetypes* as playing a central role in the development of personality. Archetypes are elaborate constructs that, although they have a biological basis, also belong to the societal realm of culture and language. Though Jung attributed a positive role to spirituality in the well-being of the person, his position tends to psychologize religion and to reduce spirituality to a "psychic phenomenon." Both Freud and Jung limit their idea of personality to various combinations of intrapsychic and interpersonal causality, ignoring God-like freedom and self-determination of the human hypostasis.

The Human Persona

Fr Sophrony suggests that if Christ's divine hypostasis took on humanity, human nature can be the bearer of the undiminished fulness of his divinity. In Christ, human nature is assumed by his divine hypostasis, and as such is shown capable of "supporting," as it were, the divine mode of being. This opens the path for the human persona to develop to God-like, infinite dimensions. As such the human persona can and should be modeled upon Christ's divine persona. Christ "in the act of incarnation took into His Hypostasis the form of our earthly existence. But the human hypostasis receives divinization through grace, wherefore the fulness of the Divine image is actualized in him."[26]

Fr Sophrony's christocentric anthropology thus challenges the idea of the incommensurability between God and man—that the infinite cannot be commensurable with the finite—which was hitherto accepted axiomatically in western theology: "Between God and man there is and must be commensurability in spite of all that is noncommensurable. To dismiss this idea of commensurability would make it totally impossible to interpret any form of cognition as truth—that is, as corresponding to the reality of primordial being." For Fr Sophrony, man is created for *full* communion with God and "non-infinity" in man would diminish the fulness of this communion: "He did not create [reasonable beings] for a part only of his bliss—any element of limitation would indicate unlikeness and rule out eternal unity with God on the highest plane."[27]

---

[26] *We Shall See Him as He Is*, 192; cf ibid., 103; *His Life Is Mine*, 43.
[27] *His Life Is Mine*, 77.

Man as persona becomes infinite, despite his "creaturehood." For Fr
Sophrony, such New Testament passages as Ephesians 3:19, 1 Corinthians
13:12, and 1 John 3:2 point to the fulness of divine-human communion and
mutual knowledge. Such anthropological maximalism constrained Fr
Sophrony to search for an adequate terminology. He is aware that the traditional patristic idea of man as a *microcosm* in the Cappadocians and Maximus
does not adequately reflect the fact of the infinity and transcendentality of
man. He goes further—man is more than microcosm: he is a *microtheos*.[28]

Man as a Microtheos

Fr Sophrony deduced his ideas on the human persona from a christological
model that sets a number of parallels between human and divine personae.
First, as in divine being, persona is not a limiting factor but a principle that
transcends all limitations, so also the human persona has the same *infinite* character. Persona in divine being is not a limiting principle, and in our created
being hypostasis is a principle that takes into itself infinity. Hence, just as the
divine hypostasis is pan-transcendent, so also the human persona in its ultimate realization transcends all finitude. As such the human persona is not subject to arithmetical counting, like the divine personae: "*Persona . . .* is not
subject to the natural elements: it transcends earthly bounds and moves in the
sphere of other dimensions. One and only, unique and irreducible, it cannot
be accounted for arithmetically."[29]

This God-like infinity and transcendence of the human persona place it
beyond definition: just like the divine persona, the human persona is indefinable.[30] These ideas of infinity and transcendence of the human persona determine Fr Sophrony's perception of the ascetic life. They imply that the task of
the ascetic is to realize his potential of infinity. Within the confines of earthly
existence our hypostatic personal spirit faces the task of breaking through the
barrier of time and space. Man is to become "supracosmic."[31]

Second, God as the first principle of being is the center of all that exists.
The human persona, though not the principal being, is nevertheless seen as a
God-like *centrum*. Persona unifies all that is by virtue of taking all into itself:

[28]*His Life Is Mine,* 77; *We Shall See Him as He Is,* 194.
[29]Ibid., 196; *His Life Is Mine,* 43. Cf Basil the Great in *Spir.* 18.45, 404.
[30]*His Life Is Mine,* 43.
[31]*We Shall See Him as He Is,* 61, 74.

[Handwritten top margin: Just as man must *worship*, so to, He must love... @ least himself, good nature, better others, best, God & by loving God he must love all 3.]

The Creator of the world, the Lord holds all that exists in the palm of His hand; and man as hypostasis is a kind of centre, capable of containing in himself not only the plurality of cosmic realities but the whole fulness of Divine and human being.[32]

Third, Fr Sophrony also makes a connection between the expression of the divine I in the biblical formula of Exodus 3:14, and the human I. "The name of God is 'I AM THAT I AM.' For man, created after the image and likeness, this word *I* . . . brings out the principle of persona within us." From the eschatological perspective, in eternity our being retains this God-like personeity according to Christ's promise: "I live, and you will live also" (Jn 14:19). Our personal spirit will abide as such and will not be diluted in the ocean of any suprapersonal absolute.[33]

Fourth, the human persona possesses the God-like attribute of freedom, so much so that for the persona there is no external authority. There is nothing and no one in the whole world, not even God himself, who can impose an alien will upon man, or force him to one choice or the other by coercion, be it in time or eternity. "Although [man] is a creature created by God the Creator treats not as His 'energy' but as objective fact even for Himself."[34]

Fifth, the human persona, like the divine, can be known only in its dynamic manifestation and in the depth of one's living communion. "The created person is also beyond definition . . . Like God, the *persona*-hypostasis cannot be throughly known from outside unless he reveals himself to another person."[35]

Having established these God-like attributes in the human persona, we proceed to examine how they assisted Fr Sophrony to draw a closer parallel between the trinitarian model and manifestations of human personae in their interrelation.

[Handwritten: If we humans cannot "be thoroughly known" (or be fully human) unless we be revealed to another person, good enough. But is this the same for God? If so, is this a "limitation"? If so, is it an]

To Be a Person Is to Love

If within the Trinity the persona expresses itself in its mutual kenosis and in its love toward the world, this is also true of the human persona. There is love toward God, other human personae and the created order. Fr Sophrony makes

[Handwritten bottom: example of "self-limitation?" (on God's part?) Can God become "more fully God" thru His self-revelation to humans? Or is this equation applicable only to the Trinity? Or is it simply a stupid example of our (my) own limitations?]

[32] *We Shall See Him as He Is*, 197; *His Life Is Mine*, 43.
[33] Cf *Birth into the Kingdom*, 22.
[34] *We Shall See Him as He Is*, 109; cf *His Life Is Mine*, 37, 66.
[35] *We Shall See Him as He Is*, 192.

an explicit and direct connection between the divine mode of being, characterized by kenotic love, and its image—the multihypostatic body of humankind. In humankind as in God love emerges as *a uniting principle*:

> The attitude of love is natural for the *persona* made in the image of God of love. He does not determine himself oppositively, by contraposing himself over against the "not I." Love is the most intrinsic content of his essence. Embracing the whole world in prayerful love, the *persona* achieves *ad intra* the unity of all that exists. In the creative act of his becoming, he aspires to universal unity *ad extra* also. In love lies his likeness to God Who is Love (1 Jn 4:16).[36]

In the human hypostasis there is the same "divine" capacity for the ultimate transference of being—the ultimate self-giving (emptying) and ultimate receiving (fulness)—the *modus patiendi* and *modus agens* in persona's existence.

Love unto the End

Fr Sophrony's teaching on persona allows him to interpret certain scriptural passages so that through them he projects the trinitarian hypostatic principle onto the level of human multihypostatic existence. Thus the ontological principle of trinitarian kenoticism is reflected in the words of Christ in Luke 14:26: the requirement for Christ's disciple is "to hate one's own life." The existential orientation of the divine *modus patiendi* is reflected in humanity in the ascetic state of *love to the point of self-hatred*. Self-hatred here is understood as the opposite of self-love, which is an egocentric concern determining the focus of one's being. *Hatred* therefore can be defined as *radically reversed existential concern*. In the Trinity "self-hatred" corresponds to the ultimate self-giving of each divine hypostasis: "The 'hate,' of which the Lord of love speaks, in its essence is the plenitude of God's kenotic love."[37]

In principle, this hatred, which is expressed in kenotic self-abasement, diverts the existential concern from self and prepares the space to receive other personae (both human and divine) into itself. Love for God and our neighbor, according to Fr Sophrony, is necessarily linked with a feeling of repulsion for oneself amounting to hatred. In this fashion the human persona, with its

---

[36] *We Shall See Him as He Is*, 196-97; cf *His Life Is Mine*, 43.
[37] *We Shall See Him as He Is*, 200.

infinite "existential" space, can receive the infinite. Its true potential is thus realized:

> Had the Lord Jesus not revealed this astonishing mystery to us, no mortal could have invented such a paradox—detest yourself because of love for God, and you will embrace all that exists with your love! . . . The I is forgotten in the transport of love for the God of love but nevertheless it is this I that blissfully contains in itself all heaven and earth.[38]

When man's self remains his ultimate existential concern, he is existentially directed toward himself and so his potential for embracing the infinite, God, and thus himself becoming infinite, is not realized. And vice versa: when his existential concern is reoriented toward the infinite, his own infinite potential opens up and comes to its realization:

> *I* is a magnificent word. It signifies *persona*. Its principal ingredient is love, which opens out, first and foremost, to God. This *I* does not live in a convulsion of egoistic concentration on self. If wrapped up in self it will continue in its nothingness. The love towards God commanded of us by Christ, which entails hating oneself and renouncing all emotional and fleshly ties, draws the spirit of man into the expanses of Divine eternity (Lk 14:26-7, 33; Jn 12:25; Mt 16:25). This kind of love is an attribute of Divinity.[39]

This idea of vacating space from the finite (self) for the infinite one (God) leads Fr Sophrony to his logically justified conclusion: it is in relation to God that the human persona's true potential is realized: "In the utmost intensity of prayer that our nature is capable of, when God Himself prays in us, man receives a vision of God that is beyond any image whatsoever, Then it is that man *qua persona* really prays 'face to Face' with the Eternal God. In this encounter with the Hypostatic God the *hypostasis*, that at first was only potential, is actualized in us."[40]

In connection with this principle, Fr Sophrony defines the ascetic practice of prayer. In the state of "pure prayer" the ascetic has no self-regard: his

[38] *We Shall See Him as He Is*, 199.
[39] Ibid.
[40] Ibid., 195.

existential attention and concern do not return upon the *self*. As soon as he
does regard himself the intensity of abiding in the sphere of divine reality is
weakened.

Fr Sophrony distances himself from the tendency, shared by many Russian religious thinkers of the nineteenth and twentieth centuries, to regard the
development of persona mainly from the view point of interhuman relationships, above all conjugal love. For Fr Sophrony, the human persona within this
context is limited to a *finite* relationship. On this psychological level, the *infinity* of the human persona is not an exigency. In contrast, in its relationship with
God, for the human persona to be fully realized, it should reach not only an
analogy, an affinity, a parallel between God and man, but even identity and
equality, which is a leitmotif of Fr Sophrony's anthropology.

In relation to God, love to the point of self-hatred manifests itself in the
state of *Christ-like humility*. For Christ, the Father was the sole basis of his
being. Christ's own I was absolutely emptied in his "taking in" of the Father's
persona so much so that he is an express image of the Father's person (Heb
1:3), identical with him (cf Jn 10:30). Silouan's concept of *Christ-like humility*
reflects a similar self-giving of the ascetic to God, so that man can say: "No
longer I . . . but Christ . . ." (Gal 2:20).

Finally, hypostatic commensurability expresses itself in love within interpersonal human relationships. This emphasis on the capacity for absolute self-
giving in the human persona opens a new dimension in the application of the
model of divine triunity to human multihypostatic being. As we shall see, this
particularly affects Fr Sophrony's understanding of the concept of "image and
likeness" (Gen 1:26).

Difficulties

Having discussed Fr Sophrony's understanding of the concept of hypostasis,
one may discover some vulnerable points in his theological framework.

One or Three Gods?

As a point of departure Fr Sophrony takes the scriptural passages Exodus 3:14
("I AM THAT I AM") and Revelations 1:8 ("I am the first and the last, Alpha
and Omega") with parallels and claims these passages to be a divine revelation
about the supremacy of I—the hypostatic principle in the divine being.

Fr Sophrony, however, never discusses the question "Who is this I?" Which hypostasis is referred to? If this is one persona, then who or which one, the Father, the Son, or the Holy Spirit, who pronounces this name? The phrase implies a *single* subject of first-personhood—the three cannot say I. Should it not be plural, as in Genesis 1:26?[41] If it is pronounced by a single I, a single one, a single God, should not this phrase be related to *some principle of unity* in the Trinity (i.e., essence), rather than to three or one of the three hypostases?

Some modern western theologians are well aware of the risk involved in consideration of the three absolute personae, and therefore attribute less significance to the importance of the hypostatic principle in the divine being. The more one emphasizes the supremacy of the hypostatic principle within the Godhead, the more one risks lapsing into tritheism with three absolute-centers. Many have therefore abandoned the idea of persona as being "misleading" and found their own ways of expressing the threeness in the Godhead: "three ways of being" (Barth), "three manners of subsistence" (Rahner), "three movements" or "modes" of being" (Macquarrie), "three distinct models, which are not reducible to each other" (Ward).

Fr Sophrony does not adopt the "safe compromise" of using the idea of the "corporate personality," as we find in Zizioulas, for example.[42] Neither does he accept Bulgakov's position, which sees in "I AM" a single absolute subject combining in himself *I, Thou, We*. According to Fr Sophrony, this multi-personality in one subject leads to the fusion of persons.

Fr Sophrony's principles of theology, however, do allow his trinitarian teaching to withstand this argument. While he does not take up this issue on the level of rational explanation, he resorts to the "existential" perception of the antinomy between the absolute distinction in divine personae (so that the Father and the Son are envisaged as personal subjects, with an element of dialogue and interaction between them) and their absolute identity (cf Jn 10:30). He writes: "Contemplation is a matter not of verbal statements but of living experience. In pure prayer the Father, Son, and Spirit are seen in their consubstantial unity."[43]

---

[41]See Ware, "The Mystery of the Human Person," 66; cf Justin Martyr, *Dialog. Tryph.* 62.2, 290; Barnabas, *Epist.* 5.5, 284 and 6.12, 288; Theophilus of Antioch, *AdAutolyc.* 2.18.2, 65.

[42]Zizioulas, "On Being a Person," 39.

[43]*His Life Is Mine*, 28.

Confusion of Created and Uncreated?

It may seem that Fr Sophrony shortens the ontological distance between God and man to the extent that the difference between God and man virtually disappears. J. Illingworth warns against such a possibility in mysticism: "Mysticism has always had its attendant danger—the danger of seeking union with God by obliteration of human limitations and human attributes."[44]

The idea of man as microtheos might be thought vulnerable to such criticism. Furthermore, in Fr Sophrony's interpretation of Mark 16:19, humanity in Christ is elevated to the extent of "equality," even "identity," with the Godhead.

Yet Fr Sophrony is careful not to obliterate the difference between God and man: "Perfection in likeness, however, does not remove the ontological distance between God the Creator and man the created."[45] Though man is a reflection of the absolute and a God-like universal *centrum*, he does not become the absolute, "the ultimate principle of all that is" in relation to other living beings. In becoming a god according to the content of life, the created hypostasis does not become God for other rational creatures. This limitation is reflected in the fact that the hypostatic freedom in man is not absolute; man is not "being-in-itself" and he cannot construct his own being in such an absolute manner as God can. Man retains his status as a creature, and he always has a beginning; only God is eternal.[46] Though man's nature is deified, it is not transformed into divine nature in such a way that the Trinity would have to be expanded to include the number of added human hypostases. Man does not become a participant of God's nature, but only of God's energies, since divine essence is incommunicable.[47] Thus, Fr Sophrony is well aware of the fact that man becomes a god (*microtheos*) and not God (*Theos*).

The Persona: Material or Noetic Reality?

Concerning the relation between the hypostatic principle and the material body, Fr Sophrony holds that persona is "spirit"—it is therefore a noetic immaterial category. This seems to imply that the body is only a kind of "shell"

---

[44] J. Illingworth, *Personality Human and Divine: The Bapton Lectures 1894* (London, 1896) 17.
[45] *His Life Is Mine*, 78
[46] *We Shall See Him as He Is*, 192; *La félicité de connaître la voie*, 32.
[47] *La félicité de connaître la voie*, 30. *We Shall See Him as He Is*, 120.

in which man undergoes the "first experience of being," as Fr Sophrony puts it. Like Descartes, Fr Sophrony believes that persons are not bodies. Does Fr Sophrony therefore adhere to the Cartesian dualistic view of human nature (mind/body) with a strong influence of the classic soul-body dichotomy?

First, the Cartesian refusal to identify the person and the body is not a weakness de facto. Though it does have its vulnerable points, Descartes' approach has been revived by some modern scholars. The most recent attempts at offering a philosophical account of the structure of personhood have revived radical forms of Cartesian dualism as the most coherent conception of personal identity. Cartesian dualism is upheld by R. Swinburne, for example.[48]

Second, in Fr Sophrony the body is seen as the material "concretization" (i.e., expression) of the spiritual persona. But instead of a holistic view of personality, Fr Sophrony prefers to dwell on the ascetical implications of the spirit-body relation. He thus explores the diastasis between the developing hypostasis and the fallen condition of our bodily nature. He does not focus on a transfigured body-soul unity in its eschatological realization. Within this context of opposition between persona and fallen nature he develops his ascetic theory of struggle with thoughts (*logismoi*). These evolve as a consequence of the impulses of the fallen nature, from which our hypostasis is called to disassociate.

Moreover he exploits the spiritual dimension of persona so as to handle much more easily the idea of the unity of humanity after the pattern of the trinitarian perichoresis. The fact that the body is only an expression of persona, and not its integral part, allows Fr Sophrony to shift the discussion of intrapersonal relations onto the spiritual level. On this level he does not have to engage with the problem of the material, bodily separateness of human beings. He thus can afford to speak about transference of being between personae in spiritual terms.

Fr Sophrony's Contribution

In any attempt to assess the extent to which Fr Sophrony's ideas contribute to the development of the concept of persona in Christian theology, it appears that many of the ideas he proposes had already been circulating in the minds of theologians before him.

---

[48]See R. Swinburne, *The Christian God* (Oxford, 1994) 16ff.

Some Precedents in Tradition

PERSONA AND LOVE. Mutual love as the core of the triune being has already been emphasised in tradition. For the Cappadocians, the unity of God lies in the communion (*koinonia*) of the Godhead.[49] Augustine contributes to the development of the idea of mutual love within the Trinity when he employs the threefold analogy of *amans, quod amatur,* and *amor.*[50] Richard of St Victor develops further the idea of mutual love within the Trinity and comes to the conclusion that "the perfection of one person requires fellowship with another."[51]

In modern thought we observe a tendency toward "theological anthropology," one aspect of which is to see the human being in terms of its relational structure, built on the holistic (as opposite to the tripartite) perception of the human person. Certainly, Fr Sophrony's teaching falls within the range of modern "new trinitarian awareness," which extends from the revitalization of Christian orthodoxy to the propagation of forms of Moltmann's "social personalism" or "personal socialism." The relational character of persona was highlighted by the stream of "dialogical personalism" in the first half of the twentieth century. More recently, a similar approach is to be found in the Scottish thinker John Macmurray. However, the same idea is ubiquitous both in Russian religious philosophy and in trinitarian theology. Thus, Berdyaev writes: "Personality is not self-sufficient, it presupposes the existence of other persons ... Human personality can only realize itself in fellowship."[52] The closest parallels to Fr Sophronty are found in Florensky and Bulgakov, whose notions of persona revolve around the same main principle: *amo, ergo sum.*

HYPOSTATIC COMMENSURABILITY. Fr Sophrony's idea of hypostatic commensurability between God and man, which points to man's microtheosity, also has its precedents. Though the term *microtheos* is not found in patristic terminology, the idea has already been present both in the east and in the west. The idea that man transcends the created order is contained in Gregory of Nazianzus' passage from *Discoursess* 38.11: God has created man after his

---

[49]Basil, *Spir.* 18.45, 406; cf Gregory of Nyssa in Basil, *Epist.* 38.4, 85.

[50]*De Trin.* 8.10.14, 290–91.

[51]*De Trin.* 3.6, 141.

[52]Berdyaev, "Report of Student Conference," *Sobornost* 3 (1935) 7.

own image, as "a second cosmos," "a great universe within a little one."[53] Gregory of Nyssa, being aware of the finitude of the created cosmos, is not content with the term microcosm: "Those who magnify human nature by comparing it to this world, saying that man is a microcosm, a little world, composed of the same elements as the universe ... fail to realize that they are dignifying man with the attributes of the gnat and the mouse; for they too are composed of these four elements ... What great thing is it, then, for man to be accounted a representation and likeness of the world—of heaven that passes away, of the earth that is subject to change?" "It is in the likeness to God," he concludes, "that our magnitude consists."[54] In Illingworth's summary of the development of the concept of persona in the west up to the nineteenth century we find an important definition pointing to the infinity of human potential: "Person is a unit that excludes all else, and yet a totality or whole with infinite powers of inclusion."[55] The idea of man's *hypostatic transcendence* is widely present in contemporary western thought.[56]

A similar tendency is found within Russian religious philosophy. Thus we find, for example, in Soloviev, that the infinity of the human I represents in man the likeness of God. We find even more striking parallels to Fr Sophrony in Berdyaev's anthropology. It was Berdyaev who introduced the term *microtheos* into the sphere of Christian anthropology. He derives the idea from the fact that man is commensurate with God as a free spirit.[57] The idea of commensurability between God and man is further elaborated in Bulgakov. Man as divine image is in fact "repetition" of God. He writes that: "God has multiplied and repeated his hypostatic image in the angelic and human worlds." This allows Bulgakov to assert *identity, equality* between man and God: "The prototype and the image, despite the infinite distance between the Creator and the creature, are united by a certain 'identity,' which determines the positive correlation between them and prepares the forthcoming incarnation."[58]

---

[53]*Or.* 38.11, PG 36:321C-324B. On Gregory of Nazianzus' maximalist statement in anthropology, see A. Ellverson, *The Dual Nature of Man* (Uppsala, 1981) 38.

[54]*Opif. hom.,* PG 44:177D-180A.

[55]Illingworth, 30.

[56]See J. Cullen, "The Patristic Concept of the Deification of Man Examined in the Light of Contemporary Notions of the Transcendence of Man," D.Phil. Thesis (Oxford, 1985).

[57]Berdyaev, *The Beginning and the End,* 36, 40

[58]Bulgakov, *The Lamb of God,* 160; cf Bulgakov, *Unfading Light,* 277-78.

TRINITARIAN ANTINOMIES. Neither is Fr Sophrony a pioneer in working with the logical contradictions of the trinitarian dogma and accepting them as antinomies. In regard to the antinomy of the trinitarian hypostases, we find ideas similar to Fr Sophrony's in Lossky, for example. He precedes Fr Sophrony in stating that "[the hypostases] are alike in the fact that they are dissimilar; or rather, to go beyond the relative idea of resemblance, which is out of place here, one must say that the absolute character of their difference implies an absolute identity."[59] Fr Sophrony's explanation of the mystery of the number "three" also has its precedents in patristic tradition and Russian religious philosophy. Thus, the significance of the number three is found in Gregory of Nazianzus: "a monad moves into a dyad and finally a triad."[60] Similarly Bulgakov and Florensky emphasize that persona, whose being is expressed in love, cannot be in isolation (as *monads*), while in the dyad of relationship each persona would be limited to a mirror reflection of the other persona. It is only in the triad that this limitation is surmounted.

PERSONA AND INDIVIDUUM. In relation to the concept of hypostasis, the important distinction between individual and person had already been stated in eastern thought, notably by Lossky and Berdyaev. The latter writes: "The individual is a naturalistic and sociological category. The individual is born within the generic process and belongs to the natural world. Personality, on the other hand, is a spiritual and ethical category... It is created spiritually and gives actual effect to the divine idea of man. Personality is not nature; it is freedom and it is spirit ... the individual is part of the race and of the society ... whereas personality is not to be thought of as a part of any whole whatever."[61] Persona is thus the opposite pole of individualism or, as Berdyaev prefers, egocentrism.

APOPHATICS OF PERSONA. Nor is the apophatic dimension in the definition of the concept of human persona an idea new to the eastern tradition. Lossky, in a summary of the patristic *datum,* says that "person" signifies the irreducibility of man to his nature—irreducibility and not "something irreducible," but *someone,* who is distinct from his own nature.[62] The same attitude

---

[59]Lossky, *Mystical Theology,* 113.

[60]*Or.* 29:2, 180.

[61]Berdyaev, *The Beginning and the End,* 135-36. See Lossky, *Mystical Theology,* 121-22. Among later writers, see C. Yannaras, *The Freedom of Morality,* tr. E. Briere (New York, 1984) 22-23; Ware, "The Mystery of the Human Person," 67.

[62]Lossky, *In the Image and Likeness of God* (New York, 1985) 118.

is found in the west. The person is something irreducible: the mystery of the fact of being a person cannot be reduced to the facts of the appropriate sciences. The eastern apophatic approach to persona, however, is not of the Sartrian type. Sartre says that we cannot define persona in the abstract, since "to begin with, man [as persona] is nothing": we can speak about it only after a certain stage of its development. In the east a negative definition of persona in man is related to the apophatic dimension of its prototype, the divine persona. As Ware rightly notes: "our negative theology demands as counterpart a 'negative anthropology.'"[63] Our hypostasis escapes definition because, as our principal reality, it is itself a starting point for any definition: it is our canon of reality, the most real thing we know and by comparison with which we estimate the amount of reality in other things. A similar apophaticism in approach to persona is found, for example, in Berdyaev's anthropology. Florensky too stresses that persona, in contrast to "thinghood," is indefinable.

Shall we therefore conclude that Fr Sophrony reproduces theological ideas that have already been stated? Such a conclusion fails to do justice to the originality of Fr Sophrony's theology.

Fr Sophrony's Originality

Fr Sophrony acts as a theological bridge between the various thought-worlds—Russian religious philosophy and the eastern ascetic tradition, which is further enriched by his own experience. This threefold spectrum in his approach to the theme of persona determines its uniqueness.

His emphasis on the idea of hypostatic commensurability opens a new dimension within the sphere of ascetic theology. Unlike Fr Sophrony, some contemporary writers who touch on asceticism do not go beyond asserting the affinity/analogy between divine hypostasis and human hypostasis. They build up their anthropology on the axiomatic statement that there is *incommensurability* between created man and uncreated God. They tend toward emphasizing the difference between them. This is particularly manifest in the discussion of the trinitarian model. The general trend in recent Eastern Orthodox writers is to treat the "as" of John 17:21 ("Even as you, Father, are in me and I am in you, may they also be in us") in a figurative sense, in terms of analogy. Thus, where persona is finite, an adequate application of the

[63]Ware, "The Unity of the Human Person according to the Greek Fathers," 198.

trinitarian model to mankind is difficult. Lossky points to such a degree of difference between divine and human hypostases that he had to redefine the concept when he applied the concept to humans: for him the human persona is not an absolute category, and he does not object to the application of arithmetical categories.[64]

Fr Sophrony, by professing hypostatic commensurability—as do Russian religious philosophers—makes more extensive use of the christotrinitarian model in terms of its practical relevance to ascetic principles. This is a point where his theology diverges from Russian philosophy. Though Fr Sophrony is certainly influenced by Florensky, Bulgakov, and Berdyaev, their framework of thought remains different. One can discern the influence of German classical idealism on Bulgakov and Florensky. Berdyaev, on the other hand, explicitly acknowledges his debt to personalistic philosophy, especially to Dostoyevsky.[65] He examines persona and individual from the point of view of social anthropology. In contrast to their approach, Fr Sophrony's theology is determined by practical ascetic considerations. It is here that the radical difference between them emerges. Thus, for example, in Fr Sophrony, individualistic egocentrism can be overcome by the fulfilment of Christ's commandments about love. For Berdyaev, the "sacrificial erosion of selfhood" is determined by human creativity. Thus, creativity for Berdyaev is the very realization of human personhood. As a result, he has no theological "space" for the ascetic practice of obedience, of which he is explicitly critical: obedience for him kills personhood—it is an easy way to avoid the "burden" of freedom. In contrast, for Fr Sophrony, creativity does not contradict obedience, so much so that obedience is a virtual expression of personhood.

Thus for Fr Sophrony the *ascetic* implications of the idea of God-likeness of the human persona are his central theological concern. The idea had already been present in religious philosophy, but as an expression of dogmatic vision in *theoria* it had not been theologically integrated into ascetic theology *in praxis*. In Fr Sophrony's approach, "every step in Christian life is inseparably related to the fundamental dogmas of our faith."[66]

[64]Lossky, *Mystical Theology*, 114-19.
[65]Berdyaev, *The Beginning and the End*, 137
[66]*Words of Life* (Essex, 1996) 11.

CHAPTER FOUR

Kenosis

I n the gospel of John, Christ, before giving himself to lifegiving suffering and death, says: "Greater love has no man than this, that a man lay down his life for his friends" (Jn 15:13). As a projection of divine love, these words describe the perfect love, which inherently presupposes the ultimate sacrifice. It is love that "seeks not her own" (1 Cor 13:5). From the times of the apostle Paul, Christ is set forth by Christian kerygma as the supreme example of this sacrificial love: "Let this mind be in you, which was also in Christ Jesus: Who, being in the form of God, thought it not robbery to be equal with God: but made himself of no reputation [Gr. *eauton ekenosen*—lit. "emptied himself"], and took upon him the form of a servant, and was made in the likeness of men: and being found in fashion as a man, he humbled himself, and became obedient unto death, even the death of the cross" (Phil 2:5-6). This drama of Christ's *kenosis* (self-emptying), depicted in the Pauline words, is abundantly featured throughout the whole of Eastern Orthodox tradition—in the patristic writings in general[1] and in the liturgical texts in particular. In Fr Sophrony, however, the theme comes to the forefront of his theological concerns. The notion of kenosis becomes a controlling feature of his entire theology, but foremost of his teaching on persona. As such it shapes immensely his vision of ascetic life and ultimately that of Christian perfection. Throughout the span of his theological formation Fr Sophrony attentively absorbs the crosscurrents of kenotic ideas related to christology, to the Trinity, and to anthropology. He then forms them into a unified teaching, where Christ in his kenosis emerges as a supreme model. The centrality of kenosis in his thought emerges more articulately if one juxtaposes Fr Sophrony's "kenotic" stance to the "pleromatic" perception of eastern spirituality among some contemporary

[1]See L. Richard, *A Kenotic Christology* (Washington, 1982); and *Christ: The Self-Emptying of God* (Mahwah, 1997).

Orthodox writers, who build their theology around the idea of "fulfilment" and of "fulness."

Within the broad spectrum of interpretation of this passage, Fr Sophrony stresses two strains of thought: Christ's temporal human–divine kenosis during his earthly life, and the eternal intratrinitarian kenosis manifested through the Logos.

The Kenosis of Christ

Kenosis in the Incarnation

Fr Sophrony's approach to Christ's earthly kenosis rests on the traditional understanding—the incarnation is an ontological kenosis per se.[2] The divine uncreated Logos enters and assumes a "lower" mode of existence, the human created order.[3] Fr Sophrony repeatedly alludes to Philippians 2:6-7 and speaks of God "belittling himself," "assuming the form of a servant," and "humbling himself to the point of death on the Cross." The Logos, in his divinity, "came down from heaven to the world and then into hell."[4] Fr Sophrony also notes that the Logos in the incarnation does not exercise his own divinity but always acts in the name and power of the Father or by the Holy Spirit. Christ avoided any act that would have a character of self-divinization. Thus Fr Sophrony highlights in scripture the role of the Holy Spirit at the conception (Lk 1:35) and at Christ's baptism (Mt 3:15). He notes that it was God who raised Jesus (1 Pet 1:21), and testified to him (Jn 5:31-32). The same principle is reflected in the liturgical formula of the epiclesis, the invocation of the Holy Spirit, from which it can be deduced that it is not Christ who of himself accomplishes the consecration of the eucharistic bread and wine by the words of institution, but the Father by the power of the Holy Spirit. Christ's consistent refusal of self-deification explains why he preferred to apply to himself the title "Son of Man" rather than the title "Son of God": "From the context of the gospel it emerges that Christ did not use this name as his proper name, but as a name, common to all men."[5] Thus, the kenosis of the Logos consists in his

---

[2]See, for example, Cyril of Alexandria, *Recta Fide ad Arc.*, 238.
[3]On the history of kenotic christology, see Richard, *Christ: The Self-Emptying of God*, 73-83.
[4]*We Shall See Him as He Is*, 131.
[5]*La félicité de connaître la voie*, 44-45.

"incarnational ontological descent" and voluntary dynamic "conformation" to the mode of human existence.

Fr Sophrony also underlines the fact of kenosis in the Christ-man (cf 1 Tim 2:5) in the course of his earthly life, that is, as a human being: "All his life, while with us, had been nothing but 'unceasing torment.' Golgotha is only the concluding act, in which everything came together as in a climactic point."[6] Fr Sophrony makes an attempt to penetrate the veil of Christ's inner world. Hence, he offers a spiritual analysis of the significant events of Christ's human life in terms of kenosis—particularly the temptations, Gethsemane, and Golgotha.

Eternal Kenosis

The eternal aspect of Christ's kenosis is perceived in the framework of the kenotic intratrinitarian love. Fr Sophrony remarks that before Christ accomplished his earthly kenosis, "it had already been accomplished in heaven according to his divinity in relation to the Father." The earthly kenosis is thus a manifestation of the heavenly: "Through him [Christ] we are given revelation about the nature of God-Love. The perfection consists in that this love humbly, without reservations, gives itself over. The Father in the generation of the Son pours himself out entirely. But the Son returns all things to the Father."[7]

As far as the kenotic "pouring out" is concerned, Fr Sophrony understands it as the Father's giving over of himself to the Son in all the fulness of his uncreated being. "And so the Son is equal with the Father in absolute fulness of divine being."[8] Fr Sophrony's idea of the kenotic "taking in" by one hypostasis of the other hypostasis (or hypostases) makes clear the meaning of the passages in the gospels that testify to the unity of the Father and the Son. This absolute kenosis of Christ—the total return of his *self* to the Father—is particularly manifested in the incarnation, at Gethsemane, and at Golgotha. The self-giving involves both aspects of Christ's being—his divinity and his humanity: "The Son in like fulness of Self-emptying love gives Himself to the Father both in His Divinity and His humanity."[9]

---

[6]"The Prayer of Gethsemane," in *We Shall See Him as He Is*, Russian ed., 233–34 (Essex, 1985).
[7]Ibid., 234.
[8]*We Shall See Him as He Is*, 139.
[9]Ibid., 139.

So, the events of Gethsemane and Golgotha involve both the divinity and humanity of Christ: "In those days He began to concentrate on the act of self-emptying that lay before Him as man [as well]"[10]—"as well" means in addition to the divine eternal kenosis of the Logos. The human kenosis merges with the divine, making the latter manifest.

This has important consequences for Fr Sophrony's ascetic theology. It is not only in the person of Christ that the divine and human forms of kenosis become one. Through the participation in the kenosis of the Logos humanity restores its capacity for kenotic divine-like love. The event of the kenosis of the God-man in all its facets explains a connection crucial for our understanding of Fr Sophrony's theology—between kenosis and deification. Christ's perfect kenosis is transfigured into the equally perfect divinization of our nature.

In this *communicatio idiomatum* through kenosis, not only does man participate in the divine order, but also God the Trinity, in kenotic love for the created world, empties himself on the cross through its incarnate hypostasis. This is implied in the question, rhetorically posed by Fr Sophrony: "Is it permissible to venture beyond one's own experience and in mental contemplation conceive of the participation of the Father and the Holy Spirit in the Son's death on the Cross?"[11] In other words, the incarnation of the second person of the Trinity shows divine condescending kenosis not only vis-à-vis another divine person, but of the Triune God toward created man.

The Roots of Kenoticism in Fr Sophrony

L. Richard's research demonstrates that the eastern fathers did not explore the kenotic dimension in the Godhead to an extent sufficient to provide the sole basis for Fr Sophony's trinitarian kenoticism. Thus, concerning the idea of kenosis in the Trinity and in its relation to the world, Richard rightly observes that "Christianity has hesitated to attribute to God that authenticity of kenotic love that it has recognized in Jesus." For the fathers the idea of kenosis implies mutability per se, and as such cannot be a divine attribute.[12]

[10]Ibid., 200.
[11]Ibid., 139.
[12]See Richard, *Christ: The Self-Emptying of God*, 105.

Russian Thought on the Kenosis of Christ

The theme of kenosis came to the forefront of christology in the eighteenth and nineteenth centuries as an attempt to reconcile the credal orthodox affirmations with the newly emerging picture of Jesus given by critical-historical study in the west. Western thought on the subject gradually penetrated the Russian intellectual scene. The kenotic dimension in Russian christology evolved articulately in the nineteenth century within the milieu usually designated as "ecclesiastical tradition." The characteristic features of this theological development were its firm scriptural and liturgical basis, with a strong monastic coloring, on the one hand, and, on the other, pastoral concern: each idea is evaluated in the light of its practical implications in the field of monastic and lay piety.

Kenoticism was a general feature of Russian Christianity of that time. According to N. Gorodetzky, the kenotic Christ was "present in the background of any Russian mind."[13] Bulgakov notes the existence of the purely Russian manner of the artistic interpretation of Christ's image, which brings together writers so remote from each other in spirit as Turgenev and Dostoyevsky. The dividing line between Russian literature and religious philosophy is often blurred. Literature fed philosophy with its images, which were then transposed into philosophical ideas, so much so that Berdyaev states that Russian religious philosophy in fact works out the subjects raised by Russian literature. Hence, the kenotic Christ of Russian literature became a theological issue. In particular, the kenotic leanings became manifest in the sphere of moral ideals as created by Russian literature. Fr Sophrony was well versed in Russian literature of the nineteenth century. This is reflected in his allusions to Russian poets and writers in his works. From Russian literature the kenotic ideal penetrated and saturated the minds of Russian philosophers and theologians, and became increasingly exploited in the pastoral sphere.

Naturally, the theological attention to the kenosis of Christ raised an issue of kenosis as an eternal attribute of the Trinity. Thus, within the Russian "ecclesiastical tradition," Philaret of Moscow envisages the cross as "an earthly image" and "the shadow of the heavenly cross of love." Analyzing Philaret's concept of the intratrinitarian mode of love, R. Williams writes: "Philaret seems to imply that the love of God is, as we might say, *absolutely kenotic*, not

---

[13]Gorodetzky, xi ("Introduction") .

so merely relatively to the economy of salvation; that God's love for the world
as revealed in the sacrifice of Christ is the same in character as the mutual love
of the Father, Son and Spirit within the Godhead."[14] Philaret expresses this
"absolutely kenotic" character of divine love in his celebrated formula:"The
love of the Father is the crucifying one. The love of the Son is the crucified
one. The love of the Spirit is the one triumphing in the power of the cross.
So has God loved the world!"[15]

Kenotic love is thus a divine attribute by which the divinity is recognized.
On Matthew 27:40 (Christ is urged "to come down from the cross") Philaret
comments:"The Son of God makes himself manifest by the fact that he would
not come down from the cross until he had utterly emptied himself in the
eager striving of his love toward his Father."[16]

However, in Philaret this love in the Trinity is still "economic," so much
so that the world emerges as *causatum* and agent of the manifestation of this
love. In one passage, where Philaret spells out the above-mentioned formula
of divine love, the world figures as its indispensable part:"If the heavenly Father
delivers his only-begotten Son out of love for the world, the Son, likewise,
delivers himself up out of love for the world; just as love crucifies, so love is
crucified also."[17]

As we have observed, the ideas of Philaret are reflected in Fr Sophrony's
thought. Thus, for Fr Sophrony, John 3:16 links the absolute kenotic love
within the Trinity with the economical divine kenotic love for the world:

> In the pre-eternal Council of the Trinity this way of redemption for
> fallen man [i.e., the kenotic incarnation] was decided on. Is not this the
> Self-emptying of the Father who "so loved the world, that [he] gave
> his only begotten Son, that whosoever believeth in him should not per-
> ish, but have everlasting life" (Jn 3:16) in the bosom of the Divinity? . . .
> Thus the Father and the Spirit eternally participate in the "work" (Jn
> 17:4) which was given to Jesus to do.[18]

[14]R. Williams, "The Theology of Vladimir Nikolaevich Lossky: An Exposition and Critique," D.Phil. Thesis (Oxford, 1975) 59.

[15]Philaret,"Sermon on Great Friday (1816)," in *Collected Works of Philaret the Metropolitan of
Moscow and Colomna* 1:90, 94 (Moscow, 1873). Fr Sophrony refers to this passage in *His Life Is
Mine*, 29.

[16]Philaret, 94.

[17]Ibid., 93.

[18]*We Shall See Him as He Is*, 139.

Fr Sergius Bulgakov on Kenosis

In the twentieth century Sergius Bulgakov—the theologian of kenosis par excellence—gave to the Russian leanings toward kenotic perception a firm dogmatic grounding, not least through their synthetic integration with the ideas of the German kenoticists, notably Schelling.[19] The latter stands out for his cosmogony of kenotic relation between God and his creation. Creation in Schelling is seen not only as "revelation" of God, but as his realization and personalization. Bulgakov integrates the Schellingian theme into the framework of his teaching on Sophia, which emerged as an attempt to tackle the problem of the relationship between the creator and his creature. It is within this sophianic scheme that Bulgakov applies the concept of *absolute kenosis* to the Trinity and Christ without reservation.

It is through Bulgakov that Fr Sophrony in the 1920s in Paris was introduced to the kenotic ideas in Christianity. Bulgakov's ideas became a theological matrix for a further integration of the kenosis theme into ascetic theology in Fr Sophrony.

Bulgakov distinguishes various levels in the kenosis of God. Kenosis is a first principle of trinitarian existence: it constitutes the being of each hypostasis. Bulgakov attempts to deduce kenotic implications from the very concepts of the fatherhood of the Father and of the sonhood of the Son: "If on the side of the Father, there is self-negation in the begetting of the Son, the Son is thoroughly emptying himself when he accepts the 'passive' state of the one who is begotten."[20]

Kenosis of the Father toward the Son is expressed in the fact of the eternal generation of the Son from the Father. Bulgakov expresses it in terms of "self-emptying," by which the Father realizes himself in the Son, and which is also his "self-actualizing." Bulgakov defines this self-emptying as "the giving of self to the other, the self-sacrificing ecstasy of burning love, which zealously cares about the other." The Son mirrors the Father's self-emptying and empties himself out for the sake of the Father: "If the Father desires to have himself . . . in the Son, the Son also does not desire to have himself for himself; he sacrifices his own self [*samost*] to the Father, and being the Word of God, he, as it were, becomes wordless of himself, making himself the Word of the Father." On the level of interhypostatic relationships in the Trinity, Bulgakov

---

[19]Nichols, *Light from the East*, 59; cf Gorodetzky, 156ff.
[20]Bulgakov, *The Lamb of God*, 468; cf ibid., 122: "The Sonship is already an eternal *kenosis*."

makes a starting point: self-emptying involves *suffering*. He manages to reconcile this element of suffering with that of all-blessedness in the divine being.
Suffering not only does not contradict the all-blessedness in the divine mode
of being: it is even identified with it in the *joy of self-sacrificing love*, which brings
suffering and *bliss* to oneness.[21]

In Bulgakov, the kenotic dimension in the Godhead necessarily affects the
perception of the creator-creature relationship. Bulgakov sees the creation as
a kenotic act of God. Kenosis of the Godhead consists in the self-diminution
of God's absoluteness because of the *relation* with creation: "The absolute God,
who has no relation to anything apart from himself, becomes absolutely cor-
relative." Each of the hypostases have their own share in the kenosis of the
Godhead in relation to the created cosmos. The kenosis of the Father is his
silence-absence in the creation: he reveals himself only in the divine Sophia—
the twosome of the Son and the Spirit—as well as in the creaturely Sophia.[22]

The kenosis of the Spirit in creation consists "not only in overshadowing
the creation in general but in accepting the measure of this creation and its
difficulty of perceiving the revelation of the Spirit." The incompleteness of
this perception, and even the resistance to it, do not force the Spirit to abandon the creation to the condition of its original nothingness. He abides in it,
sustaining it in existence. The kenosis is manifest in the long-suffering of the
Spirit. In another passage Bulgakov sees the kenosis of the Spirit in that the
Spirit, being the fulness and the depth of the Godhead, has entered the process
of formation (*stanovlenie*) in his self-revelation within the creaturely Sophia. In
Bulgakov's view, the incompleteness (*nepolnota*) of the creation is only a striving toward its intended fulness. Hence, the kenosis of the Spirit means that the
immeasurable one confines himself to measure.[23]

The kenosis of the Father and of the Spirit is further invoked by Bulgakov
in their participation in the earthly kenosis of Christ. Thus he mentions the
co-crucifixion of the Father along with the Son.[24] His triadological and christological kenoticism colors his understanding of the incarnation.

Bulgakov felt that a focus on kenoticism in christology could renew
Orthodox theology, just as it had brought new life to the theology of Protes-
tantism. In his christology Bulgakov, along with the traditional idea of the

[21]Ibid., 121–22.
[22]Bulgakov, *The Comforter*, 253.
[23]Ibid., 239, 254.
[24]Bulgakov, *The Lamb of God*, 340, 400.

"kenosis of the incarnation," perceives through the prism of kenosis various faculties of Christ: his knowledge, intellect, will. Even Christ's burial and glorification are fitted into the framework of the kenotic perception, as well as his post-Easter existence in eternity.[25]

Bulgakov believes that the Chalcedonian definition itself presupposes a kenotic interpretation of the divine nature in Christ. The correlation of human and divine natures in Christ is only possible if there is a kenotic self-diminution of the divinity as well as the deification of the humanity. As Bulgakov puts it, "God reveals himself *theandrically* ('Godmanly')."[26] It is not Christ's divinity that undergoes lessening, but it is the *morphe* (the mode of divine existence) that diminishes itself—God puts aside his divine glory and enters the categories of temporality. Though possessing divinity, Christ does not exploit it to the full extent: even the miracle stories in Christ's ministry are marked by kenotic limitations.[27]

Bulgakov believes that Christ's self-awareness of his divinity developed during his earthly life. Here his kenosis consists in the absolute undergoing of a process of formation. Bulgakov thereby rejects the patristic interpretations of those cases where Christ is said to act sometimes as man and sometimes as God. Instead he insists that all these manifestations are due to the kenotic state of Christ's divine self-awareness. As Bulgakov puts it, kenosis turned Christ's divine self-awareness into a *tabula rasa*.[28] He calls this the kenosis of the divine hypostasis. This hypostatic kenosis enabled him to co-relate the divine hypostasis (in its kenotic state) to the human hypostasis. A similar idea of leveling is crucial for Fr Sophrony's theology of persona. Bulgakov asserts that the process of formation undergone by the theandric hypostasis of Christ is similar to that of every human hypostasis.[29] This allowed Bulgakov and then Fr Sophrony to use Christ as a model for the ascetic life to the utmost extent. Bulgakov holds that in the Trinity there is no subordination, only a hierarchy in relationship. Yet in Christ's kenosis his relationship to the Father acquires the character of subordinationism (cf Jn 14:28), and in the incarnation there is a kenotic *dissolving (rastvorenie)* of the Son in the Father.[30]

[25]Ibid., 278, 410, 436.
[26]Ibid., 266, 270.
[27]Ibid., 252, 260, 264-65.
[28]Ibid., 269, 280-82, 313.
[29]Ibid., 261.
[30]Ibid., 330-31, 336-37.

Kenosis also touches on Christ's relation to the Holy Spirit. The Spirit withdraws from Christ at Golgotha (or rather does not reveal himself). The kenosis of the Holy Spirit goes in parallel with the kenosis of Christ, starting from Christ's birth. Thus, in the child Jesus the gifts of the Holy Spirit are present, but not in their fulness. At his baptism Christ receives only some gifts of the Holy Spirit. The climax of the Spirit's kenosis comes at the time of Golgotha: "In the kenosis of death on Golgotha the immutable abiding of the Spirit [upon the Son] becomes imperceptible in contrast to the [ultimate] perceptibility at the transfiguration." Golgotha, thus, is seen as the kenosis of the Spirit in his operation. Hence Bulgakov works out the difference between the kenosis of the Son and the kenosis of the Spirit. It is a difference between the *kenosis of the hypostasis* (in the Son) and the *kenosis of operation* (in the Spirit).[31]

Vladimir Lossky's Critique of Fr Sergius Bulgakov

Bulgakov seems to be aware of a human side of Christ's kenosis, which is ruled out by Lossky, who says: "Kenosis can be related neither to man, nor to the God-man, but to God alone, who for the sake of our salvation assumed 'the conditions of the life of the world' and subjected himself to them, being 'in the likeness of man.' "[32]

Lossky's stance naturally excludes any further anthropological implications of kenosis within the ascetic life. In his eyes, the idea that kenosis is inherent to the Trinity led Bulgakov to believe that the incarnation was determined by divine necessity. He refers to Bulgakov's statement that "the kenosis of the incarnation ought to be accepted . . . as the metaphysical Golgotha of the Logos' self-crucifixion . . . which had the historical Golgotha as its consequence."[33] Lossky feels that Bulgakov's concept of "metaphysical crucifixion" rules out the element of the free sacrifice on the part of God for the salvation of mankind: the incarnation is then determined not by soteriological concerns but by ontological exigency within the Godhead. Thus, to describe Bulgakov's idea of the incarnation, Lossky uses the phrase "divine suicide," toward which God has an existential drive. Instead of ontological exigency, Lossky emphasises the voluntary character of Christ's redemptive act. Lossky also accuses

---

[31]Bulgakov, *The Comforter*, 288–91; cf *The Lamb of God*, 345.

[32]Lossky, *The Debates about Sophia* (Paris, 1936) 70.

[33]Ibid., 71; cf Bulgakov, *The Lamb of God*, 260.

Bulgakov of turning the divine hypostasis of the Logos into a human hypostasis, which later "regains" its divine self-awareness through humanity.[34]

Fr Sophrony's Position

Though Fr Sophrony would agree with Bulgakov on the kenotic principle in trinitarian being, his trinitarian kenoticism hinges on the concept of persona and not on any abstract deductions from the concepts of "fatherhood" and "sonhood." Fr Sophrony's principle of persona per se presupposes ultimate kenosis in relation to other personae, since kenosis is inherent to the hypostatic mode of existence, which is love:

> The Person in God we live as the bearer of absolute fulness of Being; and at the same time the Person does not exist alone . . . Perfect love does not live locked in itself but in the other Person, in other Persons. The whole conjunction of Being obtains as the imprescriptible possession of each of the Three Hypostases. But the Hypostasis manifests itself thus in the act of perfect love which similarly implies complete self-emptying, the belittlement of self.[35]

Though Fr Sophrony supports Bulgakov in the idea of the trinitarian kenosis and the cross as its earthly manifestation, he differs from Bulgakov in the way he relates the world to its Creator. For Bulgakov, the incarnation and the cross are the factual expression of an internal divine exigency. It would have taken place even if Adam did not fall. For Fr Sophrony, the motive of the incarnation and of the cross is purely *soteriological*, determined only by the fall of Adam. He holds that Bulgakov's position deviates from the tradition, which maintains a purely soteriological purport of the incarnation, as expressed in the Nicene creed: Christ came down from heaven "for us men and for our salvation."

Fr Sophrony is on the side of Lossky in his criticism of Bulgakov's idea of Christ's "hypostatic kenosis." The hypostatic kenosis of Christ in Bulgakov is not a voluntary effort, but an ontologically "inborn" fact. In Lossky and Fr Sophrony we find that Christ voluntarily undergoes kenosis: while possessing divine power by virtue of his divinity, he deliberately avoids its manifestation.

---

[34] Lossy, *Debates about Sophia*, 72–73, 68; cf Bulgakov, *The Lamb of God*, 257.
[35] *We Shall See Him as He Is*, 230; cf *His Life Is Mine*, 29.

This is what Bulgakov calls the "kenosis of action," but he relates it not to Christ's will but to the operation of the Holy Spirit. The "kenosis of action" in Christ, as Fr Sophrony conceives it, has more direct anthropological implications for his idea of the deification of man.

This comparison allows us to situate Fr Sophrony's roots within the Russian theological scene. Fr Sophrony is more attentive and receptive than Lossky to Bulgakov's ideas on kenosis. Nevertheless, though Bulgakov's kenoticism had a significant impact on Fr Sophrony's theological framework, it does not determine it. Bulgakov's abstract idealism remains alien to Fr Sophrony's mystical-ascetic "realism."

Silouan the Athonite on Kenosis

The anthropological dimension of kenosis was demonstrated in Silouan's spiritual experience. The fulness of grace in Silouan's vision of Christ was preceded by his kenosis, so deep as to allow Fr Sophrony to draw an analogy with the kenosis of Christ.[36] The idea of self-diminution is a leitmotif of Silouan's writings and comes to its most articulate expression in the formula: "Keep thy mind in hell and despair not."[37] This implies diminishing one's self before God to virtually nothing, and seeing oneself worthy of hell. Fr Sophrony deduces from it a general principle:

> When we properly condemn ourselves to eternal infamy and in agony descend into the pit, of a sudden some strength from above will lift our spirit to the heights. When we are overwhelmed by the feeling of our utter nothingness, the uncreated light transfigures and brings us like sons into the Father's house.[38]

This ascetic self-diminution is well embedded in the eastern tradition, as J.-C. Larchet aptly demonstrates, especially in the *Apophthegmata Patrum*.[39] Silouan, however, going beyond his precedents, marks an important connection between christology and ascetic theology when he introduces the concept of *Christ-like humility*.[40] This self-diminution is seen as a divine attribute,

---

[36] *We Shall See Him as He Is*, 132ff.
[37] *St Silouan the Athonite*, 42.
[38] *His Life Is Mine*, 60.
[39] Larchet, "La formule 'Tiens ton esprit en enfer et ne désespère pas,'" 51-68, esp. 58ff.
[40] *St Silouan the Athonite*, 301ff.

transferred to the plane of ascetic theology. The utmost self-emptying is seen in the absolute surrender of self to God in one's will, action, word—that is, in every manifestation of one's being. Silouan, though, did not possess the same conceptual tools as Fr Sophrony, who was more able to "furnish" kenosis theologically. Bulgakov's idea of the kenosis of the divine hypostasis and his kenotic christology provided Fr Sophrony with a solid bridge linking the kenotic theme of Silouan's ascetic experience with the given framework of eastern theology.

Kenosis in Man according to Fr Sophrony

The Example of Christ

Within Fr Sophrony's theological framework, built on the principle of *commensurability* between God and man, the imitation of Christ as model and becoming Christ-like (God-like) emerge as a necessary goal of the Christian life. In support of this idea Fr Sophrony often resorts to the scriptural passages where *following after Christ* is stressed: the verb *to follow* is interpreted by Fr Sophrony as meaning to undergo the same ontological experiences as the Christ-man, as recorded in the gospels. He uses such passages as John 13:15, Matthew 10:38, Revelations 14:4, and Philippians 2:5 to justify the transferring of christological statements to the sphere of ascetic anthropology. Citing John 17:3, Fr Sophrony sees a living existential knowledge of Christ's own experiences as a necessary goal for the attainment of deification. This Johannine "knowing Christ" refers not so much to "intellectual information" as to ontological sharing in like experience: "Only those living an inner life like His earthly life 'know' Christ."[41] If the life of Christ is seen through a kenotic prism, then it is natural that the process of ontological cognition of his experience involves the same pain of kenosis: "Realising that for me, created from nothing, it was essential to go through fiery torture in order more profoundly to apprehend the Man of Sorrows (Is 53:1-12), I accept the sacred pain with a grateful love." If we experience Christ in his humanity, through this experience his divinity becomes accessible to our ontological knowledge as well. Fr Sophrony writes: "[This pain] initiates me into the mysteries of Being, not

[41] *We Shall See Him as He Is*, 131.

only of the created order, but also of the uncreated."[42] As we shall see further, this explains the role of kenosis in the deification of man.

Ascetic Kenosis and the Teaching on Persona

The *modus patiendi* and *modus agens* of persona presuppose the kenosis of one's being: kenosis is an actual expression of the dynamic dimension of persona's being, its capacity for *transference of being*. Without kenotic experience in man's life, his hypostatic capacities would remain unrealized. Thereby, the teaching on persona allows Fr Sophrony to assimilate the kenotic experience in the ascetic life and to see kenosis as a necessary element within it.

"PRAEPARATIO NEGATIVA": EMPTYING OUT OF THE FINITE—"PURGE ME . . . AND I SHALL BE CLEAN" (PS 51:7). For the human persona to reach its potential of infinity in God, it ought to "prepare" itself by transcending any finite category. Hence, Fr Sophrony employs the idea of "cleansing," annihilation of the "old man." This "finite" old man is seen as an obstacle to the laying of a new foundation for the persona's subsequent participation in the infinite God-like mode of being: "When we return to 'nothing' we become material which our God can create from." Kenosis as the "crossing out" of the past is more explicitly expressed in another passage, where Fr Sophrony says that when we are reduced to nought, "in this manner are we cleansed from the 'curse' of our inheritance (cf Gen 3:14-19)." "Inheritance" is to be understood as the condition of man distorted by the fall; behind Fr Sophrony's thought here lies the Pauline concept of "the law of sin," living in man (Rom 7:23). The process of discarding this "inheritance" and restoring the primeval *tabula rasa* involves therapeutic self-emptying and hence suffering. Fr Sophrony describes this "emptying out of the finite" as becoming bare of the former "attributes" of our existence: "Everything that we set store by in the past, we cast away, and find ourselves stripped of earthly ties, of our learning, even of our will."[43] Therefore, Fr Sophrony links *kenosis* with *repentance*. On the one hand, man empties/exhausts himself in his effort to turn to God and transform his own being. On the other, repentance transforms all his efforts and strivings toward God into kenosis—"all this becomes Christ-like kenosis."[44] The phrase

[42]Ibid., 224.
[43]Ibid., 123.
[44]Ibid., 187-88.

"Christ-like kenosis" signifies the ultimate character of one's efforts: in Christ's prayer of repentance for the sins of the world in Gethsemane, he emptied himself of his strength to implore the Father.

Assimilation of the divine mode of being is necessarily linked with *pain.* Therefore Fr Sophrony admits that pain is "a leitmotif of his life in God." Fr Sophrony asserts that the kenotic experience, though it involves pain, is not negative in its essence, but positive and constructive. He draws a distinction between the "spiritual suffering" in kenosis, on the one hand, and on the other, pathological pain: nervous tension, the unsatisfied urge for sensual, passionate experiences, physio-psychological conflict.[45] The main difference in the two forms of suffering is that the former arises always in relation to God, and his involvement in one way or another transforms the negative experience into the positive one, while the second is, as it were, "self-subsistent," having neither sense nor value for spiritual advance. This distinction allows Fr Sophrony to counterbalance Lossky's refutation of the "dark night of the soul" as a way to union. Lossky did not make any such distinction, seeing thereby the suffering of kenosis only as a negative, destructive experience.

"PRAEPARATIO POSITIVA": OPENING UP TO THE INFINITE—"THOU HAST ENLARGED ME WHEN I WAS IN DISTRESS" (PS 4:1). In its "positive" aspect, kenosis develops the hypostatic *modus agens*—the entire giving over of I to the other, and the *modus patiendi*—the receiving of the other in his/her fulness. To be able to "receive," one ought to "give space" within oneself by diminution of this self, so as to become an *express image* of other persona(e) in a Christlike manner, as we saw above.

Fr Sophrony's ascetic teaching brings out the link between self-condemnation (which found its ultimate expression in Silouan: "Keep thy mind in hell and despair not") and kenotic personalism. The depth of the experience of grace depends on the depth of kenosis. The kenotic "descent into hell," as "reducing of oneself to nothing," builds up the necessary space/foundation for the *perception* and capacity to contain and assimilate the infinity of divine grace. In order to justify this spiritual principle, Fr Sophrony introduces the analogy of a tree: just as in a tree, where the size of its roots corresponds to the size of its upper part in order to be able to sustain it, so negative experience allows us to receive, sustain, and assimilate the positive. This correspondence is in

[45]Ibid., 88.

direct ratio: Fr Sophrony believes that "the measure of [man's] salvation . . .
corresponds to the depth of his *kenosis*."[46]

Hence Fr Sophrony posits an ascetic "equation-formula," which puts the
two types of experience in proportionate dependence on each other and
which, he believes, lies at the root of the eastern ascetic tradition: "The fulness
of *kenosis* precedes the fulness of perfection."[47] This equation is of crucial
importance for Fr Sophrony's theory of the monastic life. He calls this equation "the mystery of the Love of God." In Fr Sophrony this formula arises in
connection with the interpretation of Christ's passion, where the fulness of
Christ's kenosis anticipates his resurrection and glorification. Fr Sophrony
then transposes the same principle to the sphere of ascetic anthropology. He
cites, as justification for doing so, the words of Christ in Luke 18:14, in which
he sees the same principle contained. The formula *the deeper–the higher* is a
commonplace in Fr Sophrony's later works, especially in *We Shall See Him as
He Is*. Hence, kenosis is linked with the idea of the *amplitude* of Christian experience. The closer one advances in one's "ascent" to God, the broader is the
diapason of one's being. Fr Sophrony illustrates this by pairs of contrasts: on
the one hand the mysterious interweaving of darkness (Mt 8:12), suffering,
pain, descent into hell; on the other, ascension into heaven, anticipation of resurrection, heavenly bliss, contemplation of uncreated light, the kingdom of
God having come in power, eternal glory, joy.[48] This twofold aspect of Christian experience is projected from the experience by Christ's disciples of his
transfiguration. Unlike Lossky, who sees in the event of the transfiguration
only the manifestation of the divinity of Christ in its positive energy (uncreated light),[49] Fr Sophrony also points out the kenotic element, witnessed by
the disciples—namely, the conversation in the Lucan narrative about Christ's
kenotic *exodos* (departure, Lk 9:31). Evaluating this event, Fr Sophrony writes:
"In a short period of time there are both the infinite glory and descent into
hell. And this is the way for Christians.'[50]

The same twofold character is seen by Fr Sophrony in the passion of
Christ. Along with the utmost depth of suffering on the Cross, Christ
contemplated the coming victory:

[46]Ibid., 128.
[47]Ibid., 53.
[48]Ibid., 77, 88, 99.
[49]See Lossky, *Mystical Theology*, 220ff.
[50]*We Shall See Him as He Is*, 77.

It would not be mistaken to suppose that His global vision included not only extreme Self-emptying to the extent of descent into hell but the spectacle of His victory over death. He beheld the multitude of them whom He had saved in the Light of the Father's Kingdom.[51]

The idea of "broadening of one's being" is a reflection of Fr Sophrony's personal mystical experience. He often describes the divine realities as an "abyss." This word conveys the sense of the immensity and infinity of what was experienced. From within the same framework he interprets the Pauline concept of "the fulness of Christ" (Eph 3:19), the Johannine notion of the "abundance" of life (Jn 10:10), and the "breadth and the length and depth and height" (Eph 3:18).[52] In these passages Fr Sophrony sees the indication of the diapason of one's mystical Christian experience, which embraces utterly negative states ("descent into hell," kenosis) and positive states (participation in divine bliss, anticipation of the future resurrection).[53]

His ascetic teaching presupposes a consecutive scheme, projected after the pattern of Christ's *exodos*. Christ's kenotic experience of Gethsemane, Golgotha, and his descent into hell precedes his exaltation. The *downward–upward* scheme is set forth as a fundamental principle of ascetic striving for perfection: "The striving for the Highest Goodness is natural to us, but our journey towards Him begins with our going down to hell." This ascetic formula has its inception in the christological statement Ephesians 4:9-10, where the apostle Paul highlights the same scheme *descent–ascent*. This scheme is taken as a pattern for men to follow: "And this is precisely our route after the fall." Fr Sophrony also interprets the descent–ascent scheme in terms of humility as reversal of pride, which allows him to view the christological scheme as the correcting reflection of Adam's fall: "Our ascent to the Most High is through humility, since through pride we fell down into the darkness of hell."[54] In varying forms this scheme often appears in Fr Sophrony's writings.

The two schemes ascent–descent and the deeper–the higher play an important role in Fr Sophrony's understanding of the deification of man. In the context of the deification this broadening entails the breaking of former limits of finitude in order to reach the infinite:

[51]Ibid., 106.
[52]Eph 3:8-19, *We Shall See Him as He Is*, 107, 137; Jn 10:10, ibid., 77.
[53]Ibid., 106, 135, 137.
[54]Ibid., 66-67; cf *His Life Is Mine*, 61, 78.

The superiority of the Father explains the necessity for our struggle to assimilate [his image] ... We grieve painfully because we do not contain His fulness in ourselves ... This [metaphysical] pain is something qualitatively different—an essential stage in our progress from earthly to cosmic, even eternal dimensions.[55]

Liturgy: Kenosis and Pleroma

Fr Sophrony's kenotic perspective has affected his comprehension of liturgical prayer. We now turn to an analysis of those points that set Fr Sophrony somewhat apart from contemporary Orthodox writers who touch upon the theme of the liturgy.

The Contemporary Theology of the Eucharist: Fr Alexander Schmemann

The most outstanding Orthodox liturgists in Fr Sophrony's milieu were Fr Cyprian Kern and Fr Alexander Schmemann. Schmemann's approach is marked by a sharp awareness of the "deviation" and "westernization" that had occurred in Orthodox theological schools. Hence he attempts to restore the distinctiveness of Eastern Orthodox liturgics by reviving the scriptural features in liturgical practice.

First, he strongly criticizes an "individualistic perception" of the liturgy. Instead he points out that "assembly (*synaxis*) was always considered the first and basic act of the Eucharist." An idea of the necessity of *synaxis* is associated with the ecclesiastical attribute *sobornost* (conciliarity). He affirms the connection between the words *sobornost* and *sobor* (the temple), where the latter is seen as a visible expression of the former.[56]

Second, for Schmemann, the liturgy makes manifest the *pleroma* of Christ's redemption and the kingdom having already come with power. Such a conception of liturgy leads to a certain neglect of the centrality of the cross in worship. Schmemann's focus on eschatological fulfilment sets the eucharist into the "forward looking" perspective: it takes place in the time of fulfilment "on the eighth day." Schmemann does point out the retrospective element,

---

[55] *We Shall See Him as He Is*, 112, 224.

[56] A. Schmemann, *The Eucharist: The Sacrament of the Kingdom*, tr. P. Kachur (New York, 1988) 19, 115, 230.

but he refers primarily to "the beginning,"[57] that is, the creation of the world, which in the act of the eucharist is deified and returned to God. The liturgy is the fulfilment of the *eschaton*. For Schmemann, the biblical eschatological promise in 1 Corinthians 15:28, "God may be all in all," comes to its realization in the liturgy. The liturgical breaking of bread is conceived primarily as "the ascent to the throne of God and the partaking of the banquet of the Kingdom."[58] Due to his eschatological stance, he sees the liturgical act of the church as "above all the joy of the regenerated and renewed creation."[59] D. Staniloae notes this centrality of joy in Schmemann, which reflects the Easter triumph: "Now all things are filled with light, both heaven and earth."[60]

Even those elements that are retrospective de facto, such as the commemoration of the historical events of Christ's life, are seen by Schmemann through the prism of eschatological reflection. The kenotic elements of Christ's redemption are dissolved in the joy of the *eschaton*. At the *proskhomidia*, when the "lamb is sacrificed," Schmemann sees "a symbol completely filled with the reality of the new creation."[61] What links the Christ-event, in general, or the last supper, in particular, with the liturgical act is not the act of retrospective remembrance, but their common prospective participation in the eschatological fulfilment.[62] Thus, the historical element of the liturgy is diluted in eschatological eternity, and consequently the importance of the actual moment of consecration risks losing its urgency: the whole anaphora is seen as one single prayer. Schmemann refuses to ascribe any specific significance to the consecratory formula, saying that the focusing of attention on this moment demonstrates the influence of western scholasticism.[63] For Schmemann, to present the Eastern Orthodox epiclesis as a consecratory formula is simply to substitute one consecratory formula for another. He believes that the very principle of locating a moment of consecration remains wrong. The liturgy is beyond time and space.

It would appear that for Schmemann "God has saved the world" already, and the goal of the liturgical service is primarily to *witness* to this salvation. Schmemann generalizes this task in the following words: "all our worship

[57]Ibid., 34-36. Schmemann calls this element *cosmic*.
[58]Ibid., 35-36, 55, 92, 163.
[59]Ibid., 53; cf 119: "joyous affirmation of the cosmic offering."
[60]D. Staniloae, "Orthodoxy, Life in the Resurrection," ECR 2:4 (1969) 371.
[61]Schmemann, *The Eucharist*, 110.
[62]Ibid., 202.
[63]Ibid., 214, 218, 226.

services therefore are an ascent to the altar and a return back to 'this world' for witness." He speaks of this ascent as a prime means for the restoration of the unity of mankind, which for him comes from above and which was lost after the fall of Adam. Thus Schmemann's liturgical theology focuses on restoration, fulfilment, and fulness of life.[64] As such it appears devoid of any kenotic element.

In contrast to Schmemann's stress on joyous triumph in the eucharist, Fr Sophrony reinstates a kenotic insight into the perception of liturgical prayer, which is characterized by an awareness of "negative" experience (i.e., of spiritual suffering and pain). The liturgy is perceived through the kenotic prism of his christology and his concept of prayer, formed on the basis of his own ascetic experience.

Fr Sophrony's Contribution

Of course Fr Sophrony's perspective does not undervalue Schmemann's emphasis on eschatological triumph. In Fr Sophrony this triumph is synthetically integrated with Christ's kenotic self-sacrifice into one scheme. Thus, Fr Sophrony echoes Schmemann when he speaks of "the anticipation of the kingdom 'having come in power' (Mk 9:1)," of the resurrection, "the foretaste of the messianic banquet in the kingdom of the heavenly Father (Mt 22:2)." He agrees with Schmemann in pointing out that in the "eucharist" as "thanksgiving" one participates in divine life with joy. He even uses the same terms when he speaks of the *cosmic dimensions* of liturgical prayer, especially when it embraces the beginning—the act of creation. Similar ideas of the temple and its role are found in Fr Sophrony: "the church, where the liturgy takes place, is the gates of the holy heavenly kingdom. This ministry is the source of delight for us."[65]

Nonetheless, Fr Sophrony's approach, marked by the sharp awareness of the kenotic dimension of hypostatic being, shifts the liturgy retrospectively toward the Christ-event and transforms it into a "Gethsemane" type of prayer, rather than a merely triumphant celebration: "Through this holy sacrament we learn to 'live' [i.e., experience] the eternal character of the kenosis of the Logos of God."[66]

[64]Ibid., 61, 99, 152.
[65]"Liturgical Prayer," in *We Shall See Him as He Is*, Russian ed., 216, 220-21, 224 (Essex, 1985).
[66]*Birth into the Kingdom*, 166.

Unlike Schmemann, for whom the liturgy is above all "ascent," Fr Sophrony's perception of liturgical prayer is characterized by his stress on the perpetual movement between God and the world. Liturgical prayer is an attempt to "unite" both of these spheres of being and as such it is characterized by the painful "tearing asunder" (*razryv*) of our being. The combination of these different existential levels within liturgical prayer is in line with Fr Sophrony's idea of the *amplitude–diapason* of Christian experience, mentioned above. Thus the liturgical "diapason" stretches from the *ascent* into the luminous sphere of the divine but also to the *descent*, merging through compassion into the suffering of the cosmos.[67]

This kenosis is determined by several theological ideas. First, Fr Sophrony sees the spiritual essence of the liturgy as "sacrifice for the sins of mankind."[68] The *hypodeigma* (example) of Christ (Jn 13:15) in his kenosis remains of prime importance for Fr Sophrony. The goal of the liturgy is "to represent Christ's earthly 'work' (Jn 17:4) in our minds as fully as possible." Fr Sophrony writes: "The obligation of the priest is the continuous 'repetition' [i.e., as "re-presentation"] in time of the divine act of redemption, so as to fulfil Christ's commandment—*Do this in remembrance of Me.*"[69]

The celebrant *recapitulates* the world in Christ-like prayer. Fr Sophrony's concept of the hypodeigma of Christ embraces all aspects of his incarnate life, the prayer in Gethsemane being one of its most significant elements. Christ's prayer for the whole world is set forth by Fr Sophrony as a supreme degree of Christian ascetic perfection, and just as Christ prayed there for the whole world, the celebrant of the liturgy should follow Christ's hypodeigma. Such prayer will indeed "embrace the fulness of cosmic being," "a multitude of lives and eons of time": both the *anabasis* (ascent) into the kingdom, as in Schmemann, and also *katabasis* (descent) into the "ocean of human suffering." The praying person is enabled to sense and assimilate Christ's taking upon himself of "our illnesses" (Is 53:3-4). In a Christ-like manner the intercessor mystically participates in the suffering of mankind. This mystical taking upon oneself of the suffering of mankind is necessary for the elimination of negative forces, the consequences of sin within mankind.[70]

Second, although Fr Sophrony does agree with the idea that liturgy transcends time and breaks through chronological barriers into eternity, this

[67]"Liturgical Prayer," 216, 224.
[68]Ibid., 228.
[69]"Liturgical Prayer," 227; cf 216, 220; cf *His Life Is Mine*, 88.
[70]"Liturgical Prayer," 216-17, 221-22, 227; cf *His Life Is Mine*, 87.

transcendence is not merely eschatological but is "the ontological entering into the sphere of Christ's spirit, in his divine and earthly dimensions." Moreover, Fr Sophrony's approach is free from "non-historicity" of the liturgy—the eucharist is not simply ascent-escape from time with a subsequent "return." In Fr Sophrony's theology the element of historical remembrance is more articulately present: the eucharist brings about "the visible presence of the Gethsemane prayer and of death on the cross on Golgotha within history."[71] For Fr Sophrony the liturgy brings time into eternity, uniting them:

> We have two ontological levels: one is "before the creation of the world" [i.e., eternal], the other is our historic time ... Such is the eternally temporal and temporally eternal character of this sacrament. Our present needs are intertwined with the eternal principles of God.[72]

Third, as far as the question of sobornost is concerned, Fr Sophrony does not ascribe to it the same significance as Schmemann. Sobornost, as we shall see in chapter five, is understood not simply in quantitative but in qualitative terms. Its quality is interpreted in terms of the fundamental attribute of hypostatic existence, that is, the capacity for the mystical embrace of other personae and of the whole cosmos in its spatial and chronological dimensions. That is why liturgical prayer is said to be "the most adequate expression of hypostatic prayer"—when the hypostasis emerges in the fulness of its kenotic embrace of others. Basing his idea on his eremitic experience, when he celebrated in the presence of only one other person, he claims that even with only a "symbolic" synaxis, the celebrant did not experience any lack of sobornost, for "the whole world was there—the cosmos and the Lord and eternity."[73]

Finally, a christocentric kenotic perception of the liturgy allows Fr Sophrony to justify the defensive emphasis on the epiclesis made by the liturgists of the eastern rite. He points out its significance on the basis that Christ has set us an hypodeigma—an example of kenosis for men to follow. Fr Sophrony, as we saw earlier, interprets this kenotic stance in the sense that Christ, though bearing the fulness of divinity, consistently avoids any manifestation of self-deification. The invocation of the Holy Spirit for the supernatural divine act of "consecration" is yet another kenotic self-belittlement on

[71]"Liturgical Prayer," 227-28; cf *His Life Is Mine*, 88
[72]"Liturgical Prayer," 221.
[73]Ibid., 224-25; cf *His Life Is Mine*, 88.

the part of Christ the Logos, whom the priest represents at the liturgy. In ascribing a consecratory function to the words "Take, eat … " (Mt 26:26), as it is found in the western tradition, and omitting an invocation of the Holy Spirit, one introduces the element of "self-deification" into Christ's action.[74]

Fr Sophrony's liturgical stance is in line with other Russian theologians who maintain the sacrificial nature of the eucharist. Here again he has much in common with Bulgakov. For Bulgakov, the eucharist is a remembrance of the last supper, a sacrifice dynamically related to the sacrifice of Golgotha. Like Fr Sophrony, he has an idea of the commemorative "repetition," of "entering into the power of the events of Christ's life on earth." As such the eucharist is a continuation of Golgotha as a testimony of Christ's com-passion with humankind.[75] Also in S. Chetverikov the eucharist is the re-presentation of the Golgotha sacrifice where God's love for the world manifests itself.[76] The twofold nature of eucharistic experience in Fr Sophrony is adequately paralleled in Florovsky. Though the eucharist is celebrated in remembrance of Christ, his last supper, and though the eucharist is Golgotha, even Golgotha is a sacrament of joy.[77] However, in Fr Sophrony this kenotic stance overtly makes the amplitude of kenosis–pleroma theologically legitimate. He achieves this by linking liturgical prayer with his teaching on persona.

We have seen that for Fr Sophrony the kenotic dimension of hypostatic being serves as a determining factor in christology, in triadology, and in ascetic and liturgical theology. His exploration on such a large scale of the implications of kenosis in the hypostatic mode of being comes as a result of his synthetic integration of kenotic ideas from various strands of thought. Fr Sophrony inherits the existential dimension of kenosis from Silouan. By absorbing these currents of ideas through the prism of his own experiences and his teaching on persona, Fr Sophrony works out the concept of kenosis on an all-embracing level. Each constituting element—christology, triadology, anthropology, and liturgical theology—works in a dynamic interaction, constituting one integral *theoria*.

[74]*La félicité de connaître la voie*, 44.
[75]S. Bulgakov, "The Holy Chalice," *Put'* 32 (1932) 28–34.
[76]S. Chetverikov, "The Eucharist as a Center of Christian Life," *Put'* 22 (1930) 3–45.
[77]G. Florovsky, "The Eucharist and Sobornost," *Put'* 19 (1929) 3–22.

CHAPTER FIVE

Image and Likeness

The concept of *image and likeness* derives from the biblical passage: "And God said, Let us make man in our image, after our likeness" (Gen 1:26). Though most of the fathers touched on the theme, they came to no single interpretation. Since substantial research has already been done on the interpretation of the concept of image and likeness in the fathers in general and on some fathers in particular, we shall mention only the main features of the patristic tradition.

When interpreting the concept of image and likeness, the fathers generally preferred not to concentrate on any isolated part of the human being. Nonetheless, some scholars highlight the platonic tendency in the fathers to confine the elements of the image to the sphere of the *noetic* part of the human being and its functions. The inclusion of the body into the image (as in Irenaeus, for example) has rarely been exploited theologically to its fullest extent. Maximus offers an important synthesis of patristic ideas: for him the *psyche noera* (noetic soul), as the image, is the spiritual apex of man, considered as an entirety. In this he integrates Evagrian and Macarian notions by way of Diadochus.

The latter also precedes Maximus in reviving the distinction between the image and likeness. Irenaeus, Clement, and Origen already saw in Genesis 1:26 a difference in meaning between image and likeness.

St Gregory of Nyssa saw the likeness to God not only in static attributes of man, but also in his ability to imitate God in living a sinless life. Maximus explores this existential dynamism of likeness on a new theological level, seeing it in terms of "a total relationship" of the *whole man* with God.

The use of trinitarian analogies by the fathers is often related to the tripartite structure of human noetic faculties. That is why the fathers, when employing the trinitarian model for man, "emphasize the unity of the Trinity" and, in contrast to the modern personalistic approach, are less inclined "to find any distinctive representation of different persons,"[1] that is, to use interpersonal human relations in their analogies for God's triunity.

Fr Sophrony on Image and Likeness

Fr Sophrony's interpretation of the concept of image and likeness marks him out as a theologian who works within the framework of the eastern tradition, and yet who at the same time advances the expression of its anthropology. Significantly new ways of expression of the traditional idea emerge in relation to the eastern patristic tradition and also in relation to some modern Russian theologians.

Image and Likeness as the Mode of Being

Fr Sophrony sees the concept of image and likeness as embracing the totality of the human being. He echoes Gregory of Nyssa's and Maximus' idea of the dynamic dimension of likeness, and introduces a new formula to express the idea of image and likeness, saying that it lies in the *mode of being*. He admits that the divine image and likeness is reflected partially in all those elements of man singled out by the fathers, but insists that the *mode of being* is the most appropriate summary of the concept, since it embraces the totality of the human being. He explains man's similarity to the Creator in terms of the capacity of the human being to participate in the divine life, and its potential "to live in the likeness of God" and to be deified.[2] While the fathers, generally speaking, tried to find some static attributes in the divine being that are reflected in man's constitution, Fr Sophrony shifts the emphasis to the dynamic attributes of the divine mode of being.

Fr Sophrony's approach to the concept of image and likeness has Christ as a focal point of theological attention. The dynamism of his interpretation of

---

[1] J. Sullivan, *The Image of God: The Doctrine of St Augustine and Its Influence* (Dubuque, Iowa, 1963) 193-94. The idea of the so-called "psychological" (J. Meyendorff, *A Study of Gregory Palamas* [London, 1959] 232) trinitarian model is employed by various fathers and is best presented in the west by Augustine and Gregory Palamas in the east (see M. Hussey, "The Palamite Trinitarian Models," SVTQ 16:2 [1972] 83ff.). However, Methodius of Olympus, Ephrem the Syrian, and Gregory of Nazianzus (see for example Or. 31, PG 36:144Df) used the image of three human beings to illustrate the Trinity.

[2] *St Silouan the Athonite*, 174; cf *La félicité de connaître la voie*, 23.

the concept derives from the Chalcedonian formula and its implications: perfect humanity and divinity concurring in one hypostasis. This makes hypostatic existence the main point of correspondence between the divine and human being. Thus, the concept of persona emerges as determinative for Fr Sophrony's interpretation of the concept of image and likeness. Just as persona is the innermost principle of the absolute being, hypostasis is also the basis of man's being as the image of God. In Fr Sophrony, even the traditional aspects of image and likeness—freedom, mind, spirit—pass through the prism of his teaching on persona, and are transformed therein into dynamic attributes of hypostatic existence. Just as persona can be manifested in the dynamics of existence, so also the divine image has a dynamic dimension. That is why Fr Sophrony emphasizes that the divine image is revealed to us by the man Christ, that is, in his active "hypostatic" manifestations. The Slavonic translation of *hypodeigma* in John 13:15 as *the image (obraz)* supports his dynamic interpretation: it is Christ's *life*, and not merely any static elements of his being, that constitutes the image. Thus, living in imitation of Christ's life is the way to realization of the image. This emerges in connection with the discussion on the monastic vow of chastity:

> For us the fundamental and incontestable justification of this vow lies in the "image" given us by the Lord himself (Jn 13:15) ... For us Christians, the problem facing us is an absolute one: if possible, to become like Christ in everything, in order, through this likeness to the man-Christ, to attain likeness to God, which is the ultimate aim and meaning of our existence.[3]

That is why he rarely applies the aspects of the image employed by the fathers in their *static* sense (such as mind, spirit, soul) and emphasizes the *dynamism* of likeness.

"Image and Likeness" of the Trinity

For Fr Sophrony, the image of God in man is not simply envisaged individualistically. Mankind is multihypostatic in like manner to God. Having established in chapter three Fr Sophrony's understanding of the life of the Trinity,

---

[3] *Principles of Orthodox Asceticism*, ed. A. Philippou (Oxford, 1964) 20.

Christ's commandments as the projections of divine life onto the level of human existence.

here we shall attempt to see how he understands mankind as modeled in the image of the triune God.

The intratrinitarian love is transposed by Christ's incarnation to the level of man and revealed in divine commandments. Fr Sophrony treats them as the self-expression of God: "In their essence Christ's commandments are the self-revelation of God."[4] As such they are the projection of divine life onto the level of human existence.

Fr Sophrony particularly singles out the "second commandment": "Love your neighbor as yourself" (Mt 12:31). Commenting on this injunction, Fr Sophrony writes that it "does not reveal so much degree or measure of love than to make apparent the consubstantiality of the human race, the sharing on an ontological level of all our human existence."[5] This rules out any interpretation of Matthew 12:31 that would treat love as a rule in a moral or ethical code of behavior. As a concrete expression of the dynamics in the triune God, the love commanded of us introduces humans into the trinity-like life, and leads mankind to singleness of being. This love, as "the inmost content and the best expression of *persona*," denotes the presence of attributes in the human persona that we find in the divine persona—namely, its existential orientation toward another hypostasis; its capacity of giving itself to, and receiving of, other personae; and the need for other personae in order to realize itself. Thus the unity in the Trinity, ensured by mutual ever-acting love, can be envisaged in humankind as well:

> We have learned to see these dynamics in the love that is the most profound moment in the fact of eternal self-determination of the persons of the Holy Trinity ... The Energy of Divine Love is poured down on us who are created "in the image and after the likeness," and we are commanded to acquire this love.[6]

The ontological meaning of love for one's neighbor as oneself is therefore that the human race becomes one single reality, one man–mankind. This love is "ontologically" expressed in *prayer for the whole world*. In eastern ascetic tradition such prayer is mentioned, for example, by Macarius and particularly stressed by Silouan.[7] However, in Fr Sophrony this experience receives explicit

[4] *We Shall See Him as He Is*, 72.
[5] *La félicité de connaître la voie*, 20.
[6] *We Shall See Him as He Is*, 205.
[7] Macarius, *Hom.* 18.8, 180.

theological justification. Following the pattern of love and consubstantiality in the Trinity, human personae are united by love in the same manner as the divine personae:

> Lively experience of the *Persona* is rarely given to people here below. It comes by praying like Christ for the whole world as for oneself. Led to such prayer by the workings of the Holy Spirit, man existentially lives the image of the Triune God. In this kind of prayer one experiences the consubstantiality of the human race. Such prayer reveals the ontological meaning of the second commandment, "Thou shalt love thy neighbor as thyself" (Mt 12:31). All Adam becomes One Man– mankind.[8]

Fr Sophrony uses the terms *Vse-chelovek* (whole man) and *Ves' Adam* (whole Adam) to express the idea of the unity of humankind and to draw a closer parallel with God, who is one in three persons.

In principle, prayer for the whole world is based on the same pattern of ultimate "giving" and "receiving" that we find in the Trinity. In ultimate self-abasement (giving) the praying person receives into himself the entire human race. This receiving is accomplished through love: it embraces the whole of mankind. The same principle is at work in God and in man: "Love transfers the existence of the person who loves into the beloved, and thus the person assimilates the life of the beloved."[9] In prayer for the world, "the beloved" is the rest of one's fellow men. In this mutual transfer (giving) and assimilation (receiving) one can detect the principle of the trinitarian perichoresis, which actualizes the absolute unity of the divine hypostases. This echo is clear from the following passage:

> Drawn by the Spirit of God to prayer for the whole world, to share in the Lord's prayer in Gethsemane, we suddenly behold in ourselves a divine miracle—a spiritual sun rises in us, the name of which is *persona*. It is the beginning in us of a new form of being, already immortal. At the same time we apprehend, not superficially, not with our reason, but in our very depth, the revelation of the hypostatic principle in the Holy

---

[8] *We Shall See Him as He Is*, 203.
[9] *La félicité de connaître la voie*, 21.

Trinity. We behold in Light the sublime mystery of Unoriginate Being—the *Living* God: One in Three Persons.[10]

This ontological state is therefore the reflection of the Trinity on the human plane. It also verifies the characteristic of the human hypostasis: as in the Trinity each hypostasis contains the fulness of divine being, so also the human hypostasis is called to "achieve the fulness of god-manhood," that is, "to become dynamically equal to humanity in the aggregate."[11]

The Roots of Fr Sophrony's Approach

Fr Sophrony and the Eastern Patristic Tradition

In the fathers there is no explicit elaboration on the theme of the human hypostasis as the image of God, but one can find traces of Fr Sophrony's approach. In seeking signs of God's image in man, the fathers sometimes refer to the soul's attributes: nonmateriality, self-determination, freedom or free will,[12] that is, those that Fr Sophrony sees as attributes of hypostatic being. As mentioned above, there is indeed a *dynamic* dimension in Gregory of Nyssa's approach to image and likeness. As various scholars have observed, he does not make a distinction between the two. Such "image-and-likeness" is understood as the God-like existence attainable through virtues: one becomes God-like through goodness, through communion, through mutual and brotherly love, through gaining control over sinful passions. Thus in Gregory of Nyssa *apatheia,* freedom from passions, largely constitutes the divine image. For Gregory, the capacity for the fulness of "good things" in human nature is an attribute of the image, which reflects the divine prototype.[13]

Maximus elaborates further on the dynamic dimension but within likeness alone. He parallels the image/likeness and nature/persona distinctions. Particularly important for our study is the implicit connection between the

---

[10] *We Shall See Him as He Is,* 195.

[11] *His Life Is Mine,* 29.

[12] Thus Gregory of Nyssa refers to the attributes of "spirit" (and "nonmateriality"): *Opif. hom.,* PG 44:137B, 181C, 192A; *Mort. Orat.,* 42; *Anima et res.,* PG 46:44A, 89A; to "self-determination": *Virg.,* 298; to "freedom": *Anima et res.,* PG 46:101C; *Opif. hom.,* PG 44:184B.

[13] *Imag.,* PG 44:276C; *Opif. hom.,* PG 44:184B.

likeness and *praxis entolon* (practice of the commandments) in Maximus.[14] It is not, though, as explicit or developed as in Fr Sophrony.

As for the trinitarian dimension of the image, there are parallels between the tradition and Fr Sophrony but they are not explicit. In scripture one may find only hints of the reflection of the trinitarian image, such as the use of plural in Genesis 1:26. In the New Testament, John 17:22 partly reflects this multiplicity-in-unity. The early church did not integrate the idea of the Trinity-image into its ecclesiological framework. Instead, it elaborated the principle of unity on the Pauline idea of the body of Christ.

With a few exceptions, such as passages in Cyprian, Cyril of Alexandria, and Hilary of Poitiers,[15] the tradition has no single direct precedent for Fr Sophrony's type of trinitarian model. He himself refers to Gregory of Nyssa's idea that image is related not to any human part but to the whole human race: "Because the image is not in any part of the [human] nature . . . but it is to the whole race that the attribute of the image is extended."[16] He points out Gregory's expression—*the universal man*, which Fr Sophrony connects with the concept of the whole Adam. Yet despite the presence of the idea of the unity of mankind, we do not find in Gregory any development of the connection between the consubstantiality of mankind and that of the Trinity.

Thus, despite some examples of "dynamism" in the concept of God-likeness in the eastern tradition, and Gregory of Nyssa's idea of the universal unity of mankind, it is difficult to see how these "passing" remarks in the fathers alone could have provided a framework for Fr Sophrony's articulate and theologically advanced interpretation of Genesis 1:26. The patristic parallels, being only partial and remote, prove inadequate to be the sole source for Fr Sophrony's understanding of the image and likeness.

Fr Sophrony and Russian Thought on Persona and Triunity

Already in nineteenth-century Russian philosophical and theological writings we find rich parallels with Fr Sophrony. T. Špidlík, in his summary of Russian personalism, rightly points out the significance of the development of the idea that "man is 'persona,' because he is the image of the personal God." Špidlík

---

[14]Maximus, *Cap. Car.* 3.25, 154; *Quest. Thal.* 53, 435.

[15]Cyprian, *Dom. orat.* 23, 105, ll 448-49: "de unitate Patris, et Filii, et Spiritus sancti, plebs adunata"; Cyril, *Ioan. Evang.* 11.11, 729-37, esp. 734; cf Hilary, *De Trin.* 8.7-17, 319-29.

[16]*La félicité de connaître la voie*, 52 (cf *Opif. hom.*, SC, 160). Cf Gregory of Nyssa, *Com. Cant.* 14, 427:22-428:2.

agrees with Olivier Clément's observation that the merit of Russian theology and religious philosophy in the nineteenth and twentieth centuries lies in its more correct approach to the mystery of man as image of God, which in the tradition until then "had been obstructed by substantialism and intellectualism."[17] Thus, Berdyaev believes that in man as persona there is a Prometheus principle—man's God-likeness. "The human persona is not complete; it ought to realize itself—to actualize the image and likeness of God, to receive in itself, in an individual form, the *universal* fulness." A somewhat similar understanding of the image of God in man is found in Bulgakov, for whom the fulness of the image of God in man is persona. Špidlík provides ample illustrations of the various dimensions of persona in Russian thought, such as "agapic" and "kenotic,"[18] which directly correspond to Fr Sophrony's concept of persona.

The societal aspect of being human is a commonplace in contemporary reflection. A recent revival of interest in triadology in the west has contributed to a further elaboration of the communal dimension of being. In Russia the dynamic trinitarian dimension of the human persona received great attention much earlier. The idea of likeness based on the trinitarian model had been current in Russian theological circles since the nineteenth century. Špidlík observes:

> The Russian church, which likes to be described as "Johannine," is particularly sensitive to this mystery of the Trinity, contemplated by the man of faith . . . Russians wish to bring to the world the ideal of the "unity of all" . . . of a multiplicity that succeeds in its unity. The Holy Tri-unity then, truly expresses the vocation of the Russian people.[19]

Though the central field of application of the trinitarian model is theology and especially ecclesiology, the idea embraces various aspects of human culture, with a special emphasis on the social dimension.[20] In Fedorov, for example, there is a celebrated expression: "The Trinity is our social project." The trinitarian model is *theologically* sketched by Khomiakov but developed by others to varying degrees, in particular by Khrapovitsky, Florensky, Bulgakov, Florovsky, and Lossky.

[17]Špidlík, *L'idée russe*, 24; O. Clément, "Aperçu sur la théologie de la personne dans la 'diaspora' russe en France," in *Mille ans du christianisme russe (988-1988)*, ed. N. Struve, 303 (Paris, 1989).
[18]Špidlík, 24ff, esp. 30-31.
[19]Ibid., 61, 63.
[20]Ibid., 62, 64.

The centrality principle of the Trinity was implanted in Russian thought even earlier, via Sergius of Radonezh. The event usually stressed is his setting up of a church dedicated to the Holy Trinity for the first time in the history of Russian Christianity. For many centuries Sergius' theological message was neglected. Only in the twentieth century did Russian theologians comment on Sergius' interest in the Trinity.

In the nineteenth century the idea of the Trinity received a new departure in Russia. One of the earliest attempts to establish a connection between the Trinity and human society (the church) is found in Khomiakov:

> The unity of the church follows necessarily from the unity of the Godhead, since the church is not a multitude of persons in their individual isolation, but the unity of the divine grace, which lives in the multitude of reasonable creatures, who submit themselves to grace.[21]

However he does not elaborate on the union, following the Trinity-model, and prefers the concept of the body of Christ.

His concept of unity is taken further by Antony Khrapovitsky (1863-1936), whose own theology is controlled by his pastoral concern. His method of theologizing consists in extracting the *moral truth* contained in each dogmatic statement of the church. As far as the dogma of the Trinity is concerned, it is "a metaphysical foundation for the moral duty to love [one another]."[22] Thus, the Trinity provides a prototype of human unity and love. Commenting on John 17:11, 21-24, he writes: "From these words of our Lord it is clear that his followers . . . are to be permeated by a close internal unity, such as that in which the Father and the Son abide in relation to each other."[23] Khrapovitsky highlighted the link between the dogma of the Trinity and Christ's words about love in John 15:13 and 17:26. "Love to the point of full communion in life and of readiness to sacrifice one's life (Jn 15:3)" is seen as the basis of unity. This unity is "the unity of many persons according to essence." The unity presupposes the identity of the content of life, unity of will. Khrapovitsky makes an important remark that unity "acts as a certain power within each person." It is difficult to discern whether he here anticipates some Russians in their

[21]A. Khomiakov, "The Church Is One," in *Collected Theological Works*, ed. J. Petrov, 39 (St Petersburg, 1995).
[22]A. Khrapovitsky, "The Moral Idea of the Trinitarian Dogma," in *The Moral Ideas of the Most Important Christian Orthodox Dogmas*, ed. N. Rklitsky, 19 (Montreal, 1963).
[23]Ibid., 11.

concept of the principle of *catholicity*—that each hypostasis bears the fulness of the whole—or has in mind a general idea of power constituted by unity.

Khrapovitsky also suggests that the principle of the divine hypostasis is opposed to the principle of the human individual. The latter is characterized by the division of consciousness, where I is opposed to that which is not I. In the Trinity there is no such opposition. "The freedom and eternity of the divine persons do not abolish the unity ... there is place for the *free persona* but no self-containing of persona." He employs the model of the Trinity mainly for pastoral reasons: to induce people to love each other and to remove the opposition between I and "not I," by growth from I into we. Yet he makes no explicit connection between Genesis 1:26 and the Trinity. Instead, he is pre-occupied with the idea of love between men. His model is not the Trinity as such, but the love revealed in Christ's relations to the Father.[24] The connection between the Trinity and mankind is not drawn from the concept of image and likeness, but from the moral significance inherent in any dogmatic statement of the church. The insufficiency of Khrapovitsky's theological tools explains why he proved unable to base the link between the dogma of the Trinity and ecclesiology on a more firm theological foundation.

The idea of the Trinity being the prototype for the church community is taken up by Georges Florovsky. Following Khrapovitsky, he refers to Cyril and Hilary. He applies the Trinity-model to the church alone[25] and is reluctant to go beyond the boundaries of the church. His anthropology does not allow him to explore in depth the implications of the Trinity-image: "Christ brings the believers into spiritual unity. Of course, the union of love and of single-mindedness does not reach the same indivisibility that is found in the Father and the Son."[26]

Thus, Florovsky is reluctant to apply the word likeness without qualifying it, and he prefers to use the vaguer term "reflection." Instead of the "consubstantiality" of the human race, Florovsky speaks of a "certain natural unity." While employing the Trinity as a model to spell out the concept of image and likeness, he wants to point out the *impossibility* of real and complete likeness.

---

[24]Ibid., 10ff.

[25]See G. Florovsky, "Sobornost: the Catholicity of the Church," in *The Church of God: An Anglo-Russian Symposium*, ed. E. Mascall, 55 (London, 1934) 55; "Le corps du Christ vivant. Une interprétation orthodoxe de l'église," *La sainte église universelle. Cahiers théologiques de l'actualité protestante*, hors-série 4 (Paris, 1948) 17; "Theological Extracts," *Put'* 31 (1931) 21.

[26]G. Florovsky, *The Byzantine Fathers of the Fifth to Eighth Centuries* (Paris, 1933) 55.

Thus, both Khrapovitsky and Florovsky hardly envisage the unity of the church in *ontological* terms and prefer to apply the Trinity as a model *analogically* so as to point to spiritual unity through love.

Original interpretations of the trinitarian model are offered by Bulgakov and Florensky. They deepen the *ontological* dimension of the concept of the unity of the church, thereby shortening the ontological distance between the image and the prototype. Also, both discern the trinitarian pattern in the human hypostasis in its self-determination, which they deduce from the very principle of relationship between personal beings.

Bulgakov, in his article "St Sergius' Testament to Russian Theology" (1926), discusses why Sergius of Radonezh, despite his renowned humility, shows such an amazing theological boldness as to name the chapel in his monastery after the divine Trinity. While commenting on Sergius' concern, Bulgakov lays down the main statements of his own theology of the image of the Trinity. Love is seen "as the very life of the divine triunity, the preeternal act of love-in-mutuality, in which three are one and one are three. Man is created after the image of God." In connection with the Trinity-model, Bulgakov speaks of every human subject as dependent on the other similar subject: "Thou is an other I, and at the same time a similar I, which is also not-I, because it is beyond I, but it is given to me as the condition of my self-consciousness, thus it is in me . . . I cannot remain in its self-enclosedness, in its metaphysical egoism, but it has need of Thou to become I, in order to realize the fulness of its self-being." On this basis Bulgakov arrives at the concept of the "undividedness of mutual reflection." He also speaks of the insufficiency of the unity where only two subjects are involved. This I-Thou unit may turn Thou into a mere "version" of I: "What if this Thou is the same I, only different in appearance, which put on the hat of not-I?" For the affirmation and recognition of I in Thou, there is a need for the third person. As an expression of I in other personae Bulgakov uses We, which is the self-realization of I in multi-unity.[27]

From this principle Bulgakov deduces the catholicity (*sobornost*) of any personal being: "Sobornost, or multi-unity, is an inherent attribute of the personal I-hypostasis, without which I cannot realize itself or even exist. Saying I, the hypostasis at the same time says also Thou, We, They." Bulgakov elaborates an important principle of trinitarian hypostatic being:

[27]S. Bulgakov, "St Sergius' Testament to Russian Theology," *Put'* 5 (1926) 5–9.

128   I LOVE, THEREFORE I AM

The intellect of created beings cannot comprehend what takes place in
the Holy Trinity: I does not proceed from I into Thou and He, in such
a way that I remains statically as it was; but I goes out-of-itself as if
extinguishing its light in order that it should light itself in the other or
the other two. The divine hypostasis is realized through the preeternal
act of one hypostasis extinguishing itself [*samoougashanie*] in order to
light itself in the other, for the other, through the other.[28]

In connection with this Trinity-model, Bulgakov points out that man, as
anthropos, was brought into being as bipartite: Adam and Eve, as a "multi-unity
that . . . leads toward the [archetypal] Triunity because of [each one's] hyposta-
sicity." The bond of unity is love, which is seen as a mode of being: "love is life
in the other, transference of one's own I into some Thou, self-identification
with it after the principle of trihypostatic love."[29] To summarize, Bulgakov
writes:

The fulness of the image of God in man, rooted in persona, goes
beyond persona as a monad, into the multi-unity of all mankind. One
may say that the image of God in its fulness belongs not even to man
in his one persona, but to humankind in its *sobornost*, in love after the
image of the consubstantial triunity of God.[30]

Bulgakov applies the trinitarian model to the monastic community. When
discussing Sergius' interest in the Trinity, he suggests that the aim of Sergius'
efforts was the gathering of people into one after the image of the Trinity.
Thus Sergius embarks on his ascetic effort "to bring together [human] souls,
in the unity of brotherly love . . . so that all would be one . . . after the image
of the Holy Trinity." It is in this context that Bulgakov proposes the principle
of the cenobitic life based on the trinitarian model: "For northern Russia
St Sergius is the restorer of monasticism, based on the principle of the strict
discipline of cenobitic life, which at the same time promotes brotherly love,
since there is nothing that would bring division; there is one will, one love and
one life."[31]

[28]Ibid., 9.
[29]Ibid., 10-11.
[30]S. Bulgakov, "The Problem of Eternal Life," *Put'* 52 (1937) 22.
[31]Bulgakov, "St Sergius' Testament," 11.

This principle, which Bulgakov mentions only in passing, is taken up and elaborated by Fr Sophrony.

Špidlík calls Paul Florensky "theologian of the Trinity par excellence" and highlights the various aspects of Florensky's thought on the Trinity: social, amical, cosmic, and gnoseological.[32] In his book *The Pillar and Ground of the Truth,* Florensky has an extensive discussion on the Trinity as a prototype of the church, and particularly concentrates on the issue of unity and *consubstantiality.* For him, the Trinity emerges as a solution for multiple theological perplexities, and he attempts to work out the more widely applicable senses of the dogma of the Trinity. Florensky criticizes rationalistic philosophy, and argues that any *true knowledge* is built on ontological communion in *consubstantiality.* He calls it the *homoousian* (i.e., of the same substance) type of philosophy. *Homoiousian* (i.e., of a like substance) thinking operates with abstract objects in terms of static comparative analysis, and as such it lacks the conceptual apparatus to account for dynamic interrelationships among beings. In connection with this principle Florensky focuses attention on the words in the Liturgy of St John Chrysostom that signify unity after the image of trinitarian unity: "let us love one another that with one mind we may confess the Trinity consubstantial and undivided." The participants of the eucharist are invited to glorify the name of the Trinity *with one mouth and one heart.* Florensky emphasizes that this is *en homonoia* (in unity of thought) and not just *en homoinoia* (in similarity of thought).[33] On the basis of this distinction he argues that the unity of the faithful is not just moral: this would mean they were *homoiousioi.* The unity that makes men *homoousioi* in relation to one another is "objective-metaphysical," after the pattern of the trinitarian unity, actualized through love:

> The metaphysical nature of love lies in the supra-logical overcoming of the naked self-identity *I=I* and in the going out of oneself . . . Owing to this going-out itself, *I* becomes in another, in *not-I,* this *not-I. I* becomes *consubstantial* with the brother, consubstantial (*homoousios*) and not just like-in-substance (*homoiousios*). And it is this *like-substantiality* that constitutes moralism, i.e., a vain, inherently insane attempt at a human, extra-divine love.[34]

[32]Špidlík, 63-67.
[33]P. Florensky, *The Pillar and Ground of the Truth,* tr B. Jakim (Princeton, 1977) 64ff.
[34]Ibid., 67.

Florensky follows Bulgakov in deducing the necessity of the trinitarian pattern (I–Thou–He) in hypostatic self-determination, though he employs a different kind of logic. While Bulgakov asserts that He is necessary to break through the binary opposition of I–Thou dualism, and to affirm that Thou is not a mere version of I, Florensky says that He is necessary to contemplate the unit I–Thou:

> Enjoying the beauty of the dyad (*I-Thou*), *He* loves this duality and thereby comes to know every *I*, affirming every one, in its hypostatic self-being . . . and restores the self-identity of the contemplated hypostases: of the first *I* as the loving and beloved *I* and the second *I* as the beloved and loving . . . Through breaking the shell of this dyad enclosed within itself, the third *I* thereby communes with the dyad . . . and the dyad becomes a trinity.[35]

Discussion of the trinitarian model emerges, as in Bulgakov, as a commentary on Sergius' setting up of the Trinity chapel. Florensky reads into it "the call of Russia to unity" and says that Sergius' purpose was "contemplation in it of the prototype of divine unity." Florensky, too, sees there the archetypal pattern that sets an example for any social unit. He believes that for Sergius the idea of the Most Holy Trinity was embedded into the very structure of society; it was a rule of communal life.

For Florensky, in each trinity-unit, the third I, which contemplates the twofold unit as an object, itself becomes a foundation for the new trinity. Via the uniting agency of these third Is the trinity units grow together into the one single body, namely the church, which is the "objective manifestation of the hypostases of the divine love."

Vladimir Lossky systematizes the idea of the church as the image of the Trinity. He mentions Gregory of Nyssa's idea that Christianity is the imitation of the divine life and his interpretation of Genesis 1:26.[36] He thus builds up the idea of the church from the universality of the trinitarian image: "the character of the Image of God . . . refers to the whole man in his integrity."[37] In Lossky the triadological dimension of ecclesiology is finally integrated into a balanced synthesis with the idea of sobornost, to which we now turn.

[35]Ibid., 68–9.
[36]*Profes. Chr.*, 136; *Opif. hom.*, PG 44:185AD.
[37]Lossky, *Mystical Theology*, 115-16.

Trinitarian Unity and the Concept of Sobornost

When discussing the trinitarian models as used in Russian theology, we notice the centrality of the concept of *sobornost*, which stands for *catholicity*. Berdyaev recognized it as a cornerstone of nineteenth-century Russian thought, unparalleled in the west. The idea was introduced into Russian theology and discussed by Khomiakov in his "Letter." His sources for the idea remain a riddle, but he had a profound impact on Russian religious thought. By justifying the translation of the Greek *katholike* as *conciliar (soborny)*, and not *universal,* in the Slavonic translation of the creed, Khomiakov was the first to assert its *qualitative* implications, as opposed to the *quantitative* ones found in the fathers. For him it reflects the harmony of the whole ecclesiastical body and the exclusion of any sort of particularism, be it nationalistic or geographical.[38] *Soborny* secures *inner organic unity through love in freedom* and not through *authority* (which Khomiakov associates with Roman Catholicism). Khomiakov does not, however, explore *soborny* in its triadological context.

Nicholas Lossky rightly praises Florensky's merit in developing further the principle of trinitarian consubstantiality and introducing it into the metaphysics of created being. It allowed Florensky to speak of love as an *ontological,* rather than psychological (*pace* Khomiakov), bond. Nonetheless, though critical of Khomiakov, Florensky follows him in explaining *katholikos.* Though he says that *katholikos* means "all-common, *universalis, generalis, das Ganze betreffend, allgemein,*" he also admits that the term "universal" (*oikoumenike*) is only a particular aspect of *katholike.* He asserts that *sobornost* means not a number of voices (votes), but "communion of being, goal, and spiritual life, bringing all together." Catholicity is the task of the church, similar to the tasks of unity and moral perfection.[39] Florensky's idea marked a step from the static interpretation of sobornost as loving unity toward the dynamic "trinitarian" sobornost we find in Ilyin, Vladimir Lossky, and finally in Fr Sophrony. Ilyin sees in the kenotic trinitarian model how the one who loves puts all his I into Thou of the beloved, and the beloved denies himself for the sake of the other. Sobornost is the earthly icon of the divine consubstantiality and the *sobor* (council) of the Father, Son, and Holy Spirit.[40]

---

[38]A. Khomiakov, "Letter to the Editor of *L'union Chrétienne* on the Meaning of the Words *Catholic* and *Conciliar,*" in *Collected Theological Works*, ed. J. Petrov, 278-79 (St Petersburg, 1995); cf Cyril of Jerusalem, *Catech.* 18.23, PG 33:1044A.

[39]"The Idea of the Church in Holy Scripture," in *Collected Works* 1:403-4 (Moscow, 1994).

[40]V. Ilyin, "The Nature and the Meaning of the Term 'Sobornost,'" *Sobornost* 1 (1935) 6.

Vladimir Lossky argues that sobornost is not quasi-organic togetherness, but the *personal* communion in the Holy Spirit after the mode of trinitarian being. The attempt to balance the common and personal elements in the unity of the church led Lossky to the formulation of a fundamental principle of sobornost: the part is never absorbed in the whole. Not only every church but every Christian believer is catholic in the sense that he fully expresses the potentiality of the whole church. The idea that one part of the whole bears the fulness of the whole grew out of the principle of the trinitarian existence, where each divine hypostasis bears the fulness of the Godhead. Lossky expresses it thus:

> As in God each one of the three persons, Father, Son, and Holy Spirit, is not a part of the Trinity but is fully God in virtue of his ineffable identity with the one nature, so the church is not a federation of parts: she is catholic in each one of her parts, since each part in her is identified with the whole, expresses the whole, has the value which the whole has, does not exist outside the whole.[41]

Lossky applies the concept sobornost only within the confines of the church, in which the capacity of the human being for such a mode of being is demonstrated. Lossky has prepared the ground for the further application of the trinitarian model—not only to the existence of the church but, as in Fr Sophrony, to the whole of mankind.

A similar understanding to that of Lossky is found in Bulgakov, who, however, does not expound it, noting it only in passing. For Bulgakov sobornost becomes a fundamental principle of hypostatic existence, which ensures the unity of the multihypostatic mode of being. This being is modeled upon the pattern of the triunity, whose wholeness is safeguarded by the ontological bond of absolute kenotic love. He explains how this principle became manifest in the life of Sergius of Radonezh: "this sobornost, the image of the divine triunity, burnt with a bright light in his [Sergius'] heart. He himself accomplished the act of sobornost in his deep inner heart, conquering his love of self, sacrificially denying self for the sake of love toward others, living not in and for himself, but in and for the other.[42]

[41]Lossky, *In the Image and Likeness of God*, 180.
[42]Bulgakov, "St Sergius' Testament," 12

Fr Sophrony sees sobornost as an attribute of hypostatic being after the image of the triune divinity. In Fr Sophrony we find a synthesis of the ideas of Florensky, Ilyin, Bulgakov, and Lossky. Fr Sophrony develops his idea of sobornost within the context of polemic concerning the nature of the unity of the church. He makes reference to Khomiakov, but though accepting Khomiakov's principle of unity as *internal* (*innere Einheit*), and a unity of love, Fr Sophrony follows Florensky in stressing the ontological character of this unity. It is not just human psychological unity, but a result of the activity of the grace of God actualizing his image. In this connection H. Ruppert noted Fr Sophrony's concern for the application of consubstantiality to the church,[43] which echoes Florensky. Fr Sophrony regards the church and its organization as built after the image of sobornost of the Trinity: each local church and parish bear the *fulness* of the whole body.

Fr Sophrony's Contribution

Fr Sophrony and the Russians

The above analysis suggests that Fr Sophrony owes much to Russian theologians in general and to Lossky in particular. However, it would be wrong to say that Fr Sophrony does not make any significant contribution of his own. Each of the above-mentioned theologians uses the trinitarian model in his own way. Fr Sophrony makes his own synthesis of some of their methods and ideas.

Fr Sophrony values Khrapovitsky's concern for the practical pastoral relevance of each theological dogma and the immediacy of its application. He views the principles of monastic cenobitic life through the prism of triadology. However, his theological system is far tighter than that of Khrapovitsky, who is more interested in the general moral principles contained in dogma rather than the organic unity of his dogmatic theology. Any "pathos of intimacy" and "psychological esoterism," for which Florovsky criticizes Florensky and which are partially present in Khrapovitsky, are absent in Fr Sophrony.

As Williams rightly notes: "Bulgakov's ecclesiology is irrevocably bound to Sophiology and any attempt to understand his thought is bound to take into consideration the doctrine of *Sophia*."[44] First, Bulgakov does not elaborate on

---

[43]Ruppert, 47-48.
[44]Williams, 35.

the implications of the trinitarian model: how exactly it is reflected in communal existence and in the link between individuals and mankind as a whole. Instead, the sophianic context of the trinitarian image transfers the whole discussion into more general issues: Bulgakov speaks about pan-unity rather than about the consubstantiality of mankind. The church is seen as the embodiment of the reconciliation of divine and creaturely Sophia, brought about by Christ's work. This reconciliation is founded upon Christ's hypostasis. It is in Christ's hypostasis that man enters the life of the Trinity: the life of unity in plurality. But in Christ, man's individuality is transcended by his sharing in a hypostatic life not of his own (i.e., Christ's).[45] Bulgakov's anthropology is focused on the idea of man being a microcosm. In man the world is perfected and articulated; through man alone can it be brought to sophianic fulness.[46] Thus Bulgakov, due to his sophianic speculations, is less concerned with human trans-relationships according to the image of the trinitarian triunity.

Second, the concept of Sophia colors the whole theological framework with an element of gender dualism, alien to Fr Sophrony. In his *Unfading Light* Bulgakov envisages Sophia as a fourth "hypostasis," symbolizing the eternal femininity in God.[47] Bulgakov's sophianic perception of the Trinity affects his understanding of the human being as the image of God. The principle of man's multi-unity is found not only in the fact of the general multiplicity of persons, as in Fr Sophrony (Adam is the whole mankind), but also in the conjugal dyad of man and woman. Thus, Bulgakov always interprets the term Adam as a proper name, along with Eve.[48]

Yet Fr Sophrony is very close to Bulgakov's maximalist anthropology. Their shared anthropological absolutism allows Fr Sophrony to explore more fully than does Lossky the model of the Trinity in its application to mankind.

In respect to the consistency of his theological system, Fr Sophrony stands much closer to Lossky, whose theology and anthropology are insolubly linked. Also from Lossky Fr Sophrony inherits a reserved attitude to the speculative elements in Florensky's and Bulgakov's theological methods, especially their sophianic theologoumena.

Yet, much more than Lossky, Fr Sophrony treats the biblical formula of Genesis 1:26 in its *absolute* sense, and not through the prism of ecclesiology

[45]Bulgakov, *Unfading Light*, 348.
[46]Ibid., 269.
[47]Ibid., 212–14.
[48]Bulgakov, "St Sergius' Testament," 10.

alone. This absolutism expresses itself in two points of difference with Lossky: its universal extent, and the existential depth of the application of the trinitarian model.

If, for Lossky, Gregory of Nyssa's idea of the universality of the divine image in humanity provides a basis for the concept of the church, Fr Sophrony shifts theological attention to the universality of the image as inherent in *the whole of mankind,* even beyond the boundaries of the church. For Lossky the radical distinction between the concept of image and the concept of likeness *presupposes* the limit of likeness to the confines of the church. The image is the in-built potential and the likeness is the realization of this potential in the new unity of human nature, purified by Christ, within the church, the body of Christ. Its realization depends on human cooperation with the Holy Spirit. The function of the Holy Spirit is the bestowing of *koinonia,* which happens exclusively within the confines of the church—the rest of mankind (its non-Christian part) not being accounted for. As a result, Lossky's ecclesiology presupposes the old unredeemed part of mankind and the new redeemed members of the church—the old and the new Adam, somehow dividing the single Adam (mankind) of Genesis 1:26.[49]

Fr Sophrony would not object to any of this, but his theological concerns are different: he prefers to dwell on the *universalism* of the image, rather than on the perfection of likeness. Fr Sophrony is closer to Gregory of Nyssa than is Lossky in that he uses the *Adam*-terminology to express the consubstantiality and unity of the whole humanity—the whole Adam. He stresses that Christ came to redeem the whole Adam. This universalism manifests itself in that, in contrast to Lossky, Fr Sophrony, as Ruppert notes, does not employ the idea of the church as the body of Christ.[50] Of course, Fr Sophrony does not reject this traditional idea, but he himself prefers to use the idea of the body to express the unity of the whole human race: "*All mankind* is one body," and each one of us is its single cell. This unity as *inherent* may manifest itself, albeit negatively, even outside the post-Pentecostal *koinonia:* thus, one cell of this body (be it in the church or outside) *suffers* because the whole body is afflicted with illness. It also explains the fact of consubstantial responsibility for Adam's sin.[51]

---

[49]V. Lossky, *Orthodox Theology: An Introduction,* trs. Ian and Inhita Kesarcodi-Watson (New York, 1978) 70; *In the Image and Likeness of God,* 177ff, 184ff.

[50]Ruppert, 48.

[51]*St Silouan the Athonite,* 121.

This universalism has significant implications for Fr Sophrony's reinterpretation of sobornost. He sees it as an inherent principle of the whole humanity, where each particular human can bear the fulness of the whole Adam. This
universalism of Fr Sophrony's application of the trinitarian sobornost has been
noted by G. Dejaifve.[52] As such, sobornost becomes an indispensable attribute of persona, related to all and each human being. In Fr Sophrony the
dynamic dimension of sobornost reaches its ultimate limit and becomes
equivalent to the trinitarian perichoresis: *each* human persona can bear the fulness of all. Fr Sophrony's idea of the universality of sobornost was taken up
and developed by some Russian theologians, as we find, for example, in
Zenkovsky.

Why is he different from Lossky on the point of universalism?

In Fr Sophrony's anthropology, *every* man has an in-built image-model, and
hence a longing to perceive the divine reality: "We, who are in the divine
image, bear within ourselves an insuperable urge to find the meaning of the
self-existent divine being that is revealed to us." As such, every man is capable
of having a partial understanding of truth: "the Verity of God Himself is
implanted in us, for we are made in His image."[53] This has practical implications, which go beyond the sphere of Christian theology: any social unit of
men has the trinitarian pattern of relationship as its prototype. Thus, the intu-
itive perception of the contrast between the present state of mankind and its
Prototype gives birth to a tragic understanding of the world in philosophers,
artists, and writers.

Can the perichoresis of hypostatic love on the human level be as total as
in its trinitarian prototype? Lossky, like Florovsky, gives a negative answer,
pointing to the ontological difference in mode of being between the human
and divine hypostases. As created and limited beings, men do not have the
same capacity for perichoresis as the Trinity. Lossky spells out this difference
by referring to John of Damascus. Moreover, in later years Lossky was more
reserved in referring to the doctrine of perichoresis even in triadology, as it
seemed to him to endorse the *filioque*.[54]

---

[52]Dejaifve, 81f: the Trinity is "the perfect model of that unity of the human race, the
absolute perfection of charity of which the mystery of unity is the realization of the incomprehensible pledge of a total co-penetration of distinct persons."

[53]*We Shall See Him as He Is*, 104 and 247.

[54]Lossky, *Mystical Theology*, 53f; transcript of lectures delivered from 1955 to 1957, in
possession of Canon A.M. Allchin (January 12, 1956), 32.

Fr Sophrony states that the barrier between human hypostases does not disappear to the extent that it does in the Godhead.[55] However, the context of this passage suggests that Fr Sophrony has in mind mankind in its present imperfect state, rather than in the final realization of its potential. When Fr Sophrony speaks of the unity of humankind ("The Man is one, in the image of the Holy Trinity"), he goes so far as to say that "the *whole fulness* of human being becomes a possession of each human hypostasis";[56] and this is, in fact, a mirror of the absolutism of trinitarian dogma, applied to men. Why is this bold application possible in the framework of Fr Sophrony's theological system and impossible in that of Lossky? The crucial difference lies in their different estimations of the potential of human nature: Fr Sophrony speaks of the *God-like infinity* of man-persona,[57] while Lossky points out man's *limitation*. Thus, in connection with the concept of image and likeness, Fr Sophrony uses Bulgakov's striking expression, that in the creation of man "God *repeats* himself": man is deified to the point of equality with God.[58] From this argument, based on the model of Christ, Fr Sophrony concludes: "When each human hypostasis by the fact that it rests in the fulness of the consubstantial unity becomes the bearer of the whole of human existence, it is dynamically equal to all humanity, to the image of Christ, the perfect Man who contains all mankind in Himself."[59]

The Trinity and the Monastic Community

The difference between Fr Sophrony and other Russian theologians is not confined to anthropology alone. Fr Sophrony develops further the implications of the concept of image and likeness in the sphere of the practical ascetic theology of cenobitic life. None of the above-mentioned theologians relate the triunity in the Godhead to the ascetic practice of prayer for the whole world, while Fr Sophrony's trinitarian concern renders such prayer the supreme aim of ascetic endeavor. Neither do those fathers who mention the idea of prayer for the whole Adam-humanity relate it to the idea of the trinitarian image of mankind.[60] For Fr Sophrony the potential of persona is not

---

[55] *We Shall See Him as He Is*, 216.
[56] *La félicité de connaître la voie*, 21f.
[57] *His Life Is Mine*, 78.
[58] *We Shall See Him as He Is*, 192–93.
[59] *La félicité de connaître la voie*, 21.
[60] See Macarius, *Hom.* 18.8, 180.

fulfilled until it is expressed in this Christ-like prayer, since "to the persona it is given to embrace all creation in the flame of Christ-like love."[61]

Fr Sophrony also explores further the theological implications of the application of the trinitarian model to the monastic community. It finds its clearest expression in his final "Testament" to his brethren: "the monastic community sets out to achieve unity . . . in the image of the oneness of the Holy Trinity . . . Each one of us, in some sense, within his own hypostasis, is the center of all . . . There is no one greater, no one lesser."[62]

Already in Silouan we find the ascetic principle that Fr Sophrony would later situate in the framework of trinitarian reflection: "Our brother is our life."[63] This formula expresses the characteristic element of persona, whose existential concern can be defined as "being-toward-the-other." It presupposes the trinitarian pattern of conveying the fulness of one's being to another hypostasis. It reflects persona in its *modus agens*; it is the projection of the second commandment into the sphere of ascetic cenobitic principles. The priority of other personae in respect to I expresses itself in the notion of ascetic *humility*: *I* is last in the community. In his "Testament" this principle is expressed thus: "All that he has and his whole self, he surrenders to each and all." On the empirical level, the *modus agens* of persona expresses itself in the practice of poverty, which Fr Sophrony understood not only as a deprivation of material goods, but as denying one's possessions (spiritual, material, intellectual) for the sake of sharing with others.[64]

In the same "Testament," the *modus patiendi* principle is expressed positively as "everyone and everything exists for him [i.e., for each member]."[65] The fulness of life on every level becomes the property of each member of the community. Each member is the focus of existential concern for each and for all, and this is expressed on every level—spiritual, material, psychological. The *modus patiendi* in community also has another aspect: the capacity for the ultimate "receiving" of another persona expresses itself in the practice of obedience, which is the self-abasement of I in order to give space in my persona to the other persona, appropriating thereby his/her being into I. Fr Sophrony considers obedience as the most adequate expression of the trinitarian mode

---

[61] *We Shall See Him as He Is*, 204–5; *His Life Is Mine*, 95.

[62] "Testament," in *Birth into the Kingdom Which Cannot Be Moved*, ed. N. Sakharov, 187 (Essex, 1999).

[63] *St Silouan the Athonite*, 47.

[64] "Testament," 187.

[65] Ibid.

of kenotic love. This principle explains why in eastern monasticism the vow requires obedience not only to the superior but to all members of the community. Fr Sophrony's concept of obedience goes beyond the common understanding of the concept as simply "deadening your will": it is the hypostatic "taking into oneself" of the other *personae*.

Fr Sophrony stresses theologically the importance of the *unity* of the community as a significant goal of the ascetic life. The ultimate unity of the community is realized through mutual perichoresis, which is expressed in Silouan's formula. The majority of ascetic practices are concerned with maintaining and striving for unity. The principles of trinitarian existence, when transferred into the community, presuppose the capacity on the part of each member to "take into himself" all *personae* of the community, which finds its expression above all in prayer: "Everyone, bearing in his prayer all the members of the community, strives to achieve what the commandment sets before us: 'Thou shalt love thy neighbor as thyself'—that is, as 'one's own' life."[66]

The unity of the community on the spiritual level comes about through the spiritual tradition of the monastery. One assimilates "the spirit of life" of the community, that is, the mode of life accepted in a particular community. Through this oneness in being, the Trinity-like unity of will with coordinated actions and mind is achieved. In the image of the Trinity, where one aspect of unity is the Father being the kenotic source of the Godhead, so the life of the community is coordinated by the abbot. Singlemindedness is achieved through obedience to him, as well as through the sharing of a common aim. Fr Sophrony also assigns an important role to the practice of ascetic struggle against unloving thoughts, which might create a negative predisposition toward another persona and result in the break of existential mutuality. The empirical expressions of trinitarian consubstantiality are the communal events of daily life: church services, meals, work, meetings, and other activities.

Thus Fr Sophrony advances the eastern ascetic theology of cenobitic life to a new level by exploring further implications of the trinitarian message of Sergius of Radonezh. His attention to detail in this area broadens the scope for the potential application of the trinitarian model to a wider range of social units. The monastery is an example or, in his words, "a school of life."

---

[66]"Testament," 187-88.

Difficulties

Perichoresis and the Human Persona

How problematic is Fr Sophrony's attempt to extend the idea of the complete ontological *perichoresis* to the human level? He emphasizes the spiritual dimension of the human hypostasis; though he does not dismiss the body, he mentions it more often in the context of ascetic struggle rather than as a glorified temple of grace. Thus, he writes, "persona is spirit," and being spiritual, non-material, perichoresis is then possible. This idea is fully supported by Nicholas Lossky's eschatological vision. It is likely that Fr Sophrony was acquainted with his article "On the Resurrection of the Body," which would assist him in making the fuller application of the trinitarian model. Nicholas Lossky speaks of the new potential of man in the deified state and the communion, even of bodies, among the members of the kingdom of God—their *complete mutual coinherence*. Fr Sophrony's position finds its further support in Ephrem the Syrian, who solves the question of "space" in paradise for the resurrected bodies by pointing to their immateriality.[67]

Universalism versus Ecclesiology

Does Fr Sophrony's universalism lead to the obliteration of the concept of the church, its uniqueness? Indeed the sacraments of the church do not occupy a significant position in his immediate theological concerns. The Holy Spirit is mentioned predominantly within the scope of ascetic experience rather than in an ecclesiological context. However, one ought not to read into Fr Sophrony's "silence" on this subject the absence of theological concern for the institutional church: tradition on many points is taken for granted by Fr Sophrony. Moreover, he stresses that the church is the guardian and revealer of the undistorted vision of the divine reality, which reflects his concern for dogmatic orthodoxy. He stresses that any deviation in the vision of the prototype results in the distortion of its human image.[68] Second, he sees the church as the bearer of the *fulness of grace*. The deification of man, man's attaining to the likeness of God, and his participation in God-like love and universality are not achieved "pelagianistically" by man's own efforts: it is the result of *synergeia*, of

---

[67]*Hymn. parad.* 5.7–10, 17–18.
[68]*La félicité de connaître la voie*, 23–25.

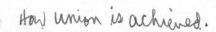
How union is achieved.

the cooperation of man and divine grace. Thus the perfect realization of persona-image also comes as a result of the action of the Holy Spirit.[69] The trinity-image, though inherent in all mankind even in its distorted form, may be restored fully to its original ideal only through the grace of the Holy Spirit, which "lives in the church." The healing of one of its parts benefits the condition of the whole Adam-mankind. This universalism is manifest in Fr Sophrony's liturgical theology: the eucharist, as we discussed earlier, is an offering for the whole of mankind, which has a cosmic effect. Thus the church remains an indispensable condition for the full realization of the divine image and likeness in mankind.[70]

The Whole Adam and Origenism

The unity of the whole of mankind in the image of the Trinity brings about a theological tension within Fr Sophrony's thought. On the one hand he condemns Origenism and believes in the reality of eternal perdition.[71] On the other hand, if at the last judgment the single body of mankind is split into the lost and the saved it appears theologically impossible to maintain the idea of the whole Adam. This unsolved tension emerges also in Silouan: after death he will not be in bliss and will not cease to pray for all mankind until God will have mercy upon all.[72]

As we saw in this chapter, in his theology of the image and likeness, Fr Sophrony, along with traditional elements, introduces a fresh interpretation, enriching thereby the eastern tradition. The newness is largely due to his teaching on persona, which he sees as the core of the divine image in man. The divine image in man is seen in *dynamic* terms: as man's capacity for assimilating the hypostatic divine mode of being. The Trinity is seen as a multi-hypostatic model for mankind, where the multiplicity of hypostases does not exclude absolute unity, so that mankind is seen as one single entity. Although such thinking was already present among other Russian thinkers, Fr Sophrony develops its implication beyond the confines of ecclesiology. His distinctive treatment of the formula in Genesis 1:26 licenses the application of the model to asceticism. It finds its most significant expression in the concept of the

---

[69] *We Shall See Him as He Is*, 231-32, 186.
[70] *St Silouan the Athonite*, 89ff; *We Shall See Him as He Is*, 205.
[71] *Birth into the Kingdom*, 186.
[72] *St Silouan the Athonite*, 259.

monastic community, where the ultimate goal of monastic life is perceived through the prism of the trinitarian model. The trinitarian model allows him to give a theological foundation for the mystical state of prayer for the whole world, and to explain why it is a prime goal of the ascetic practice of prayer. His theological exploration of the dependence of ascetic practices on dogmatic teaching marks him out as an original and creative theologian.

CHAPTER SIX

The Deification of Man

"I said, ye are gods" (Jn 10:34)—these words of Christ, quoting the psalm *théosis*
(82:6), set *deification* as the ultimate goal for the Christian life. They
opened up a new dimension in anthropology, unknown to the ancient world.
This *christological* dimension introduced notions that ran counter both to rab-
binical thought and to that of the Hellenistic world. Following the example
of the Johannine gospel, the Christian fathers applied the word *god* to man in
the context of deification, often with reference to Psalm 82:6.[1] In Christian
anthropology the concept of the deification of man carries a new principle—
the nullification of the opposition between the divine and human worlds. This
derives from the fact of the incarnation of God and is expressed in the so-
called "*tantum-quantum* formula": Christ the Logos became what we are in
order to make us what he is. This principle lies at the heart of the teaching on
deification in Ireneaus, Athanasius, the Cappadocians, Maximus, and others.[2]

The deification of man is expressed in various ways by Christian authors.
In 2 Peter 1:4 we read: "Whereby are given unto us exceeding great and precious promises: that by these ye might be partakers [*koinonoi*] of the divine
nature." This idea of *koinonia* (communion) is taken up by Ignatius, who speaks
about "participation in God."[3] Origen attempts to give a more elaborate theological account of how men participate in God, developing thereby a concept of dynamic participation in God through the Logos. The Alexandrian
theologians favored the concept of mystical participation in the deified body
of Christ. From the time of the Cappadocians the distinction between divine

[1]See Basil the Great, *Eunom.* 3.5.20, 164; *De Spir.* 9.23, 328; Macarius, *Hom.* 34.2, 261; John
Chrysostom, *Psalm.* 4.5, PG 55:46–47; *Psalm.* 2.3, PG 55:148; *Eutrop.* 2.8, PG 52:403; *Hom. Gen.*
22.2, PG 53:187–88; *Iohan. Hom.* 3.2, PG 59:39.
[2]Irenaeus, *Her.* 5, prooim, 15; cf *Her.* 3.19.1, 375; ibid., 4.33.4, 811–13; cf Athanasius, *Incarn.*
54.2, 458; *Adelph.* 4, PG 26:1077A; Gregory of Nazianzus, *Or.* 29.19.9–10, 218; Maximus,
Ambigua, PG 91:1113B; *Cap. theol.* 2.25, PG 90:1136B.
[3]*Ephes.* 4.2, in *Epist.*, 60.

ousia and *energeia* assisted the further development of the idea of participation in God, so much so that in Gregory of Nyssa the concept of participation tends to replace that of *theosis* (deification).[4] The idea found its ultimate completion in Gregory Palamas. The patristic tradition often speaks of participation in divine attributes, such as immortality and incorruption. *Participation* embraces the totality of the human being, its entire material and noetic constituents. Body, soul, mind, will—all these are the subjects of deification. This integrality is found, for example, in Palamas, as Mantzaridis convincingly shows: deification embraces the "moral" and the "material" aspects of man.[5] Despite this integrality, the fathers focus on the God-receiving capacities of *matter*, which gave rise to John Meyendorff's subsuming term *Christian materialism*.[6] That is why in the fathers the concept of deification frequently emerges within the context of bodily asceticism: they often referred, for example, to chastity as a means to deification.[7] Hence comes a connection that the fathers commonly make between the participation in the Godhead and the participation in the eucharistic body and blood of Christ: the divine mysteries are seen as the source of our deification.[8]

The deification of man was often expressed in terms of God's indwelling in man: "And the Word . . . dwelt among us" (Jn 1:14; cf 1 Cor 15:28; 1 Cor 3:16). When God permeates the human being on all levels, both material and spiritual, man becomes God's dwelling.[9] In the eastern tradition the imagery of the divine presence in/among men is reflected in the term *theophoros* ("God-bearing"), which was coined by Ignatius.[10] Since then the term became a common epithet for the saints—who, according to John of Damascus, possess God indwelling in their bodies, which become his temples.[11]

Patristic tradition usually sees man's potential for deification in the fact that man is created by God in his own image. Because of this natural affinity, the fathers spoke of man as potentially a son of God. The process of deification involves the realization of the status of *son of God* through the process of

[4]Cf Gregory of Nyssa, *Orat. dom.* 5, 60; cf *De beat.* 5, 124.

[5]G. Mantzaridis, *The Deification of Man* (New York, 1984) 61–84.

[6]J. Meyendorff, *A Study of Gregory Palamas*, 156.

[7]Cf Athanasius, *Decr.* 14.5, 12; (Pseudo-)Athanasius, *Contr. Arian.* 3.53, PG 26:433B; Methodius, *Symp.* 9.4, 276; ibid., 10.6, 302; Gregory of Nyssa, *Virg.*, 258.

[8]Cf Gregory of Nyssa, *Cat. Orat.* 37, 151–52.

[9]Gregory of Nazianzus, *Or.* 2.22.

[10]*Ephes.* 9.2, in *Epist.*, 66.

[11]Cf Athanasius, *Vie.* 14.1, 172; John of Damascus, *Exp. fid.* 4.15.13–34, 203–4; *Imag.* 1.20, 96.

hyiothesia ("adoption of sons"). The idea is present already in the New Testament. Christ gave power to those who receive him "to become the sons of God" (Jn 1:12), that the faithful might "receive the adoption of Sons" (Gal 4:5; cf Rom 8:15). This adoption of sons was accomplished through Christ's incarnation. Athanasius represents one set of ideas when he asserts that "Christ made us the sons of the Father and deified man by becoming himself a man." His thought hinges upon the idea of the incarnation: humanity is deified in a *natural* (*physikos*) manner, being assumed by God in the incarnation. Due to this understanding—our becoming God's children as a natural consequence of God the Son becoming man—he uses the concept of *hyiothesia* as synonymous with "deification":[12] to be a son or daughter of God is to be deified. Another set of ideas is presented by Basil, who speaks of our adoption not so much through natural deification at the incarnation as through its subsequent effects: the descending and indwelling in man of the Holy Spirit.[13] This emphasis on the Holy Spirit as the agent of *hyiothesia* is linked with the idea of deification as God's dwelling in man. Finally, the concept of divine adoption becomes a controlling feature of the theology of deification in Maximus,[14] due to his concern to maintain *dyothelism* in christology, as well as in ascetic anthropology. For him deification through *hyiothesia* is seen as a result of the dynamic communion of divine and human will.

While proposing these modes of deification, Christian tradition did not often tackle in fine theological detail the question of how deification is actually manifested in a human being. The fathers favored making reference to participation in the uncreated light and the deification of the human body, so much so that Florensky summarizes the concept of deification as "the holy body."[15] Therefore, on the basis of the deification of the human body the fathers could speak of the *empirical* effects of deification.[16] Maximus though does go beyond the empirical effects, and stresses human freedom and the moral effect of deification. The reservations on the part of the fathers concerning other aspects of deification are linked with the fact that the deification of man is conceived by them in eschatological terms, as a process that

---

[12]*Contr. Arian.* 1.43, PG 26:100D–101A; ibid., 1.38, PG 26:92B.

[13]*De Spir.* 15.36, 370; *Eunom.* 3.4.20, 158; ibid., 3.6.39, 170.

[14]Cf Maximus, *Lib. ascet.*, PG 90:953B; *Orat. dom.* 266–69, 42.

[15]Florensky, *Pillar*, 213.

[16]On the deification of the bodies of the saints, see Macarius, *Hom.* 5.8–9, 60–61; John Climacus, *Scala parad.* 30, PG 88:1157B; Maximus, *Cap. theol.* 2.88, PG 90:1168A; John of Damascus, *Exp. fid.* 4.15.13ff, 203f.

begins in this life and has its full completion in the life to come. These reservations were taken to extremes within the Russian ascetic tradition, which was more concerned with the aspect of humility and kenotic self-abasement. The concept of the deification of man is far from being a significant theme in the works of Russian authors who touched on asceticism. The proper introduction of the theme of deification within the Russian milieu came about as a result of the attention to the theology of Gregory Palamas in the twentieth century. Palamas' teaching provided an effective spectrum of ideas for the interpretation of the earlier patristic thought on deification. In Palamas, deification is generally interpreted in positive terms: as participation (*metousia*), communion (*koinonia*), and unity (*henosis*) with divinity through the divine energies. Within the three aspects of divine being (i.e., *hypostasis-physis-energeia*) the twentieth-century neo-Palamites concentrate their discussion largely at the level of *energies* in the divine being when dealing with deification. This neo-Palamite setting results in the "insistence upon the Spirit-bearing potentialities of the material body"[17] and, we may add, of the soul.[18]

Fr Sophrony on the Deification of Man

The doctrine of the deification of man is seen by Fr Sophrony as one of the central points of the Christian message, indeed as the very meaning of "salvation," and therefore a crucial element of the theology of the Eastern Orthodox Church. The attitude to man and his ultimate destiny is one of the most significant points on which the west and the east disagree. Within the eastern contemporary approach, Fr Sophrony's theology provides a framework within which the theme receives a fresh interpretation. Along with *energeia*, he also deals with the subject on the level of hypostasis-persona within the divine being, with the result that the concept of the deification of man goes beyond the idea of participation. He has enriched the eastern tradition through introducing his own teaching on persona into the theme of deification. On the one hand, this allowed him to speak of human deification in a more radical manner (i.e., to the extent of equality with God) than is often the case. On the other, the focus upon the hypostatic principle in his approach to the theme

[17]K. Ware, "Foreword," in Mantzaridis, *The Deification of Man*, 9 (he takes a similar line throughout his "The Transfiguration of the Body," *Sobornost* 4:8 [1963] 420–34).
[18]See Gregory of Nazianzus, *Or.* 7.21.

has brought two key perspectives into closer link with the idea of deification: these may be termed *communal* (multihypostatic) and *self-denying* (kenotic).

In contrast to the Russian ascetic writings of the nineteenth century, Fr Sophrony sets forth the idea of the deification of man as an indispensable motif of his ascetic theology: the concept of deification is a frequently recurrent theme throughout all his writings. Here the direct influence of the patristic ideas is obvious. Thus, Fr Sophrony makes use of the traditional modes of deification, understood as *indwelling*: man is deified through the indwelling of the Holy Spirit, the adoptions of sons, and participation. We may also note the traditional connection between deification and the experience of permeation by uncreated light.

Fr Sophrony also employs various set phrases, which expose the influence of Byzantine tradition: "to become a god,"[19] "to be a god."[20] These terms are widely used by the eastern tradition, notably Gregory of Nazianzus,[21] and Fr Sophrony also chooses to quote Basil, Maximus, and Gregory Palamas, where the phrase *to become a god* is used.[22] In Fr Sophrony we also find the traditional "*tantum-quantum*" formula, which is expressed in various ways. However, in his insight into the traditional expressions a new dimension emerges: "In the same way as Christ, being in the form of God, in his incarnation was made in the likeness of man, so also man, being in the form of a servant, in Christ puts on the form of divine being."[23]

The use of the term "form of divine being" instead of the rather general "god" introduces two new significant advantages: it is a more specific way of expressing the human potential; and "form of being" is an indication of the dynamic dimension within the idea of deification.

The Ultimacy of Human Potential

The patristic formula—"man becomes god"—often assumes a rather general, even rhetorical sense, which requires further qualification. In Fr Sophrony's formula—that man assumes the *divine form of being*—the traditional scheme becomes a concrete revelation that proclaims human potential for assuming

[19] *La félicité de connaître la voie*, 42 (reference to Maximus' *Cap. theol.* 2.88, PG 90:1165D).
[20] *La félicité de connaître la voie*, 43.
[21] Cf *Or.* 1.5; 7.22; 7.23; 14.23; 17.9; cf *Or.* 2.73.
[22] Cf Maximus, *Ambigua*, PG 91:1088, in *La félicité de connaître la voie*, 50; Gregory Palamas in *La félicité de connaître la voie*, 37; Basil in *We Shall See Him as He Is*, 194.
[23] *St Silouan the Athonite*, 98.

the divine mode of being. The tantum-quantum formula now points clearly to the fact of commensurability between two modes of being. This revelatory element is even more evident in the following rephrasing of the formula: "If the Creator in all things was made like unto man (cf Heb 2:17), it follows that man was created with the possibility of being like unto God in all things: 'We shall be like Him; for we shall see Him as He is' (Jn 3:2)."[24]

Thus, the incarnation is the vehicle of the divine revelation not only about God but about man as well: "In Christ, incarnate Son of the Father, we contemplate God's preeternal idea of man."[25] The kerygma of the Christian message, therefore, is not just about God becoming man—it is also about man *being able* to assimilate the divine life. Fr Sophrony regards the deification of man as a significant element of the Christian creed, so much so that belief in one's own deification is a necessary condition of being a Christian: "He who believes in Christ believes in his own divinization. Belief or disbelief depends on an elevated or depreciated conception of man."[26]

Once it is accepted that the incarnate Son is the preeternal ideal of man, then we are justified in raising the question of *the scope of the deification of man*: what does it mean "to assume the divine mode of being"?

In answering this question, Fr Sophrony's position proves to be more overtly maximalist than is the case in patristic tradition. Speaking of the extent of deification, Fr Sophrony uses the term *identity* between God and man: the latter is to inherit the *fulness* (*pleroma*) of the divine being to the extent that he becomes *equal* with God. He points out that deified man becomes "like God in all things."[27]

Hence our next question: Does such a "pleromatic" view render itself "problematic" when put to the test against the background of the Eastern Orthodox tradition?

To answer this question, we ought to follow the roots of Fr Sophrony's view on deification. On the one hand, the Chalcedonian formula (two complete natures in one hypostasis) suggests commensurability between the human and the divine.[28] To the Chalcedonian type of argument, Fr Sophrony adds that this commensurability is also determined by the fact that human *physis* is God's own creation: the divine fatherhood can be maintained not only

[24] *We Shall See Him as He Is*, 194; cf *His Life is Mine*, 77.
[25] Ibid., 193.
[26] Ibid., 73–74.
[27] Cf *His Life Is Mine*, 21; *La félicité de connaître la voie*, 44; *We Shall See Him as He Is*, 193.
[28] *His Life Is Mine*, 77; cf *La félicité de connaître la voie*, 35.

in relation to Christ, but to the whole human race. The implications of this commensurability and compatibility can be subsumed under a single term *the-andric* (divine-human) *being.* Fr Sophrony employs the term in order to show the fully integrated communion of divine and human being in the ultimate realization of the latter. ✓ *This is the (true) New Man! (The "new Adam")*

On the other hand, the concepts of commensurability and equality arise as a result of Fr Sophrony's interpretation of the scriptural datum. Fr Sophrony draws attention to some passages where the ideas of the equality and commensurability of human and divine natures are present implicitly, enriching thereby the traditional catena of passages on deification. In so doing, he employs an exegetical method, used by various fathers, where one passage of scripture acquires its meaning when juxtaposed with the other. This exegetical method of cross-reference is based on the traditional attitude to scripture, which regards it as being divinely inspired. Such an attitude to scripture Fr Sophrony inherits above all from Silouan.

The cornerstone of Fr Sophrony's idea of the deification of man is the passage stressing Jesus' humanity in 1 Timothy 2:5, where Jesus is called *anthropos*.[29] It is noteworthy that English translations usually render the Greek *anthropos* as "the man," adding, by the use of the definite article, a savor of particularity, while the Slavonic retains the expression as a more general category: *a man* as a single "typical" representative of the human race. This point is taken up by Fr Sophrony as a pivot for his christocentric anthropology. From this perspective, the interpretation of some other passages acquires a profound meaning in relation to the potential of all humans. First and foremost, this understanding of 1 Timothy 2:5 allows us to look afresh at Colossians 2:9: "for in him dwelleth all the fullness [*pleroma*] of the Godhead bodily [*somatikos*]."[30] The juxtaposition of the two passages suggests that it was "the man Jesus" (*somatikos*), and not the God-Jesus, who contained the undiminished fulness (*pleroma*) of the Godhead. This scriptural evidence leads to the following corollary: humanity can contain the *fulness* of the divine being—a statement ✓ that is an axis of Fr Sophrony's anthropology.

Another passage, Mark 16:19, which describes the event of Christ's ascension: "the Lord . . . sat on the right hand of God," points to the idea of commensurability between two natures. Fr Sophrony attributes much significance to the wording chosen to register the event. In biblical language "the sitting

[29]See *We Shall See Him as He Is*, 61, 102, 128, 173.
[30]Cf *La félicité de connaître la voie*, 35.

on the right hand," as Fr Sophrony points out, means *equality*.[31] Fr Sophrony transforms this equality, which had a "legalistic" savor—into an ontological category, designated by the term *identity*. It was Christ as man-Jesus, and human nature in his person, that "was seated" on the right hand of God, since as the Logos he is God preeternally, and ever belonged "at the right hand" of the Father: "Christ manifested the perfection of the divine image in man and the possibility for our nature of assimilating the fulness of divinization to the very extent that, after his ascension, he placed our nature 'on the right hand of the Father.'"[32]

This commensurability and equality find their further expression in the application of the vocabulary of the divine attributes to the human being. According to Fr Sophrony, despite the fact of their being created beings, men inherit the fulness of the uncreated divine life. He indeed pushes to the limit the extent of human deification when he says that men become "without beginning" (*anarchoî*):

> The imparting to us of this uncreated Energy effects our likening to the Creator—our divinization. Love, being the pre-eternal and immutable life of the Triune God, when it comes to dwell in us makes us not only immortal, in the sense of living for evermore, but "without beginning," too, since the love that is in the Trinity is pre-eternal.[33]

This key anthropological principle derived from 1 Timothy 2:5 and Mark 16:19 allows Fr Sophrony to read into the words of scripture various aspects of man's equality with God. The summary covers the following divine attributes: eternity, omnipresence, omniscience, truth, universal love, without-beginningness, omnipotence, perfection, and life.[34]

Fr Sophrony points to the fact that because in Christ the feebleness of bodily existence coexists together with the divine *omnipotence*,[35] this reflects also *our own* capacities. To confirm this he refers to the Pauline expression "I *can do all things* through Christ who strengthens me" (Phil 4:13). An echo of this idea can be traced in the way Fr Sophrony estimates the capacities of deified humans: the saints are seen as possessing divine power, which would enable

---

[31] *La félicité de connaître la voie*, 45.
[32] *We Shall See Him as He Is*, 193.
[33] Ibid., 205-6.
[34] *La félicité de connaître la voie*, 32-33, 43.
[35] *We Shall See Him as He Is*, 88; *La félicité de connaître la voie*, 43.

them to control mankind and the course of historical and even cosmic events, yet in their likeness to Christ they follow the opposite, self-effacing way— "theirs is the *reverse* method."[36]

If the being of God is not determined by any external elements, one of the aspects of deification is to attain such being, free of any external determining causes, which Fr Sophrony, following Silouan, calls "true freedom."[37] In order to back up his opinion on this aspect of deification with scriptural passages, Fr Sophrony refers to 1 Corinthians 15:47–50: liberty emerges as one of the aspects of the likeness of man to God. Deification is seen as the realization of this potential within the human being: free will is an essential condition for the created persona in his progress toward the assumption of divine life. A Christian is "to bear the image of the heavenly man," that is, of Christ: "Where the Spirit of the Lord is, there is liberty" (2 Cor 3:17). The same passage, along with the following verse ("But we all, with open face beholding as in a glass the glory of the Lord, are changed into the same image from glory to glory, even as by the Spirit of the Lord") is quoted in connection with the function of the church. The church is designed not to "enslave" her members by imposing any kind of "form" by disciplinary means, but "to lead her children into the sphere of divine being... Those who have matured in her bosom ... to find the liberty of the sons of God are no longer bound by any geographical situation or local tradition."[38]

Thus, the promise of Christ "to make his disciples free" (Jn 8:31) is seen in the light of the juxtaposition of the freedom of the Spirit of God (1 Cor 3:17) and the liberation of the human spirit, as the latter becomes conformed to the former.[39]

The New Testament references to life, especially in the Johannine corpus, are interpreted by Fr Sophrony in terms of the life/being of God, which men are to receive (Jn 1:4; 3:36; 5:24, 26, 29, 40; 6:33). Fr Sophrony reads these passages in connection with the idea of deification. The Johannine expression "the abundance of life" (Jn 10:10) is illustrated by the Lucan account of the transfiguration, which reflects the ultimate diapason of the Christian life: the ultimate bliss of the divine glory and at the same time suffering unto death (Christ's exodus is referred to). This has been discussed in chapter four. This

---

[36] *St Silouan the Athonite*, 225.
[37] Ibid., 341ff.
[38] *We Shall See Him as He Is*, 95–96.
[39] Ibid., 110f.

amplitude of experiences is what makes man universal in his "existential dia-pason" and therefore God-like.[40]

Fr Sophrony points to the scriptural expression that "Jesus Christ is the same yesterday and today, and forever" (Heb 13:8) to indicate that the eternal being, attained by Jesus the man, is not subject to any change. Likewise the believer is to experience Christ's *unchangeability* (or to anticipate it through prayer), if he or she "follows" Christ. Christ's being "the same" in eternity cor-responds to the biblical concept of "that which cannot be shaken" (*ta me saleuomena*), which is found in Hebrews 12:27. The latter passage refers to the eschatological destiny of the whole creation, which is to remain unshakable. "The kingdom which cannot be moved" (Heb 12:28) is frequently quoted by Fr Sophrony, and he charges the term "unshakable" with new theological meaning: it reflects a divine attribute of immutability or "rest." The term "unshakable" as a divine attribute is extensively used in his later writings.

This idea has its place in Fr Sophrony's vision of the eschatological state of the deified human being. The deification of man implies an abiding in divine permanence, which a man is to attain through different existential experi-ences, so that "the things which are shaken" (*ta saleuomena*) can be transformed into "those things which cannot be shaken" (*ta me saleuomena*): "To man will it be given to dwell in the 'Divine fastness' which is ever dynamic to the utmost extent. And this is verily 'eternal rest.' "[41]

As far as the idea of the *adoption of sons* within the context of the deifica-tion of man is concerned, Fr Sophrony points to passages that are not usually invoked by the eastern tradition: Luke 1:35 and John 5:21. These have usually been regarded as referring to Christ the Logos. However, Fr Sophrony puts them in a new context, where the term *the Son of God* is rendered by *a son of God*, relating it thereby to any deified man. In the first instance, the passage Luke 1:35 is cited to illustrate how we become alike to God through Christ's incarnation, his teaching and example, and finally receive the adoption of sons, which is manifested by the indwelling of the Holy Spirit in the believer. As for the Johannine passage (Jn 5:19-20), if *ho hyios* is interpreted as "a son" (the Russian and Slavonic translations do not distinguish between the definite and indefinite articles), the deified man becomes godlike in his potency and the manner of his actions.[42] This interpretation is placed in the context of the task

---

[40] *La félicité de connaître la voie*, 43.

[41] *We Shall See Him as He Is*, 63.

[42] Ibid., 101.

of the church: the latter is designed to deify her children, that is, to bring them to the sphere of the divine being.

These texts from scripture, which serve to support the idea of equality between God and man, have not been previously exploited by the eastern tradition to the same effect. Therefore, one is justified in wondering whether the boldness of Fr Sophrony's approach to the theme of deification, introducing as it does a maximalist transcendent anthropology, verges upon the point of a break with the whole eastern tradition. His absolutism and the expressions used for it—identity, equality, commensurability—are not commonly found in the Byzantine patristic tradition, which carefully safeguards the ontological distance between the Godhead and the creature, the finite and the infinite.

The Roots of Maximalism: Fr Sergius Bulgakov?

Does Fr Sophrony indeed encroach upon the traditional ontological distance between God and man, as Bulgakov does? The abolition of this ontological distance, with subsequent confusion of the human and the divine, was one of the points that led to Bulgakov's condemnation by the Russian Orthodox Church in the persons of Metropolitan Sergius and Vladimir Lossky.

In order to answer this question we ought to touch on the relation of Fr Sophrony to nineteenth- and twentieth-century Russian religious thought. Russian religious philosophy indeed proved very effectual in providing him with a terminological apparatus. Russian idealism makes much of the "ontological" dimension of the incarnation. The proof of this is the development of the concept of *Godmanhood*, which Berdyaev believed to be one of the characteristic features of Russian religious thought.[43] This concept, as a philosophical theme, was introduced by Vladimir Soloviev in his *Lectures on Godmanhood*. There are different opinions concerning the origins of Soloviev's idea of Godmanhood. F. Copleston challenges Berdyaev's opinion that the concept is "specifically Russian" and points to the New Testament for the roots of the idea. Le Guillou argues for Soloviev's dependence on Maximus, while P. Zouboff attempts to trace Hegelian influence.[44] Soloviev, for whom the concept is a controlling feature of his philosophical framework, interprets

[43]Berdyaev, *The Beginning and the End*, 35.

[44]F. Copleston, *Russian Religious Philosophy* (Turnbridge Wells, 1988) 59: he refers to Eph 1, Col 1, Rom 8; P. Zouboff, "Introduction," in V. Soloviev, *Lectures on Godmanhood*, tr. P. Zouboff, 42ff (New York, 1944).

it in terms of Christ's cosmic role and his function as head of a universal divine-human organism, developing through history. As such, Godmanhood is the principle of universal unity, which plays an important role in Soloviev's outlook.

In Soloviev's successors the development of the theme embraces anthropology. Thus, S. Frank aims "to affirm the indissoluble connection between the idea of God and the idea of man." For him the fact of the incarnation "bears testimony to an affinity between God and man."[45] As a corollary of the doctrine of Godmanhood, the idea of commensurability between God and man is strongly present in Berdyaev's anthropology.[46]

Yet it was Bulgakov who offered a theological integration of Godmanhood (along with other of Soloviev's ideas[47]) within the dogmatic teaching of the Eastern Church. His trilogy—*The Lamb of God, The Comforter, The Bride of the Lamb*—employs Godmanhood as a key concept for its theology of the incarnation, and the whole trilogy is dedicated to the theme. It is tempting to infer an immediate dependence of Fr Sophrony on Bulgakov here, since they indeed seem to share many common points in their concepts of deification.

Bulgakov seems to precede Fr Sophrony in asserting the ontological possibility of the correlation of the two natures—divine and human. As far as the potential of human nature is concerned, the necessary prerequisite of the incarnation was the capacity of human *physis* to bear the infinity of the divine *hypostasis*: Bulgakov characterizes human nature as "God-receptive" and summarizes the potential of human nature as *humana natura capax divini*.[48] In connection with this, like Fr Sophrony, he pays particular attention to Colossians 2:9-10, where the God-man Christ is said to possess the fulness of divinity.

On the ontological level, Bulgakov, like Fr Sophrony, promotes the idea of commensurability of the human and divine natures. On this ground Bulgakov asserts identity-equality between man and God. Bulgakov goes so far as to credit humanity with an element of uncreatedness (*nesotvorennost'*): man both *is* and *is not* a creature. The creation of man by God for Bulgakov is not only creation as such, but also *generation* and *emanation*. The breathing of the divine spirit into Adam signifies in some way man's preeternal existence in God, and as such man is of divine origin, that is, eternal: "Man consists of the uncreated

[45]S. Frank, *Reality and Man: An Essay in the Metaphysics of Human Nature*, tr. N. Duddington (London, 1965) xiii, 141.

[46]Berdyaev, *The Beginning and the End*, 36.

[47]Nichols, *Light from the East*, 59.

[48]*The Lamb of God*, 207-9, 215, 258, 279.

divine spirit, which is enhypostasised by the created 'I.' " Can this be related to Fr Sophrony's idea of *without-beginningness*?

We find in Bulgakov as well as in Fr Sophrony the idea that human and divine nature are originally correlated. The incarnation presupposes not only humanity being modeled upon the divine but also that humanity in some way is already contained within the Godhead. Bulgakov asserts that in God everything is *man-like*: just as man carries the image of God, God also has man's image. Thus there is a *humanness* in the divine order and in the cosmos.[49]

The common key points suggest the immediate influence of Bulgakov upon Fr Sophrony's understanding of the deification of man and his radical maximalism with regard to the scope of human deification. Such maximalism would appear to abolish the ontological distance between God and the deified man. This abolition indeed takes place in Bulgakov's anthropology, where the scope and extent of human deification is taken to the limit. In his assertion of the divine-like character of human nature he goes as far as to say that "if man could be free from his *natural essence* he would simply be God, and his life would merge into the divine life."[50] This is indeed a break with the eastern patristic tradition.

However, Fr Sophrony remains faithful to the patristic heritage. Furthermore, careful analysis leads us to the conclusion that his approach comes from a different perspective than Bulgakov. The same maximalist vocabulary in Fr Sophrony does not carry the same meaning. He still operates within the bounds of patristic anthropology.

This is revealed if one considers two major points of difference between Bulgakov's and Fr Sophrony's understanding of human deification. First, Fr Sophrony takes explicit care to safeguard the ontological difference between God and man. Second, we find that Fr Sophrony's maximalism comes not from the stock of philosophical ideas, as in Bulgakov, but from the patristic tradition, confirmed by ascetic experience.

Along with his maximalism, Fr Sophrony mentions several points that challenge any impression that his anthropology puts in question the ontological difference between God and man. It embraces both levels of being: essence and hypostasis.

[49]Bulgakov, *Unfading Light*, 278, 283; *The Lamb of God*, 158–61, 209; cf "The Lamb of God: Concerning the God-Man," *Theology* 28 (1934) 24.
[50]*The Lamb of God*, 117.

On the level of essence, Fr Sophrony maintains that although man does inherit the uncreated mode of being and may even forget his creaturely origins, his status as creature remains as a fact for eternity.[51] The maximalism of *identity* concerns only the act and the content of the life of God, but not his essence. The fact of human origin—man's being a creature—is a testimony that, in contrast to God, man is not "being-in-itself."[52]

On the level of hypostasis, Fr Sophrony proposes the following distinction: the deified man as persona is never to become the divine absolute for his other fellow creatures. The human persona remains only a reflection of the divine absolute. He maintains the distinction on the basis of the scriptural passage Mark 12:30-31, where the attitude to God and to one's neighbor are defined in a differentiated manner. In the distinction of the commandment "love your neighbor as yourself" from the other commandment, "love God with all one's being," he sees a sign of the "ontological distance" between God and man.[53]

Thus, when Fr Sophrony uses the term Godmanhood, we ought to have in mind the total picture of his anthropology, where the above-mentioned points play an important role.

The Roots of Maximalism: Tradition?

It would be wrong to suppose that Fr Sophrony's maximalism is alien to the eastern tradition. As we have examined above, the idea of man being God-like is already present in the New Testament. Thus we find in Matthew 5:48 the divine measure of human perfection, which, as Fr Sophrony notes, ought to be interpreted not in a relative sense but in the sense of living reality.[54] Even the idea of man being "without beginning" is already present in Hebrews 7:3, where Melchizedek is said to have no "beginning of days."

When employing maximalist vocabulary—such as *fulness of divinity* and *unoriginate*—to describe the deified human being, Fr Sophrony makes reference not to Bulgakov but to Gregory Palamas and Maximus. The first reference to *anarchos* (unoriginate) in relation to the deification of man appears as early as in the letters to Balfour (C6, May 11, 1935), while Fr Sophrony was on Mount Athos. He refers to Gregory Palamas (and not to Bulgakov) as an

---

[51] *We Shall See Him as He Is*, 190.
[52] *La félicité de connaître la voie*, 32.
[53] Ibid., 20.
[54] Ibid., 45.

authoritative source. He reiterates Palamas' idea that man participates in the divine life, becoming thereby "without beginning." In *Triads* 3.3.8, Palamas ponders how man becomes unoriginate through grace. Also, Palamas speaks of "gods by grace [i.e., deified men], whom the saints call unoriginate and uncreated through grace." Palamas himself explicitly refers to Maximus' use of *anarchos*.[55] In his *Ambigua* Maximus speculates on Hebrews 7:3, which characterizes Melchizedek as "having neither beginning of days, nor end of life." Maximus points out that he is such "not according to his nature, which was created out of nothing, according to which he would have to begin and cease to be, but according to the divine and uncreated [*aktistos*] grace, which abides above every materiality and time." Fr Sophrony singles out the passage where Maximus applies the word *anarchos* to describe the state of the deified man: he is one who possesses the divine life of the Logos who came to dwell in him *without beginning and without end*.[56]

Maximus' anthropology serves as a source for Fr Sophrony also in the case of his other maximalist statement, which has Colossians 2:9 as its focus, that man can contain the fulness of uncreated being. Maximus writes: "In Christ, who is God and the Logos of the Father, there dwells the whole fulness of the Godhead bodily, but in us the fulness of the Godhead [*to pleroma tes theotetos*] dwells by grace."[57] It is true that Maximus does not develop this striking statement, which he mentions in passing. In contrast to Fr Sophrony, he underlines that it is Christ as Logos, Christ-God, who is endowed with the fulness. However, the idea of man containing the fulness of divine being is more articulately expressed by Palamas in *Ag. Tom.* 2.[58] John Meyendorff notes the anthropological maximalism in Palamas: man by grace possesses the infinite attributes of God—man becomes uncreated, omnipotent.[59]

As for the fulness and absoluteness of man's likeness to God, we find that Fr Sophrony draws on Symeon the New Theologian. The passage in question is from *Hymns* 44: "If we are not such [as God] and not like unto him exactly [*en akribeia*], then how shall we be united to him, according to his word?"[60]

---

[55] *Triads.* 3.3.8, 686; *Triads.* 3.1.31, 642; *Triads.* 3.2.12, 666. Cf Sophrony, *La félicité de connaître la voie*, 37.

[56] *Ambigua*, PG 91:1141AB, 1144C; cf *La félicité de connaître la voie*, 40.

[57] *Cap.theol.* 2.21, PG 90:1133D; cf *La félicité de connaître la voie*, 53.

[58] *Ag. Tom.* 2, 571.

[59] Meyendorff, *A Study of Gregory Palamas*, 176–77.

[60] *Hymns* 44, 100; cf *La félicité de connaître la voie*, 43.

A further indication of Fr Sophrony's dependence on Maximus, Gregory Palamas, and Symeon the New Theologian, rather than on Bulgakov, is the way in which he applies the adjectives used for the divine attributes to man. Thus, if Bulgakov asserts the inherent "uncreatedness" and "beginninglessness" of man by nature, as it were, Maximus asserts that man *participates* by virtue of his communion with God in divine uncreatedness.[61] For Maximus and Palamas man becomes unoriginate only through participation in God through divine grace.[62] The same application of the terms *uncreated* and *unoriginate* is found in Fr Sophrony: man always participates in the uncreated mode of being through grace.[63]

This capacity of humans for the infinity of the divine pleroma and man's participation in the divine attributes of uncreatedness and beginninglessness, on which Fr Sophrony's anthropology revolves, fit well within the framework of patristic anthropology. This anthropological maximalism, however, does not play such a controlling role in patristic thought as it does for Fr Sophrony.

It well may be that it was Bulgakov's maximalism that drew Fr Sophrony's attention to the embryo of maximalism in patristic tradition, notably in the above-mentioned fathers. Despite the fact that Bulgakov's maximalism was condemned by official church theologians, it created a useful matrix for a far more attentive assessment of the maximalist expressions in the writings of the fathers. Furthermore, in defense of Bulgakov, we may demonstrate that even where he goes allegedly beyond the limits of tradition his ideas find some echo in the fathers. As far as Bulgakov's interpretation of Genesis 1:27 is concerned, a similar idea is found in Gregory of Nazianzus: "The soul is a breath of God [aema Theou], for all its heavenly form, it has endured mingling with that which is earthly, light hidden in a cave, yet divine and immortal." Certainly, Bulgakov's idea of man being endowed with the divine spirit echoes the anthropology of Gregory, who believes that at the creation of man God "took a portion of the new-formed earth and established with his immortal hands my shape, bestowing upon it a share in his own life. He infused Spirit, which is a fragment of the Godhead without form."[64]

St Gregory speaks of man as a particle of God (*moira Theou*), which is torn from above.[65] A. Ellverson is not astonished to find in the Nazianzen that "the

---

[61]Maximus, *Cap. car.* 3.25, 154.
[62]Mantzaridis, *Deification of Man,* 104ff; Meyendorff, *A Study of Gregory Palamas,* 177–78.
[63]*We Shall See Him as He Is,* 45, 85, 172.
[64]*Poem. Arc.* 7.32, 36.
[65]*Or.* 14.7, PG 35:865C; cf Maximus, *Ambigua,* PG 91:1080A, 1081C.

soul of man is something divine and heavenly. It is, he says in Or. 2. 17, 'from God and divine.' Sometimes Gregory with the language of Gen. 2:7 talks about the soul as a breath of God . . . In Or. 14. 7 he talks in a similar way about we 'who are a part of God.' "[66]

The idea of commensurability between man and God is present in the fathers, who envisage human nature as having the potential for participation in the divine nature.[67] The exaltation of human nature to the divine "level" is present in the thought of Gregory of Nyssa and Maximus. In *Contr. Eun.* 6 Gregory stresses that Christ is exalted in his humanity, indicating thereby the elevation of man to union with and likeness to the divine nature.[68] Gregory interprets the concept of *dextera Patris* quite in line with Bulgakov's approach: even Christ's body becomes Christ and the Lord. Some scholars are puzzled by the boldness of Gregory's language, and are eager to put up safeguards against maximalistic "misinterpretation."[69] Yet Gregory's maximalism here seems to be in line with his other texts. In *De professione Christiana* he refutes the objection that human nature cannot reach the perfection that our Lord demanded.[70] This idea is well articulated in Maximus, who believes that man became god as much as God became man, because man is elevated by the divine ascension in the same measure in which God emptied himself in his incarnation.[71]

Thus, on the question of the scope of human deification according to a maximalist view we may draw a conclusion. The agreements on this point between Fr Sophrony and Russian religious philosophy lead us to believe that through the prism of his ascetic experience Fr Sophrony integrates into a balanced synthesis the Orthodox elements within the maximalist anthropology of Russian religious thought (notably Bulgakov's) on the one hand, and on the other hand the patristic concept of deification.

[66]Ellverson, *The Dual Nature of Man*, 22; cf ibid., 43; cf Gregory of Nazianzus, Or. 38.2.
[67]Gregory of Nyssa *Opif. hom.*, PG 44:184B; cf *De beat.* 4, 122–23.
[68]*Contr. Eun.* 3.4.56, 155.
[69]See L. Wickham, "Soul and Body: Christ's Omnipresence," in *The Easter Sermons of Gregory of Nyssa*, ed. S. Klock, 290 (Philadelphia, 1981), where he comments on Gregory of Nyssa's *Contr. Eun.* 3.4.43, 150.
[70]*Profes. Chr.,* 138.
[71]*Ambigua*, PG 91:1385BC.

Deification and Persona

The Dynamism of Hypostatic Deification

The patristic idea of "becoming god" is often interpreted in the sense of Palamite mysticism, above all as the permeation of man by the uncreated light through prayer.[72] Christ's transfiguration serves as the dogmatic basis for the eastern perception of deification. Created matter can be permeated by the uncreated energies. Mantzaridis writes: "For Palamas and the Orthodox tradition, the flesh of Christ, being the body of the Logos of God incarnate, is the point of man's contact with God and furnishes the way to the kingdom of heaven."[73] This "insistence upon the Spirit-bearing potentialities of matter" in neo-Palamite "Christian materialism" suggests a certain static understanding of deification. The Palamite view of deification revolves upon what Fr Sophrony calls the "moment énergétique." But Fr Sophrony raises an interesting point: how did the deification of human nature take place in the incarnate Logos? To Fr Sophrony, the Palamite perspective (participation in the uncreated energies) suggests that it happened from the moment of the union of the two natures, namely, from the "precise moment" when the divine Logos physically assumed human nature. In this "physical theory" there is an element of "once and for all." To support such an assessment Fr Sophrony refers to John of Damascus.[74] Yet, as Fr Sophrony notes, the completion of deification takes place only after Golgotha in the ascended Christ. This allows him to employ the concept of *hypostatic deification*,[75] which runs together with the moment énergétique. It is with the hypostatic dimension of deification that his prime concern lies. The concept of persona being the controlling feature of his theology, Fr Sophrony gives more attention to the dynamic manifestation of the deified persona. Fr Sophrony states that the prime "contact" of deification is not the body (*pace* the neo-Palamites) but the persona.

Thus, the tantum-quantum formula is reinterpreted through the prism of the teaching on persona. Hence, the main thesis of Fr Sophrony's concept of deification: Christ-God assumes into his hypostasis our nature, and our

[72]Mantzaridis, *The Deification of Man*, 41-60.
[73]Ibid., 30; cf Meyendorff, *St Gregory Palamas and Orthodox Spirituality*, 149; Florensky, *Pillar*, 213.
[74]*Exp. fid.* 3.17, 156; cf Maximus, *Quest. Thal.* 62, 117-19.
[75]*La félicité de connaître la voie*, 43-44.

hypostasis undergoes the process of assimilation of the dynamic attributes of the divine existence. "Christ . . . in the act of Incarnation took into His Hypostasis the form of our earthly existence. But the human hypostasis receives divinization through grace . . . In other words man *hypostatizes* divine attributes such as eternity, love, light, wisdom, truth."[76]

The exchange of the attributes between the divine and human hypostases is conceivable since in its dynamic manifestation persona is not "determined" by the essence. Christ's divine hypostasis acts within the confines of human nature, showing thereby that the created hypostasis may in turn act as the divine. That is why for human deification it is important to assimilate the dynamic manifestations of Christ's persona. This "freedom" of the person from the "control" of the essence can also be observed on the trinitarian level. In God the essence is not of primary or even of preeminent importance in defining persons–hypostases in their reciprocal relations. Divine being contains nothing that could be external to the hypostatic principle.

Persona thus becomes the prime agent of communication of attributes: the human to the divine and vice versa.

This dynamism leads Fr Sophrony to introduce a new terminology in trinitarian theology. The traditional concept of the deifying interaction between God and man expresses it in terms of human participation in divine energy. Fr Sophrony introduces dynamic and personal synonymous concepts: *act* and *life*, instead of *energy*.[77] As such, the terms *act* and *life* denote dynamic manifestations of the divine being, which is communicable to the creature. Therefore, deification is understood as a dynamic entry into and participation in the divine *act-life*: "The saints, deified to the utmost by the gift of grace, are included in the eternal act of God to such an extent that all the properties of the divinity (all the divine attributes) even to identity are communicated to them."[78]

The idea that the saints enter the divine act is best illustrated by Fr Sophrony's interpretation of John 5:19-20, which we have discussed above. If we accept such a generalized interpretation, the traditional concept of the adoption of sons is understood as assimilation of the divine act.

The use of act-life for energy carries further the hypostatic dimension of deification, because act (as realization of one's will) and life highlight the

[76] *We Shall See Him as He Is*, 192.
[77] *La félicité de connaître la voie*, 27.
[78] Ibid., 32.

personal (as dynamic), rather than natural (as static), aspect: it is hypostasis, not nature, that lives and acts. In contrast to act and life, energy is "proceeding from nature"[79]; it thus focuses on nature. In Fr Sophrony's approach, deification implies that man also acts and lives like God. Thus when Fr Sophrony says that man can live the same life (mode of being) as God,[80] he has in mind man as a hypostasis.

The idea of dynamic participation in the divine being was spoken of by Origen. He speaks of "supernatural" dynamic participation in the Godhead,[81] in its life, rationality, virtue. In Origen the trinitarian dimension of participation plays a significant role. A similar dimension is noted by D. Winslow in Gregory of Nyssa, for whom the deification of man is above all "a dynamic relationship between man and God."[82] Similarly, Mantzaridis in his study of Palamas' thought writes: "The uncreated and divinizing grace does not stagnate in him [man] . . . but operates and is dynamically manifest in a life lived according to Christ.'[83] Garrigues stresses the importance of the idea of filial adoption for Maximus' idea of deification.[84] In such a perspective deification is not linked with any "moment précis," but presupposes a dynamic process, based on the communion of the divine and human will. Commenting on the passage from Maximus' *Orat. dom.*, Garrigues writes: "But the filial adoption in the hypostasis is not a dignity acquired once and for all, it is a communion with the Father, who in view of the dynamic resemblance to himself causes all the natural energies of man to come into operation."[85]

This Father-son dimension of deification highlights what Fr Sophrony calls the "moment hypostatique." The concept of sonship points to the idea of *relationship*, which is a hypostatic category rather than one of nature—nature cannot have relationship, hypostases can. The adoption of humans as children also implies elevation to the same status of life, their acquisition of rights and capacities like the Father's, which would allow one to *act* and *live* as he does. Thus, we may conclude that Fr Sophrony carries further the hypostatic

[79]Lossky, *Mystical Theology*, 86.

[80]*La félicité de connaître la voie*, 23.

[81]*Princ.* 1.3.5, 54-55.

[82]D. Winslow, "The Concept of Salvation in the Writings of Gregory of Nazianzus," thesis (Cambridge, Mass., 1967) 172.

[83]Mantzaridis, *The Deification of Man*, 61-62.

[84]J. Garrigues, *Maxime le Confesseur: la charité, avenir divin de l'homme* (Paris, 1976) 116-18, 133f; cf *Lib. ascet.*, PG 90:953B

[85]Garrigues, 121: see Maximus, *Orat. dom.* 266-67, 42.

dimension of deification that was delineated by Maximus. In fact, Garrigues even reads the similar principle of "divinisation hypostatique" into Maximus' ideas. However, he sees deification largely in terms of "la communion intentionelle" between the will of God and the will of man.[86] In Fr Sophrony, a conformation of the human will to the will of God similarly comprises the idea of hypostatic deification, but does not exhaust it: the "moment énergétique" remains indispensable. Thus Fr Sophrony would agree with the criticism of Yannaras, who accuses Garrigues of reading the sources through Thomistic spectacles, demeaning thereby the scope of Maximus' notion of man's participation in God.

Persona in Pleroma: Deification through "Taking All into Itself"

Having stated that Fr Sophrony stresses the dynamic aspect of deification, based on the principle of *persona*, rather than the "static" permeation of the created *physis* by the uncreated *energeiai*, we must now complete this account by discussing how the idea of the dynamic modes of persona's being affects the reinterpretation of deification, and what this implies for the practical application of this reinterpretation within the framework of the ascetic life.

The development of persona includes its infinite capacity to take into itself the other. On the basis of this principle Fr Sophrony introduces a new aspect in the concept of the deification of man, that is, the "communal" one. Along with the realization of the hypostatic principle of being in the human individual, deification implies a likeness in humanity to the multihypostatic mode of being after the manner of the Trinity. The deified man "gives" himself to the whole of mankind, and takes into himself the entire human race. In our discussion of the "image and likeness" we already referred to its implications for the idea of deification. However, we ought to note here practical implications of this relational multihypostatic aspect of deification, and how in this respect too Fr Sophrony has expanded the traditional catena of New Testament deification passages.

For Fr Sophrony, Philippians 2:5, "let this mind be in you, which was also in Christ Jesus," is a commandment to assimilate the existential orientation of the divine hypostasis. The attuning of the human mind to the mind of God becomes an important ascetic practice for Fr Sophrony. A similar dimension is found in Nicolas Cabasilas, as highlighted by Nellas. The latter writes about

[86]Garrigues, 286ff.

"the permanent . . . communion of the human intellect with the intellect of
Christ," when an intellect is "attuned to the intellect of Christ."[87] However,
there is a difference between Cabasilas and Fr Sophrony. Cabasilas speaks about
a general tuning of the mind into the divine will through the practice of constant prayer, which is rather *subjective*, as it is based on one's individual mystical experience. Together with this Fr Sophrony presupposes also a more
concrete *objective* manifestation of the existential orientation of Christ's
hypostasis, which is revealed in scripture. The christological aspect of deification presupposes conformity to the earthly "dynamic" manifestations of
Christ. His thoughts, reactions, ideas, and actions ought to be assimilated by
the ascetic. The significance of the Pauline statement (Phil 2:5) is summarized
by Fr Sophrony in the following formula: if we conform to and become like
Christ in his humanity, his earthly manifestations, we become alike to his
divinity as well.[88] This formula reveals the fundamental principle of *hypostatic
deification*: through the dynamic assimilation of the manifestations of Christ's
divine persona, one's own persona undergoes the process of deification.

This can be related to Bulgakov's idea of Christ's hypostatic growth, mentioned in chapter five. For Bulgakov the process of formation that the "the-
andric hypostasis of Christ" underwent is similar to that of the human
hypostasis.[89] Bulgakov thus prepares the theological ground for Fr Sophrony's
use of Christ as a model for the ascetic life to the utmost extent. Yet despite
the similarity between Christ's divine persona and the human persona agreed
upon by Bulgakov and Fr Sophrony, they differ on one significant point: Fr
Sophrony, in accord with the eastern tradition, nowhere mentions that Christ's
divine hypostasis underwent development. The kenosis of Christ's divine
hypostasis is *voluntary*;[90] Christ chooses to withhold the manifestation of his
divine fulness. In Bulgakov, the hypostatic kenosis is involuntary in the sense
that "humanness" in Christ (for example his ignorance, his prayers to God the
Father) is due to the kenotic diminution of his divine self-awareness. In
Bulgakov, kenosis implies that awareness of the fulness of his Godhead is not
present in Christ's consciousness from his birth: it grows gradually.[91] The difference between the two Christ-models suggests that Bulgakov can use Christ

[87]P. Nellas, *Deification in Christ* (New York, 1987) 134.
[88]*We Shall See Him as He Is*, 85.
[89]Bulgakov, *The Lamb of God*, 261.
[90]*La félicité de connaître la voie*, 44.
[91]Bulgakov, *The Lamb of God*, 282, 313.

as the model for deification only with certain reservations. His Christ-model is divine, but the divinity is "kenotically distorted," deficient. Fr Sophrony's christology, on the contrary, allows for the fulness of deification: the fulness of divinity is in him, but it is concealed *voluntarily*.

This difference allows Fr Sophrony to apply those New Testament records of the manifestations of Christ's existential orientation (through his mind, will, and reactions) to demonstrate the full extent of ascetic deification. That is why for Fr Sophrony, the deification of the mind emerges as one of the supreme goals of a Christian ascetic. He develops the tradition by asserting that the deified human mind appropriates the mode of thinking inherent in the divine persona. The scriptural passages that speak about the will of God find an anthropological application. In the context of ascetic theology, they reflect the existential orientation that the deified man ought to have appropriated.

Let us examine two particular examples. First, Fr Sophrony draws out practical implications of deification in connection with the trinitarian model. This derives from John 17:21:"That they all may be one; as Thou, Father, art in Me, and I in Thee." Here we may discern how persona takes into itself the fulness of being. From this prayer Fr Sophrony derives the idea that striving for unity as an existential orientation is one of the traits of the deified mind. He qualifies John 17:21 by the following interpretation:

> Reasonable man has to become perfect after the image of the Triune Divinity. This is the meaning, the purpose and the task of Christ's Church ... It is clear that every member of the Church must come to fulness of likeness to Christ, even to identity. Otherwise, there will be no unity of the Church in the image of the oneness of the Holy Trinity.[92]

Second, the all-embracing universalism of persona reveals itself in 1 Timothy 2:4, which speaks of the will of God, "Who will have all men to be saved, and to come unto the knowledge of the truth." Fr Sophrony sees this universal dimension reflected on the human plane in the commandment to "love our enemies" (Mt 5:44). When these scriptural ideas are appropriated by the human mind and become a natural mode of thinking, Fr Sophrony calls this "the perfection of likeness to God"[93] in reference to Matthew 5:48.

[92]*We Shall See Him as He Is*, 108.
[93]*St Silouan the Athonite*, 232.

The idea of the deification of the mind colors Fr Sophrony's ascetic teaching on purification of the mind and on prayer for the whole world. The ascesis of the mind presupposes the filtering of one's thoughts (*logismoi*), and subsequently one's actions, through the criterion of the divine will, both the particular-immediate and the general-eternal. As for the will of God in particular cases, in the initial stages of the monastic life it is discovered through the principle of monastic obedience: the elder's supervision/control acts as such a filter of thoughts. It introduces the novice to the sphere of the divine will. (This principle is rounded out further in chapter eight.) In the more advanced stages of ascetic life, the ascetic reads the immediate will of God through prayer, according to the principle formulated by Silouan: "Better defer each and any undertaking on which the soul is not prepared to solicit God's blessing—abandon any project that cannot be prefaced by untroubled prayer."[94] In a more general sense, any thought/idea that lacks accordance with the principle of love for one's enemies is an indication of the presence of a will alien to God.[95]

Persona in Kenosis: Deification through Emptying

Fr Sophrony's idea of persona adds considerably to the usual approach to deification, which is based on participation in the divine being through the divine energies. This usual approach does not give as much space as Fr Sophrony does to the kenotic aspect of deification.

Fr Sophrony follows Bulgakov in seeing kenosis as an inherent attribute of the divine love and of the divine personae. Building upon this divine model, Fr Sophrony, with his stress on the importance of the personal dimension in deification, introduces a "negative" mode that is linked with the idea of kenosis and abandonment by God, in addition to the traditional concepts of fulness and participation. In the state of abandonment by God's grace the persona reveals the extent of its assimilation of the divine dynamic attributes. When grace is withdrawn (or hidden), the persona is expected to act in the same way as if grace were present. Fr Sophrony expresses it as "following everything that grace has ever taught."[96] God's attributes become really the human's, for even "without God" the human acts as God acts. This understanding justifies the idea of the abandonment by God as a necessary stage in the ascetic life: "In the

---

[94] *We Shall See Him as He Is,* 97.

[95] *St Silouan the Athonite,* 232.

[96] *We Shall See Him as He Is,* 219; *St Silouan the Athonite,* 103.

main these infrequent instances of providential abandonment by God must be seen as an immeasurably great divine gift. Otherwise, it is difficult to understand the promised divinization of fallen man."[97]

The kenotic dynamism of the divine existence finds its reflection on the human plane in the state of God-like humility. The concept of Christ-like humility presupposes a God-like and existential orientation toward other persona(e): self-oriented concerns are entirely absent. The attaining of Christ-like humility means realization of this kenotic capacity of one's persona, that is, the capacity for its absolute self-emptying in "giving its being" to other personae. That is why Fr Sophrony offers a quite original deification formula: "the completion of our deification lies in perfect God-like humility." A reflection of the same principle is noted by Fr Sophrony in Matthew 5:3. Christ's words lay the foundation for our lifelong ascetic endeavor. If we juxtapose Fr Sophrony's concept of ascetic humility and the Matthean expression "poverty of spirit," the latter is understood as the poverty (or lack) of *self*-interest: "I am nothing."

At the crucifixion Christ manifested the absolute extent of his hypostatic orientation toward the other: total abandonment of "self" for the sake of the Father. This total kenotic obedience made the intratrinitarian hypostatic principle manifest to the world in the flesh. The human aspect of Christ's kenosis on the cross signified the deification of humanity: its capacity for kenotic hypostatic love is restored. That is why kenosis is such a vital stage in ascetic growth.

This interdependence of kenosis and deification can be understood only in the light of the teaching on persona, which explains the connection between Christ's being abandoned by God on the cross and the completion of the deification of his humanity:

> Such complete "self-emptying" on the part of "the man Christ Jesus" (1 Tim 2:5) is transfigured into equally perfect divinization of our nature . . . The Christian must somehow approximate to this state before he can assimilate the measure of salvation that corresponds to the depth of his self-emptying.[98]

Though asserting Fr Sophrony's originality in his approach to "deification through kenosis," we ought to mention the partial parallels in the fathers.

[97] *We Shall See Him as He Is*, 135.
[98] Ibid., 128.

Thus, the connection between deification and kenosis is found in Gregory of
Nyssa, particularly in relation to his teaching on christology and soteriology.[99]
However, a comparison between them suggests that, unlike Fr Sophrony,
Gregory is hesitant to draw out significant anthropological implications of
Christ's kenosis.

If one accepts Garrigues' analysis, the closest parallel to Fr Sophrony's link
between kenosis and deification is found in Maximus. Garrigues demonstrates
that Christ's kenosis plays a key role in the deification of the human race by
the revelation of divine love:

> The man in Christ appears as "new," set free not only from his sin, but
> also from the limitation of his nature in the grace of his "adoption of
> sons." This double modality of the hypostatic communion of God and
> his adopted creature, as the human kenosis of the incarnate Son and
> the "new" sonship of the deified man, is displayed in the unique and
> truly theandric mystery: love.[100]

Garrigues argues that Maximus holds Christ's kenosis (in his love to
mankind, to enemies, and to God) to be a revelation of trinitarian love. He
writes that "the personal kenosis of the Logos manifests love, as the intimate
life of the Trinity, which transposes hypostatically the essential attributes of the
perfect being."[101] However, Garrigues seems to be reading into Maximus'
texts the kenosis within the intratrinitarian hypostatic relationships, which is
not referred to in Maximus. The latter works out the idea of the "economic"
kenosis of the second hypostasis of the Trinity as an expression of the divine
philanthropia. As far as kenosis on the human level is concerned, Maximus
mentions "the kenosis of passions," which is paralleled by Christ's kenosis in
the incarnation. By the kenosis of passions one appropriates the divinity in the
same measure as the Logos voluntarily put aside his divine glory.[102] In this passage kenosis means "elimination" of passions, and it cannot be taken as a point
of departure for Fr Sophrony's idea of human and divine kenosis on the hypostatic level. The basis for his idea is not the concept of *apatheia*, but the eternal kenosis within the Trinity, which made it possible to transfer such kenosis

---

[99]*Contr. Eun.* 3.4.45, 155.

[100]Garrigues, 154–55.

[101]Ibid., 156–57. Cf *Epist.* 44, PG 91:641–4B; *Theol. pol.*, PG 91:156C.

[102]*Orat. dom.* 102–4, 32–333.

to the human plane through the prism of christology. However, the general line is delineated by Maximus: he speaks of the restoration of the unity of the human race, where love works as the uniting principle.[103] Garrigues even reads the idea of the trinitarian perichoresis into Maximus' *Epist.* 2, that is, that love puts the mutual communion of human personae into effect.[104] Garrigues' interpretation of Maximus thus appears to anticipate Fr Sophrony's idea of hypostatic deification, but Garrigues is not flawless in his assumptions. Thus, he passes over in silence the fact that Maximus never uses the concept of perichoresis in the context of trinitarian theology. In the passages that Garrigues quotes, Maximus never uses the Trinity as a multihypostatic model for mankind. In fact, he seems to rule out such affinity between the unity of hypostases in the Trinity and human hypostases.[105] Maximus speaks rather about the general providential *philanthropia* of the Godhead, as expressed in the kenosis of the Logos.

As a result of the integration of traditional ideas concerning the deification of man into the framework of Fr Sophrony's own thought, his approach is marked by a bold maximalism, on the one hand, and on the other, by an unusually high awareness of the hypostatic dimension of deification. This integration makes possible an innovative concept of hypostatic deification.

The idea of deification through kenosis, experienced in the state of abandonment by God, significantly enriches the eastern tradition, which sees the way to deification largely as participation in the divine energies. These communal and kenotic aspects of hypostatic deification, which evolve as the result of Fr Sophrony's distinctive teaching on persona and his spiritual experience, introduce a new application of the doctrine of the deification of man to the understanding of ascetic practice and his spiritual experience.

[103] *Cap. car.* 2.30, 106; *Epist.* 2, PG 91:400AB.
[104] Garrigues, 181–82.
[105] *Cap. car.* 2.29, 104–6.

CHAPTER SEVEN

Godforsakenness

The Christian revelation professes "God is love" (1 Jn 1:4), which is absolute and unconditional love. Why then does God abandon man? Different Christian traditions solve this question in various ways. In the west this phenomenon is known as the "darkness of dereliction." In the ascetic *imitation of Christ* a Christian experiences godforsakenness similar to that of Christ in Gethsemane. Modern Orthodox theologians sometimes take it for granted that the "darkness of dereliction" is alien to the eastern theological framework. Eastern theology was largely "codified" by Gregory Palamas, as É. Mélia puts it,[1] and thus "the illumination by the uncreated light of Mount Tabor is the ultimate ideal of spirituality."[2] Yet in reality, Orthodox ascetics, as Fr Sophrony witnessed on Mount Athos, do experience abandonment by God.

Fr Sophrony's teaching on persona provides the necessary theological tools to account for these "negative" ascetic experiences. The vision of the uncreated light, so much spoken of in the east, is an evident antithesis to the experience of abandonment. Fr Sophrony builds a theological bridge between the two contrasting sets of experiences of Tabor and Gethsemane. He does so by merging these experiences into one ascetic scheme, which reflects the growth of man as persona. Fr Sophrony differs from some of his Russian contemporaries, notably Vladimir Lossky, in his approach to the themes light/divine presence and darkness/divine absence. On the other hand, though using terms familiar in some western mystics, notably the Carmelites, Fr Sophrony is not translating their spirituality into eastern theological language. His distinctive theology of abandonment derives from the eastern ascetic tradition. However, as we shall see, the full theological integration of this theme within the eastern tradition becomes possible only through his theology of persona.

[1]É. Mélia, "Le thème de la lumière dans l'hymnographie byzantine de Noël," in *Noël-Épiphanie, retour du Christ, Semaine liturgique de l'Institut Saint Serge, Lex Orandi* 40:255 (Paris, 1967).
[2]P. Evdokimov, *La nouveauté de l'esprit: études de spiritualité* (Bégrolles-en-Mauges, 1977) 57.

Setting the Perspective: Godforsakenness and Lossky's Neo-Palamism

Kenotic Godforsakenness as the Crux of the Matter

Fr Sophrony dedicates to the theme of godforsakenness a significant number of pages in *St Silouan the Athonite* and a whole chapter in *We Shall See Him as He Is.* He subsumes this wide-ranging experience under one single term: godforsakenness (*Bogoostavlennost*). His impetus for a more detailed explanation of godforsakenness came partly from misunderstandings of this phenomenon within the Orthodox ascetic theology of the twentieth century. Thus, Lossky believes the darkness of *derelictio* to be an attribute of exclusively western spirituality, especially that of the "dark night," of which John of the Cross is a typical exponent.[3] He fails to make a connection between what Williams calls the "kenotic view of *personality*," on the one hand, and the state of godforsakenness, on the other. In Carmelite spirituality Lossky sees the idea of abandonment of the soul by the Spirit as a consequence of distorted dogmatic vision in general, and of an erroneous concept of persona in particular. He concludes that godforsakenness is "never thought of by the mystical and ascetical writers of the eastern tradition as a necessary and normal stage in the way of union."[4]

In contrast, Fr Sophrony works out a strong theological connection between the kenosis of persona and the experience of godforsakenness. In fact, they are so interdependent that they are used almost as synonyms, merging into one phenomenon. Moreover, for Fr Sophrony, godforsakenness is not *alien to* but even *inherent* in the eastern tradition. As a result, Fr Sophrony is more reserved in his criticism of John of the Cross. Despite their dogmatic divergence, he notes a certain affinity between his own mystical experiences and those of John.

Lossky's Interpretation of Gregory Palamas

On the whole, Lossky underestimates the validity of using Christ's example as a model for human ascetic life. The fundamental difference between human and divine hypostases—between Christ the Logos and men—prevents Lossky

---

[3] *Dark Night* 2, 5f, 94ff; see A. Louth, *Wilderness of God* (London, 1991) 84-103.
[4] See Williams, 189; Lossky, Lectures (March 8, 1956), 27; *Mystical Theology*, 225-27.

from making more extensive use of the idea of the imitation of Christ, which in his eyes is essentially alien to the east.[5] For many of his contemporaries, such as Fr Cyprian Kern, the appeal to Christ as a "moral" model was a trait of Protestant puritanism and moralism. Instead, Lossky understands the ascetic life largely within the perspective of the relationship between God and man on the level of divine energies. This focusing upon the "moment énergétique" in fact led Lossky to underestimate the importance of the hypostatic level. Lossky's criticism of western *derelictio* is based upon his stress on the immanence of divine presence through divine energies according to the Palamite teaching. Thus, he emphasizes that the energies are processions of the divine nature, while "the Son and the Holy Spirit are, so to say, personal processions."[6] For Lossky, the eternal divine energies unwaveringly permeate the created order, "making the greatness of God to shine forth in all things, and appearing beyond all things as the divine light which the created world cannot contain."[7] The energies are seen as sanctifying grace, which gives holiness to all things: animate and inanimate, personal and impersonal. Hence, the hypostatic element is not clearly brought into the framework of his distinction between *essence* and *energy*.

If the energies proceed from and manifest forth the divine nature like rays of light shining from the sun, are these energies and their manifestation under "hypostatic control," or, as in the sun, which cannot adjust the strength of its rays, are they uncontrollable "natural" proceedings? When touching this question, Lossky seems to stick to the sun analogy, with its overtones of "uncontrollable natural proceedings," which leads him to the underestimation of the hypostatic-*personal* dimension of the divine energies: "Even if creatures did not exist, God would none the less manifest Himself beyond His essence; just as the rays of the sun would shine out from the solar disk *whether or not there were any beings capable of receiving their light*."[8]

Such an approach overlooks the element of *personal love* in God's manifestation of his energies, and consequently God's freedom with regard to man. In Lossky's perspective, for the divine light to become visible depends somehow on man's will. If only one purifies oneself, the "certainty," as it were, of

---

[5] Lossky's assessment of the eastern tradition concerning the ascetic imitation of Christ (in *Mystical Theology*, 215) has been successfully challenged by I. Hausherr in "L'imitation de Jésus-Christ dans la spiritualité byzantine," in *Études de spiritualité orientale*, 217-46 (Rome, 1969).

[6] Lossky, *Mystical Theology*, 86.

[7] Ibid., 73-76.

[8] Ibid., 74 (my emphasis).

communion and transfiguration is a logically inevitable conclusion. Thus we find also in Cyprian Kern that the ascetic path progresses straightforwardly to deification, "illumination, glorification, transfiguration," "participation in the glorified body of Christ." Hence, darkness has no part of this ascetic scheme.

As a result of the underestimation of the level of hypostatic relationship between God and man on the level of energies, Lossky is unable to find any explanation for the "dark night of the soul" other than failure on the *human part*, whether it be "distorted theology" or sin. Lossky is bewildered at ascetic experience similar to Christ's at Gethsemane, and finds it incompatible with the Palamite idea of ascetic life. For him, Palamism rules out godforsakenness de facto.

Fr Sophrony and "Hypostatic Palamism"

Palamas and his predecessors were well aware of the mysterious antinomy between divine immanence and divine transcendence, as well as of the antinomy between the divine ever-omnipresence and the personal freedom of God. This antinomy is exposed in the oft-used prayer of the eastern church to the Holy Spirit. He is believed to be "everywhere present and to fill all things," and yet the faithful pray to him "to come and abide" in them. Thus when Palamas and Gregory of Nyssa used the sun analogy, they were well aware of its imperfection precisely because it does not reflect this mysterious antinomy. Gregory of Nyssa expresses his *aporia* (puzzlement) thus: "Here is something that would be worth lengthy research, namely, understanding how he who is always present comes."[9] Balthasar comments on this antinomy: "It is a mystery of the presence that has never finished coming."[10] This antinomy led Frank to suggest two modes of presence of God in the world:

> When He [God] enters the world ... through the gracious presence of the Holy Spirit in the depth of the human soul, He descends, as it were, from His far-off transcendent abode. But in another aspect of His being He is the immanent ground of universal life. That aspect is creative dynamism and "omnipotence." Reality is the derivatively-divine substratum of existence.[11]

[9]*De paup. amand.* 2, 22.
[10]H. Balthasar, *Presence and Thought: Essay on the Religious Philosophy of Gregory of Nyssa* (San Francisco, 1995) 161.
[11]Frank, 209-10.

Lossky solves the antinomy differently: he rationalizes the Palamite frame-work of thought by virtually ignoring this antinomy in favor of *immanence*, and thus he verges on an almost impersonal, "essentialist," metaphysics. Georges Florovsky rightly warns against such misinterpretation of Palamas:

> [St Gregory's theology] should be described in modern terms as an "existentialist theology." Yet in any case Gregory was definitely op-posed to all kinds of "essentialist theologies" that fail to account for God's freedom, for the dynamism of God's will, for the reality of divine action . . . It was the predicament of Greek impersonalist metaphysics. If there is any room for Christian metaphysics at all, it must be a meta-physics of persons.[12]

In Fr Sophrony the patristic antinomy is maintained. His theology pre-supposes the Palamite framework with the hypostasis-essence-energy dis-tinction, where the energies are seen as immanent. Along with this, however, he uses the language of the divine "coming and going." This presence-and-absence scheme reflects Silouan's living experience, confirmed by Fr Sophrony's own experience and the experience of his contemporary ascetics.

The key to the theological integration of kenotic godforsakenness is the principle of commensurability between the divine and human on the level of hypostasis. In contrast to Lossky, Fr Sophrony extends the possibilities for the application of the divine model of Christ on the human plane. His approach is determined by his theocentric interpretation of the human persona, based on the Christ-model, where the hypostatic principle within the relationship between man-Jesus and God the Father emerges as the starting point for the explanation of any "human" ascetic experience. He succeeds in providing a theological explanation for godforsakenness in ascetic life, because along with the *moment énergétique* he explores extensively the hypostatic level. In such a "hypostatic" perspective, Christ's abandonment by God at Gethsemane and Golgotha has immediate relevance to ascetic life as well as transfiguration.

In contrast to Lossky's and Kern's emphasis on *participation* in divine ener-gies as the way toward union with God in eastern spirituality, Fr Sophrony

---

[12]G. Florovsky, "St Gregory Palamas and the Tradition of the Fathers," *Sobornost* 4:4 (1961) 176. D. Staniloae takes a similar position in "The Cross in Orthodox Theology and Worship," *Sobornost* 7:4 (1977) 241: "[sanctification] does not come about by an impersonal magic force, immanent in nature. It is always Christ as a person who through nature invisibly communicates his personal energies to men."

prefers to stress that living knowledge of and union with God is based on the "personal" principle, which includes freedom on both sides. God, as a personal being, and not solely man himself, controls the manifestation of grace. According to Fr Sophrony, this light is given to men in varying measures. It cannot be opened up within us by any ascetic means. It comes exclusively as a gift of God's mercy.

Thus, when one includes this *moment hypostatique*, it follows that the withdrawal of grace is not determined solely by any human error. In Fr Sophrony's interpretation of the phenomenon as an act of divine providential involvement, godforsakenness is not only *a mode of divine presence,* but even *God's gift.* Fr Sophrony calls it "another pole of Divine Love."[13] Hence, periods of godforsakenness are seen as *normative* within ascetic experience.

Godforsakenness in Fr Sophrony

The Example of Christ: Gethsemane and Golgotha

The normativeness of godforsakenness is derived from the Christ-model. Fr Sophrony stresses the *Gethsemane event* no less than the event of the cross as a redemptive moment, and devotes a whole chapter in *We Shall See Him as He Is* to the former. In his estimation, it is one of the most invaluable revelations about God and man. It is eternal as a spiritual act. Here Fr Sophrony makes a clear distinction between the external and internal aspects of Christ's suffering. He points out that the physical sufferings of Christ on the cross do not have exclusive significance in his redemptive act: they make his suffering *total,* embracing his being at all levels. The passion implies that Christ's prayer in Gethsemane remained without answer on the part of God, and shows that the abandonment by God on the cross is a continuation-completion of the agony in Gethsemane. Gethsemane emerges as a redemptive "inner sacrifice" of primary importance. The superiority of inner sacrifice over external is deduced from the story of Abraham and his son. Attachment to his son Isaac diminished Abraham's love toward God. When this was restored internally by Abraham's readiness to sacrifice his son, the external sacrifice was no longer necessary. With this concept of "inner sacrifice" in mind, Fr Sophrony believes that in Gethsemane the Lord accomplished his sacrifice *internally.* However,

---

[13] *We Shall See Him as He Is,* 136.

he, for the sake of "the work" (Jn 17:4), had to suffer "to the end," *externally* as well, otherwise no one would have been able to penetrate the mystery of redemption. Therefore, it is only on Golgotha, before death, and not in Gethsemane, that Christ cried out "It is accomplished."

Despite the fact that Fr Sophrony looks at the cross as a partly revelatory event (so as to allow men to penetrate the mystery of redemption), one should not regard the cross in Fr Sophrony's interpretation as a kind of "show." Christ's bodily crucifixion and death are the crowning moment of the completion of *kenotic* godforsakenness. In order to unveil the spiritual reality of Golgotha, Fr Sophrony juxtaposes the scriptural passages in the following order. The cry "My God, My God why hast thou forsaken Me?" (Mt 27:46) is the testimony to Christ's being abandoned by God. Yet, as a response to such a "forsaking Father," Christ remains *faithful* to him "even unto death" (Phil 2:6) by committing himself to God—"Father into thy hands I commend my spirit" (Lk 23:46). This faithfulness in total abandonment marked the completion of Christ's kenosis—"It is finished" (Jn 19:30).

The Teaching on the Three Stages of Ascetic Life

This scheme of Golgotha sayings has a bearing upon Fr Sophrony's theory of the three stages of ascetic life, where the "ascent to heaven" of communion with God is always preceded by the "descent to hell" of godforsakenness. In the Christ-model, the descent of the Spirit at theophany and Christ's consequent glorious ministry eventually lead Christ to Calvary and to hell, which in turn precede the resurrection and the glorious ascension. Hence, within ascetic experience there is also a threefold scheme.

The first stage—palpable visitation by grace—is described in slightly different terms in *St Silouan the Athonite* and in *We Shall See Him as He Is*. Thus in *St Silouan*: "The initial experience of divine visitation strikes man to the core and draws his whole being into the inner life of prayer and struggle against the passions. His heart is alive with feeling during this initial stage, which abounds in such powerful experiences that the entire mind is drawn to take part in them."[14]

Among other traits of the first period, Fr Sophrony points out that requests in prayer, whether small or great, are miraculously granted almost before they are uttered. In *We Shall See Him as He Is* the same sort of experience is

---

[14] *St Silouan the Athonite*, 188.

described in more general terms. There Fr Sophrony interprets the parable in Luke 16:9-12 in terms of the three stages. The first stage is when God bestows grace upon man and draws him to himself with love. He calls it "the unrighteous [i.e., 'undeserved'] mammon" (Lk 16.11): man is "given the real experience of divine eternity," but grace is not yet assimilated ontologically so as to become inherent.

The second stage is named in various ways: "godforsakenness," "period of spiritual trials," "the withdrawal of grace." In *St Silouan the Athonite* Fr Sophrony describes this period in the following terms:

> When the time of trial starts, everything alters. It seems as if heaven had closed up and become deaf to all our prayers. For the fervent Christian everything in life gets to be difficult . . . And finally—the most painful and unbearable of torments—God deserts him. His suffering is complete—he is stricken on every level of his being.[15]

"Assaults from demonic powers" are experienced particularly at the time of prayer: "the mind . . . is darkened and sees demons; they haunt and trouble the monk in an attempt to distract him from prayer or affect, at least, the purity of prayer." One experiences dryness of heart, and is inclined to reestimate past experiences of divine love. He then tends to interpret their visitation from on high as some temporary psychological elation. The perception of God is distorted; speaking of the thoughts of the ascetic at the time of godforsakenness, God appears as "hard-hearted," "merciless." As Silouan puts it: "God cannot be moved by entreaty!" Fr Sophrony only partly puts to writing such "thoughts and feelings," for, he says, it is better to cover them with silence. The enemy in such cases incites the soul to the point of revolt against God. The enemy has power to penetrate the innermost parts of our soul, and there he begins to accuse God for all the torments of our world, since *he,* God, created this world. The perplexity becomes like prison fetters: the heart and mind revolt. The tempter tries to push man to extremes: to do everything against God.

The state of godforsakenness is often described as the feeling of a curse cast upon the ascetic. The soul feels it as a spiritual death. It seems that there are various degrees of this state of godforsakenness: on the one hand it may last for decades, on the other hand its climactic depth can last, according to Fr Sophrony, only for a very short time, and not often. Fr Sophrony follows

[15]Ibid., 200-201.

Silouan here, asserting that the human being cannot endure such a state for any extensive time. Silouan is said to have experienced this state in its ultimate form only twice in his life. Fr Sophrony describes Silouan's first experience in terms of the darkness of eternal death and infernal anguish. The second time, having exhausted himself in the struggle for pure prayer, he lost hope of achieving what he desired and his soul was grievously tormented.

What happens during the event of abandonment—does God really depart, really become absent? If so, the experience of abandonment by God indicates his real withdrawal. Fr Sophrony adopts a different perspective: "Objectively it is not a complete withdrawal of grace but rather subjectively the soul experiences even the smallest reduction of grace as abandonment by God."[16] It is an event of divine providence, where God does not withdraw but only diminishes the active power of grace within the ascetic, leaving thereby the darkness of the aroused passions within the soul.

God remains present and even "most attentive." He exposes the ascetic to demonic attacks by "permitting" (*parachoresis*) them to act on the ascetic: those attacked are still within the frame of divine providence. Furthermore, God *actively* disposes situations that involve not only the ascetic himself, but other people and circumstances as well:

There is a change in people's attitude toward him—he is no longer respected. What is willingly forgiven to others is held against him. His resistance to physical ills is lowered. Nature, circumstances, people—all turn against him. He finds no outlet for his natural talents, though they are no less valuable than other people's. On the top of all he has to endure the assaults from demonic powers.[17]

The third stage of spiritual life is characterized by a "mature and complete dogmatic consciousness." Fr Sophrony describes it as man's discovering in himself "the light of the knowledge of the ways of the spirit." It comes secretly and unobserved (cf Lk 17:20). "This knowledge, which is called dogmatic consciousness, is the deep-set life of the spirit, having nothing to do with abstract gnosis." In this third phase man assimilates divine life as his own, as is clear from Fr Sophrony's interpretation of Luke 16:12. Divine life is given as "one's own" for an "eternal possession."

[16]Ibid., 28.
[17]Ibid., 200-201.

Theological Integration of Godforsakenness

Fr Sophrony's insistence on the total freedom of the hypostatic being allowed him to integrate the experience of godforsakenness within the framework of eastern theology.

Without freedom there is no person and without person there is no free-dom: the man who experiences godforsakenness is left in total freedom to manifest his existential orientation, because the influence of grace is no longer palpably present. In this complete freedom man has an opportunity to develop his potential as a hypostatic being: "The purpose behind this withdrawal of grace is to give him the opportunity to manifest his freedom and fidelity to God . . . Without this testing of our freedom we cannot realize ourselves as truly free persons."[18]

Godforsakenness serves "to educate and bring to the point of perfection, if possible, the gift of freedom for our self-orientation in the sphere of eter-nity." Thus, faithfulness is the positive realization of human freedom. Godfor-sakenness may bring a man to the kenosis of love for God, analogous to that of Christ on the cross. It can even be called the kenosis of faithfulness: despite the withdrawal of God, man is expected to "abide in love toward him." Fidelity grows through a succession of experiences of godforsakenness, into unshak-able stability, which is associated with salvation. Man attains to the state of eternal rest (*katapausis*) in his faithfulness to God. Thus man abides in the "unshakable kingdom":

> When love is stronger than death, it is perfect love. After such a "try-ing out," which none of us can avoid, love through death on the earthly plane conquers death in eternity and makes man an inheritor of a "kingdom which cannot be moved" (Heb 12:28).[19]

Thus, in Fr Sophrony the concept of godforsakenness is integrated as a theological exigency of hypostatic development. The potential of hypostatic freedom for self-determination can only be realized if God's "intervening sus-tenance," as it were, is removed. Fr Sophrony's predecessors did not possess a sufficiently articulated teaching on human persona to explain this ascetic phenomenon as an integral part of the overall dogmatic vision.

---

[18] *We Shall See Him as He Is*, 129, 93–94.
[19] Ibid., 72.

The Roots of Fr Sophrony's Teaching on Godforsakenness

Fr Sophrony and John of the Cross?

It is tempting to see in Fr Sophrony a borrowing from Carmelite spirituality, largely because of the emphasis he places on godforsakenness. Fr Sophrony, as we mentioned in chapter one, was acquainted with the writings of John of the Cross and, in contrast to Lossky, estimated them rather positively. Some commentators have indeed drawn parallels between Silouan and John of the Cross. As we mentioned earlier, Fr Sophrony himself admits a certain affinity between John's experience and his own. For example, John sees the dark night as "a mark of God's intimacy" (Williams), "a part of the relationship" (Cugno); for Fr Sophrony godforsakenness is a gift of God's love.

The question of the potential dependence of Fr Sophrony on John fits well within the context of the debates about the place of dark-night spirituality in the east. Lossky's opinion, outlined above, has been contested by Hausherr, Balthasar, and Daniélou, who highlight the similarities concerning godforsakenness in the east and the west. Hausherr concludes that the east possesses all the elements that constitute these purifying nights.[20] Others, however, are more careful in drawing such parallels. Puech argues that the patristic use of the terms *gnophos* (gloom) and *skotos* (darkness) is metaphorical: they do not represent an experiential reality, as they do in the dramatic and affective mysticism of John.[21]

Any attempt to subsume John's mysticism of the dark night under a single definition fails to do justice to the complexity of experience. The association of dark night merely with the dereliction/absence of God, or an unqualified equation of dark night with Dionysius' and Gregory of Nyssa's *gnophos* and *skotos* as the manifestation of God, would be onesided and thereby misleading. To begin with, John distinguishes *different types* of dark night on various experiential levels. In *Ascent of Mount Carmel* it signifies purification and purgation. He distinguishes between a night of the senses and the night of the spirit, as well as between active and passive purification. He thus calls the journey toward union with God a "night." He further extends the imagery of night

---

[20]I. Hausherr, "Les Orientaux connaissent-ils les 'nuits' de saint Jean de la Croix?" in *Hésychasme et prière*, 125 (Rome, 1966).

[21]H.-C. Puech, "La ténèbre mystique chez le pseudo-Denys," *Études carmélitaines* 23:2 (1938) 53.

and its application to faith:"for the intellect faith is also like a dark night." The notion is also related to God himself:"God is also a dark night to man in this life." In the *Dark Night* he also relates the night to contemplation, when the soul is watching in darkness, divested of thoughts and images.[22]

Some of these multiple experiences can certainly be paralleled in Fr Sophrony. He praises John for his determination to follow the hard path: the way toward union with God is through trials, kenosis, and abandonment. There are striking parallels between the dark night of contemplation in John and the second period of ascetic life in Fr Sophrony, discussed above. For John, the soul feels that all creatures have forsaken it, and that it is condemned by them, particularly by its friends. Inasmuch as God is purging the soul according to its interior and exterior faculties, the soul must be in all its parts reduced to a state of emptiness, poverty, and abandonment and must be left dry and empty and in darkness. Dark night "has hindered its faculties and affections in this way; it is unable to raise its affection or its mind to God, neither can it pray to him, thinking that God has set a cloud before it through which its prayers cannot pass. . . . it thinks that God neither hears it [soul] nor pays heed to it." The soul believes God to be against it, that God has cast it away.[23] Finally, John and Fr Sophrony both know of the darkness of divestiture, when the mind is stripped of any thought or image.[24]

We may nonetheless rule out any immediate dependence on John of the Cross. Fr Sophrony's ideas on kenosis and godforsakenness must have taken shape before he read John of the Cross. The first extant mention of John is in 1932, but he read the whole book *Dark Night* only in 1943. His interest in John's experience was stimulated by the intensity of his own experience of godforsakenness. In connection with kenosis and godforsakenness, Fr Sophrony points rather to the experience of his teacher, Silouan, than to John. Among the books he recommended as reading for advice on spiritual life, he never mentions John.

Furthermore, Fr Sophrony is eager to emphasize the difference in his approach to godforsakenness. On the theological level, their respective backgrounds are different. John of the Cross is rooted in the western medieval mystical tradition with its "dramatic and affective character,"[25] while Fr Sophrony

---

[22] *Ascent* 1.1.1-1.2.1, 17-20.; cf *Dark Night* 1.8.1, 55 and 2.5.1, 94: "This dark night is an inflowing of God into the soul." Cf Louth, *Wilderness of God*, 95.

[23] *Dark Night* 2.6.3-4, 99-100.; ibid., 2.5.5, 96 and 2.8.1, 109.

[24] *St Silouan the Athonite*, 179ff.

[25] A. Louth, *The Origins of the Christian Mystical Tradition* (Oxford, 1981) 184.

has patristic tradition as his roots. If we pursue further our comparison of the dark night and the darkness of godforsakenness in Fr Sophrony, we discover that the actual experience of God is conceived in different tones. In John the terrible sufferings—agony, pain, dryness of the soul—are caused by "the assaults of divine light":

> And when the soul suffers the direct assault of this Divine light . . . it believes God to be against it, and thinks that it has set itself up against God. This causes it sore grief and pain, because it now believes that God has cast it away . . .
>
> When the Divine assails the soul . . . the soul feels itself to be perishing and melting away, in the presence and sight of its miseries, in a cruel spiritual death.[26]

In Fr Sophrony the divine light "brings humble love," "banishes all doubt and fear," "makes the soul safe from everything that hitherto weighed her down." "Aches and pains disappear . . . Anxieties are absorbed into a sweet peace." This light does not "assault" but is "quiet and gentle." Though in Fr Sophrony, like in John, this light purges the soul, it does so "calmly, hardly making itself felt."[27]

As for the pains and agonies, in Fr Sophrony those negative states are brought about by demonic assaults by divine permission, while in John they are inflicted directly by God: he hardly ever mentions the enemy, or demons. It is noteworthy that Hausherr makes the same point when he compares St John of the Cross to the eastern fathers.[28] Thus, according to Fr Sophrony's experience, in those "dark moments" it is the enemy "who penetrates the inmost parts of our soul," sets it against God, and obstructs prayer. Perhaps this point may be partly related to Lot-Borodine's assessment of the difference between the east and the west. She points out that in contrast to John of the Cross' "great stress on the soul's learning to be passive," the idea of synergism in the east presupposes active struggle of the soul. Thus, in the east this "active-ness" of the soul at the time of godforsakenness is linked with the idea of spiritual warfare: God allows negative forces to act on the soul so the soul can actively wage battle against them, making its self-determination manifest.

[26]*Dark Night* 2.5.5, 96; ibid., 2.6.1, 98; cf ibid., 2.5.6, 97: the experience of agony.
[27]*We Shall See Him as He Is*, 166f; cf *His Life Is Mine*, 79.
[28]Hausherr, "Les Orientaux," 123.

These qualifications allow us to assert that the theme of divine light is the most significant point of divergence, and this proves Fr Sophrony's lack of theological dependence on John. John also speaks of divine light, but it appears to the soul as darkness: "when this Divine light of contemplation assails the soul, which is not yet wholly enlightened, it causes spiritual darkness in it; for not only does it overcome it, but likewise it overwhelms it and darkens the act of its natural intelligence."[29] In line with his time, John's flight from the senses and the intellect to the *principalis affectio* as the highest point of the mind (*apex mentis*) and the sole agent of contact with God[30] neglects man's participation in God. The result is that neither sense perception nor intellectual acumen, but only faith, will find the way to union with God. Faith, then, deepened by intellectual effort, plunges the soul into the very darkness of the divine mystery. For Fr Sophrony man is plunged into the divine light of communion with God, which embraces the *totality of man's being*, its sensual, spiritual, noetic/intellectual, and bodily constituents. This disparity points to the further difference in their respective backgrounds. John's darkness derives from his concern to maintain divine infinity, transcendence, and thus incomprehensibility. For Fr Sophrony *homo capax Dei*, and the deified man is capable of "seeing God as He is" (1 Jn 3:2), that is as "light, and in Him is no darkness at all" (1 Jn 1:5). His idea of knowledge and contemplation of God rests on the Palamite framework, which asserts immanence and, thus, the possibility of knowing God through his energies. This Palamite "bridge" between God and man was alien to the John's theological milieu. Therefore, for Fr Sophrony God *always* manifests himself as light: darkness is clearly associated with God's absence, light with God's presence. Thus Fr Sophrony is in line with the hesychasts, for whom, as Wunderle observes, the union with God is *luminous*: "God manifests himself to the mystic in all his splendor, if the latter succeeds in shutting out all that darkens it.'"[31]

As for the darkness of divestiture, for Fr Sophrony it is not yet the contemplation of God, but only a temporary stage: "If we would 'situate' the spiritual whereabouts of this darkness, we could say that it is to be found on the outskirts of uncreated light ... but God is not in [this] darkness of divestiture." He warns against mistaking this darkness for divine presence, because the

[29]*Dark Night* 2.5.3, 95; cf ibid., 2.5.2, 94.

[30]See Louth, *The Origins of the Christian Mystical Tradition*, 185.

[31]G. Wunderle, "La technique psychologique de l'Hésychasme byzantin," *Études Carmélitaines* 23:2 (1938) 67; cf *St Silouan the Athonite*, 179.

darkness of divestiture can become a stronger barrier between the ascetic and God than darkness brought about by demons, loss of grace, or the uprising of gross passion. The possibility of such an error is enhanced by the fact that the mind, if it turns in on itself, can perceive its own natural light, which is not the divine light.[32] John seems to be unaware of a distinction between the divine light and the natural light of intellect.

In his theology of light Fr Sophrony is in accord with the eastern fathers, in whose spirituality the symbol of light is more frequent than that of darkness. In the eastern framework, even for those fathers who use the concept of divine darkness as a metaphorical expression of divine incomprehensibility, the concept of God as light is still indispensable, as for example in Dionysius.[33] Fr Sophrony notes that unlike in the Old Testament, where light symbolism of the glory of the Lord (*Kabod Yahweh*) is used along with the "divine darkness," the New Testament always uses only light terminology for the divine theophany.[34] This light symbolism is also of prime importance for the hymnography of the eastern church.[35] Therefore, Fr Sophrony's integration of light and darkness into a single theological scheme is essentially different from that of John. Darkness, as godforsakenness, neither signifies nor coexists with light at the same time, as in John of the Cross; they are two different, successive experiences. Fr Sophrony's principle of persona serves as a theological bridge between these two experiences. In contrast to Lossky's confusion over *derelictio*, Fr Sophrony explains the "coming and going" of light not on the level of energies but of persona. His vocabulary gives less space for any nonpersonalist interpretation of the phenomenon. It is perceived by man's hypostatic principle. Fr Sophrony also stresses that visions of light contain an element of personal "recognition": it is impossible not to recognize God in this light. The vision of light is seen not just as a bestowal of illumination upon the spiritual senses by divine energy, and certainly not by an impersonal energy. It is rather the closest *personal* contact with hypostatic being. Thus Fr Sophrony asserts that in this light is our personal communion with God: face to Face, person to Person. This light names himself I AM THAT I AM. Interpersonal love emerges

---

[32]*St Silouan the Athonite*, 179.

[33]*Myst. theol.* 1.1, 142; cf *Epist.* 5, 162. Cf Gregory Palamas, *Triads* 2.3.51, 584; *Triads* 1.3.18, 429; Puech, 53

[34]*La félicité de connaître la voie*, 38.

[35]Cf Mélia, 237ff. However, there are examples of darkness imagery, such as "the innermost darkness" in the Great Canon (*The Lenten Triodion*, 222).

as a leitmotif of these experiences.[36] Fr Sophrony writes: "'Lovest thou Me? Yea, Thou knowest I love Thee' (Jn 21:15). In this there is the whole purport, the whole wisdom, the uncreated light—*everything*."[37]

The "personeity" of divine light allowed Fr Sophrony to highlight the difference between the vision of God (when man is the "perceiving and reflecting object"), and of the nonpersonal created light of the human intellect (when man himself is the source of some luminous sensation), which is achieved in some non-Christian mystical and intellectual disciplines. This distinction is not unknown in the eastern tradition.[38] Finally, the vision of uncreated light is linked with hypostatic prayer, when the persona embraces/takes into itself all, even enemies. In compassion toward "those who wrong us," our human love "merges together" with the divine energy of light. This all-embracing hypostatic love is seen as that uncreated light that shone upon the apostles on Mount Tabor. Fr Sophrony recalls that under the influence of this light, prayer for mankind in travail possessed his whole being.[39]

Thus the ascetic experiences of both light and darkness are situated by Fr Sophrony in the context of personeity divine and human. In this integration of the darkness of godforsakenness he does not depart from the Palamite basis of his theology: he is fully in accord with the theology of the divine energies. The Palamite framework guarantees that for Fr Sophrony the divine darkness/godforsakenness is only a stage on the way to the fulfilment of communion with God in divine light, and not the fulfilment itself. This analysis demonstrates that Fr Sophrony's theology of abandonment is not dependent on John of the Cross.

Fr Sophrony and Russian Thought?

A potential source of Fr Sophrony's stress on godforsakenness can be traced in the christology of nineteenth- and twentieth-century Russia in its approach to Calvary. Thus, Metropolitan Philaret sees an anticipation of the external cross internally in the struggle of Gethsemane.[40] His line of thought was taken

---

[36]*We Shall See Him as He Is*, 163, 167ff, 189. A similar view is found in Maximus, *Cap. car.* 1.10, 52.

[37]*Letters to Russia*, 155.

[38]Similar distinction is drawn in Evagrius, *Antirrh.* 6.16, 525; *Gnost.* 1.35, 33; Isaac the Syrian, *Syr. Hom.* 1.80, 560; Diadochus of Photice, *Chapt.* 40, 108; cf *We Shall See Him as He Is*, 155.

[39]*We Shall See Him as He Is*, 162-63, 183-84; *St Silouan the Athonite*, 232.

[40]Philaret, "Sermon on Great Friday (1813)," in *Collected Works of Philaret the Metropolitan of Moscow and Colomna* 33 (Moscow, 1873).

up by Khrapovitsky, for whom Gethsemane is the internal manifestation of the physical cross.[41] The theme received its theological crystallization in the teaching of Bulgakov. He says that although the acceptance and the willingness of Christ to be sacrificed is due to the help of the Holy Spirit, the joy of their relationship is extinguished in the night of Gethsemane. The Holy Spirit, who always reposes on the Son, seems also to have abandoned him. Gethsemane is seen as an act where Christ "suffered through and did away all the sins of mankind."[42] Godforsakenness is related to the kenosis of the Holy Spirit in his *operative faculty*, which takes place at Golgotha: "In the kenosis of death on Golgotha the immutable abiding of the Spirit [upon the Son] becomes imperceptible in contrast to its [ultimate] perceptibility at the transfiguration."[43]

It is tempting to see Fr Sophrony as a follower of Bulgakov. The principle of the *variable perceptibility* of the Holy Spirit, which Bulgakov works out on the basis of the scriptural narrative about Christ, is, as we saw, found in Fr Sophrony. Yet there are some significant differences between them. Bulgakov does not go beyond a strictly christological application of the term godforsakenness, while Fr Sophrony extends its application to the sphere of ascetic theology.

The stress of Russian thought on godforsakenness in christology led Fr Sophrony to be more attentive than Lossky to the elements of godforsakenness already inherent in the eastern ascetic tradition. The theological integration of his own living experience of the long "second phase" of ascetic life made godforsakenness as central to his ascetic theory as it was to redemptive christology among his fellow Russian theologians.

Fr Sophrony and Patristic Tradition on Godforsakenness

Fr Sophrony recognized a vivid presence of godforsakenness in the eastern patristic tradition. When we see that in the east godforsakenness is a normative stage in spiritual development, we can demonstrate that Fr Sophrony's approach to ascetic theology follows a precedent set by the eastern fathers.

In the eastern tradition, behind the concept of *enkataleipsis* (abandonment by God) lies a distinctive cosmological outlook. First, as far as the role of the demons is concerned, they are believed to seek influence over human beings

[41]Khrapovitsky, 33.
[42]*The Lamb of God*, 75, 383.
[43]*The Comforter*, 288–89; cf *The Lamb of God*, 345.

as an ever-active negative force as much and as far as divine control allows this to happen.[44] In ascetic literature God's role is expressed in the term *parachoresis*,[45] which can be translated as "withdrawal" with overtones of "allowing" or "leaving space." Second, without divine intervention and support, man himself is incapable of overcoming this negative force.[46] These two points explain *why* enkataleipsis is conceived in terms of the struggle with the demons. For Macarius, for example, when God withdraws from man "[man's] mind is expelled and excommunicated from spiritual joy, since the divine grace and love are diminished in him as well as every good action of the Spirit, and [as a result] he is delivered to suffering, temptations, and evil spirits."[47] The eastern tradition uses a specific term for this struggle: *polemos*—"warfare," "fight."

Hausherr points out that the two concepts *enkataleipsis* and *parachoresis* are used as synonyms in such authors as Evagrius, Diadochus, and Maximus: they are both associated with *polemos*. The whole event often emerges under the headings of either *thlipsis* (tribulation) or *peirasmos* (temptation).[48] Fr Sophrony uses Russian equivalents for all these words, which emerge in connection with the event of godforsakenness. Silouan also refers to his own experience of godforsakenness: "the Lord let the enemy create strife in my soul."[49] However, in Fr Sophrony's later writings, "godforsakenness" is preferred to other terms as more appropriate for his perspective of spiritual life, where the God-man relationship in terms of *I-Thou* prevails over any other ascetic concern.

Generally, the eastern tradition distinguishes two types of *parachoresis*: God's actual withdrawal from man; and God's educative apparent withdrawal from man, without depriving man of his presence. This distinction is spelled out in Diadochus of Photice. On the one hand, Diadochus points out the possibility of the actual withdrawal of God, that is, when God "turns away" from man (*kata apostrophen parachoresis*). On the other hand, God's apparent withdrawal may be in fact only a concealment of grace: divine grace remains present and effective, "supporting the soul in an ineffable way." He calls it *paideutike* (pedagogical) *parachoresis*.[50] The same distinction is found in John of Damascus,

[44]Cf 1 Pet. 5:8; cf Evagrius, *Epist.* 28, 585; John of Damascus, *Exp. fid.* 2.29, 101-2; cf John Cassian, *Conf.* 7.22, 265.
[45]See Diadochus, *Chapt.* 86, 87, 99, 146-47, 161; cf Maximus, *Cap. car.* 2.67, 124.
[46]Macarius, *Hom.* 21.4, 193; cf *Hom.* 20.7, 190; cf *Anecd.* 56.5, 45.
[47]*Brief.* 52.2.7, 141.
[48]For example, see Evagrius, *Orat. cap.* 37, PG 79:1176A.
[49]*St Silouan the Athonite*, 434.
[50]*Chapt.* 85-87, 144-47.

who defines the first type as *teleia apognostike* (complete despair), when "man is given over to perdition as Judas," and the second as *oikmomike* (providential) and *paideutike*, for "correction, salvation, and glory of the one who suffers it."[51]

The idea of God's complete withdrawal is found in Evagrius. When commenting on Ecclesiastes 5:6, he describes the plight of man, whose "works are destroyed by God's abandonment, which came upon him through his own iniquity."[52] In Macarius we find a similar idea of separating abandonment by God, which comes about because of one's sins: he illustrates it with the example of Judas. The withdrawal of grace takes place either because of one's high opinion about oneself, or when "man goes astray from a life pleasing to God, and offends the divine Spirit."[53] For Diadochus, God turns away from the soul when the soul is not willing to receive God in itself. Such a soul "is delivered to the demons as if in bondage."[54] Dorotheus of Gaza believes that such godforsakenness comes as a result of man's acting against his *katastasis* (state).[55] Maximus the Confessor echoes the same idea.[56] For John of Damascus the story of Judas in Matthew 27:5 provides an example of *enkataleipsis* unto perdition.[57] However, for these authors there is no ultimate rejection by God. Thus, in Macarius the diminution of grace is always educative, and lasts "until the soul begins to walk justly, pleasing the Spirit."[58] Diadochus provides instructions showing how to overcome the state of "complete" godforsakenness.[59] For Maximus every godforsakenness is "salvific and full of divine goodness and wisdom," since even the Jews, having fallen away from God, could have turned to repentance.[60] Thus the fathers generally allow for the possibility of restoration. This, in fact, greatly reduces the sharpness of the contrast: God never turns away from man in a definitive manner.

When Fr Sophrony distinguishes the two types of godforsakenness, he seems to draw a strict demarcation line between them, the criterion being the fact of *faith*. Thus, complete godforsakenness is experienced by nonreligious people. Here, Fr Sophrony uses the same reason as Diadochus: it is not God,

[51] *Fragm. Mat.* 27.8, PG 96:1412AB.
[52] *Schol. eccl.* 37, 126.
[53] *Anecd.* 54, 40–41; *Brief.* 51.5, 136; *Brief.* 52.2.7, 141.
[54] *Chapt.* 86, 146.
[55] *Instr.* 12.136, 398.
[56] *Cap. car.* 4.96, 236.
[57] *Fragm. Mat.*, PG 96:1412B.
[58] *Brief.* 52.2.7, 141.
[59] *Cap.* 87, 147.
[60] *Cap. car.* 4.96, 236.

but the soul itself, who is responsible for this break of union. In comparison to Diadochus, in Fr Sophrony there is a real possibility of ultimate rejection, but on the part of man. As *persona* and a *fact* even for God himself, he is totally free in his self-orientation. In rejecting God, the soul per se gives itself over to pride and to the devil. If the soul abides in God, the "enemy" has no access to that soul, unless God providentially allows the enemy to act: "The suffering occasioned by the despair that arises out of pride differs from that of the pious soul when God allows Satan to wage war against her."[61]

In the former case the breach is not static but dynamic and ever-increasing, due to the process that takes place in the soul itself:

> The proud soul, plunged in the torments and shades of hell, sees God as the cause of her sufferings and considers Him immeasurably cruel. Deprived of true life in God, she sees everything through the spectrum of her own crippled state, and begins to detest her own life and, in general, everything that exists in the world. Outside the Divine light, in her despair she begins to consider even the existence of God Himself as hopeless absurdity. And so her estrangement from God and her detestation of everything that exists grows and grows.[62]

This process is believed to happen to nonbelievers. As for the people of faith, "they escape such despair and hatred" through trust in God's love and mercy, in his word, in the testimony of the fathers of the church.

The idea of providential withdrawal is often derived by the fathers from scripture. In the Old Testament the question of abandonment by God receives particular theological attention in the "psalms of laments." Most of the laments are expressions of complaint regarding God's disposition or action, which the psalmists in their distress interpret as being indifferent or hostile. The ideas in the psalms undoubtedly influenced patristic thought, since the psalms were an indispensable element of the ascetic rule of prayer, and of the Byzantine rite as a whole. Israel's writings of the exilic period, too, were an attempt to provide an intelligible comment upon God's apparent abandonment of the chosen people. As for the theodicy of the wisdom literature—the most vivid example being the book of Job—it wrestles with the problem of the *purport* of divine abandonment of the righteous man into Satan's hands. Job was often

---

[61] *St Silouan the Athonite*, 202.
[62] Ibid. 201–2.

regarded by the fathers as a model for the faithful to follow.[63] Similar references to Job in Fr Sophrony's writings indicate his interest in how the question of abandonment is solved in scripture.[64] In the New Testament the idea of providential abandonment is linked with the Calvary event. The actual verb *enkataleipo* (to forsake) is used in Matthew 27:46. Christ's agony is sometimes seen as parallel to the pedagogical godforsakenness, as we find, for example, in Maximus, who calls it "economic abandonment."[65]

It is this type of providential abandonment that came to be associated with the concepts *parachoresis, polemos,* and *peirasmos.* The characteristic trait of this type of abandonment is that it is a mode of divine *presence,* although the ascetic subjectively experiences God's *absence.* Some Fathers prefer to speak of grace "being concealed" or "diminished" and not "withdrawn." In Athanasius' life of Anthony of Egypt we find that Anthony felt as if God had deserted him in his war against demons. When God's light appeared to him, Anthony asked: "Where were you? Why did not you come in the beginning to quench my suffering?" "I was here, Anthony," God replied, "but I tarried as I wanted to see your own struggle." This matches Fr Sophrony's experience that God is "most attentive" during such times.[66]

The development of the idea of "economic" abandonment in the east begins with Origen. In *The Homilies on the Song of Songs* he describes his experience of God's temporary withdrawals.[67] He offers the following reasons for God's "economic" abandonment of men:

> in order that the habits of each may be examined, so far as it depends upon ourselves, and that the virtuous may be made manifest in consequence of the test applied; while the others . . . may afterward obtain the means of cure, seeing they would not have known the benefit had they not condemned themselves.[68]

Due to Origen's theology of *apokatastasis* (punishment), godforsakenness is always remedial, a means of correction. Indeed, godforsakenness means to

[63]John of Damascus, *Exp. fid.* 2.29, 101; Maximus, *Cap. car.* 4.96, 236; Macarius, *Anecd.* 54.9, 40.
[64]*We Shall See Him as He Is,* 81-82, 151-52.
[65]*Cap. car.* 4.96, 236.
[66]Athanasius, *Vie* 10.1-3, 162-64; cf *St Silouan the Athonite,* 203, 433.
[67]*Hom. Cant.* 1.7, 94-96.
[68]*Princ.* 3.1.12, 70-72.

be left without divine chastisement.[69] It is within this wider apocatastatic scheme of divine providence that he allots a place to "complete" abandonment and "eternal" punishment.

Further development of the reasons for economic godforsakenness is found in Evagrius, whose ideas are echoed in other ascetic writers. He believes that godforsakenness reveals hidden virtues and humbles the ascetic, who comes to realize his lack of virtues when God withholds his divine assistance. As such, godforsakenness exterminates pride.[70] Both of these reasons are found in Fr Sophrony. Evagrius' "realization of the hidden potential" matches Fr Sophrony's idea of the realization of the hypostatic principle through the positive actualization of freedom in faithfulness. As for the second reason, the overcoming of pride, Fr Sophrony writes: "As soon as I began to perceive with my reason what was happening to me after God had condescended to me, the Light forsook me . . . I suffered the state of being abandoned by God at the approach of vainglory."[71]

As a further reason for godforsakenness Evagrius points out the restoration of virtue, lost through negligence. This idea that godforsakenness serves as a spur to ascetic life is paralleled in Fr Sophrony, where godforsakenness enhances repentance. Evagrius also connects godforsakenness with dispassion, labeling the former as "the daughter of dispassion." The result of godforsakenness is such that man comes to detest evil, being established in his self-orientation.[72]

The actual experience of godforsakenness in Evagrius, as Balthasar suggests, is linked with *akedia*—the feeling of futility and despair. However, *akedia* in Evagrius does not exhaust his concept of abandonment. *Akedia* is not a state but an active negative force, the heaviest demon.[73] Some of the characteristics Evagrius attributes to the demon of *akedia* do nonetheless demonstrate striking parallels with the state of godforsakenness, as described by Fr Sophrony. Thus, Evagrius describes it as a "languishing of the soul." Evagrius describes how the soul in *akedia* "becomes feeble and fatigued," "faints in its bitterness," "its strength is consumed because of its exhaustion," it "comes to

---

[69]*Princ.* 3.1.12-13, 70-78.

[70]Evagrius, *Gnost.* 28, 134; cf Macarius, *Anecd.* 54.9, 40; Maximus, *Cap. car.* 4.96, 236; John of Damascus, *Fragm. Mat.*, PG 96:1412A.

[71]*We Shall See Him as He Is,* 199-200.

[72]*Gnost.* 28, 134.; cf Sophrony, *We Shall See Him as He Is,* 31, 93-94.

[73]*Prat.* 12, 520. On *akedia* in Evagrius, see *Prat.* 12, 520-26; *Antirrh.* 6, 520-31; *Tract.* 13-14, PG 79:1157C-1160C.

the edge of despair because of the violence of this demon."[74] The reference to exhaustion here is particularly important, since it corresponds to Fr Sophrony's idea of kenosis, which is often linked with godforsakenness. Not only do the manifestations of *akedia* correspond to the state of godforsakenness, but so does the description of their aftermath as well. Just as Silouan experienced the ineffable joy of the contemplation of Christ after undergoing godforsakenness, in Evagrius we find that when the struggle with *akedia* is over, "the state of peace and unspeakable joy embraces the soul."[75] Yet a fundamental difference between the state of *akedia* and the event of *enkataleipsis* remains—*akedia* is one of the passions, while for Fr Sophrony *enkataleipsis* is an event in the relationship between God and man, when that man is affected on every level of his being.

The idea of providential abandonment is found in Isaac of Nineveh. In his writings "godforsakenness" comes under the term *mestabqanute d-men alaha.* This state is given so that man should learn the weakness of his nature.[76] Sometimes it comes as a result of negligence or when man despises either prayer or fear and awe before God.[77] On the other hand, it is "a hidden trial of the mind's virtue and growth." Isaac highlights the same reason as Fr Sophrony does—the revelation of the inadequacy of our condition—so that we appreciate the extent of divine assistance and man's dependence upon God: "the intention is that a person should receive the awareness of the weakness of human nature, and realize what his own nature is, and how weak, feeble, stupid, and childish it is."[78]

In Isaac, just as in Fr Sophrony, the necessity of godforsakenness is not limited to the traditional retributive theory, according to which abandonment is God's response to sin: "Let us not be troubled when we are found in darkness, especially when the cause of this is not in us. But reckon this as the work of God's providence for a reason which he alone knows." Isaac, like Fr Sophrony, postulates the inevitability of such trials: "By this temptation are tried especially those who are willing to walk in mental discipline and who in their course are running toward the consolation that comes from faith."[79]

---

[74]*Tract.* 14, PG 79:1157C; *Antirrh.* 6, 527.
[75]*Prat.* 12, 526.
[76]*Syr. Hom.* 2.14.3, 56; *Syr. Hom.* 2.9.11, 29–30.
[77]*Syr. Hom.* 1.39, 302; *Syr. Hom.* 2.14.3, 56.
[78]*Syr. Hom.* 2.9.11, 29–30; cf *Syr. Hom.* 2.34.3, 135.
[79]*Syr. Hom.* 1.48, 340.

In Isaac, it is not only the principle that "the vouchsafed experience of temptations is a gift of God" that corresponds to Fr Sophrony's idea of godforsakenness as gift. Isaac also anticipates Fr Sophrony in his "equation formula": the deeper/the higher. For Isaac, the greater man's spiritual development, the greater the trials he ought to expect.[80] Further striking parallels between Fr Sophrony and Isaac are found in the way they both describe the experience of godforsakenness. They both speak of the reestimation of the experiences of God in the past. The ascetic's perception of the goodness of God and trust in divine providence are distorted. In Isaac, "it is also accompanied by strong abuse"; in Fr Sophrony, by the thought of acting against God. Both Isaac and Fr Sophrony point out that there are some things "whereof we have no need to speak."[81] In Fr Sophrony man experiences "eternal death and darkness"; in Isaac man has a foretaste of Gehenna.[82]

Fr Sophrony describes Silouan's state of godforsakenness in terms of the actual experience of Gehenna. In his own experience Fr Sophrony describes the pain of God's abandonment as being "like agony." The depth of godforsakenness can be such that "even short moments may seem to be eternal." It is seen as "the soul merging into the shadow of death" and "descent into hell." When assessing this state Fr Sophrony, Silouan, and Isaac agree on the fact that man cannot last in this state for long. Thus, Isaac writes that "never will God leave the soul a whole day in this state, otherwise it would lose life and all Christian hope." In Fr Sophrony and Silouan we find the same idea: "the soul has no strength to endure it for long."

In Macarius we find both the vocabulary of testing and of separation. Macarius avoids speaking of God's rejection and abandonment of man—grace *always* works in various ways in man for his benefit: "Sometimes stronger, sometimes weaker does the fire burn in man; also the light shines in greater measure, or sometimes diminishes and glows dim, according to divine providence."[83]

He anticipates Diadochus' explanation as to why degrees of manifestation of grace vary: grace is said to "build up" one's salvation. The purpose for such rejection is punitive-educative. The tribulation inflicted upon the ascetic is designed also to "tame" the soul by the Spirit, "with subsequent gradual clearing out and extermination of sin." He also speaks of the diminution of grace

[80]Issac, *Gr. Hom.* 50, 207.
[81]Isaac, *Syr. Hom.* 1.48, 339-40.
[82]Isaac, *Syr. Hom.* 1.39, 302.
[83]*Brief.* 4.9.1, 50.

in small degrees, but not of its radical withdrawal: "It happens often that man attains at this time the perfect measure, and becomes free from all sin and impeccable, but after this grace somehow is diminished and the veil of the opposing force descends upon man."[84]

This Macarian scheme also reminds us of Fr Sophrony's teaching on the three stages of ascetic life. As in Fr Sophrony's second period, the soul may be engaged in spiritual warfare for many years, thinking that God had forsaken it. Finally monks, after a period of spiritual trials, become "rooted in grace" and "unshakable."[85]

The purport of *parachoresis* in this context is, according to Macarius, "to make the self-determining of man manifest." As in Fr Sophrony, grace will step aside to allow freedom of choice, without grace itself being weakened in any way.[86] Again we also find in Macarius the idea of the expanding diapason of Christian experience: "So that by the experience of the two natures, tasting the bitterness of sin and the sweetness of grace the soul becomes more sensitive and vigilant, so as to flee entirely from evil and to attach herself wholly to the Lord so that she becomes one Spirit with him."[87]

Diadochus describes providential abandonment in terms of grace *concealing itself.* This may be the reason why he does not use the term *enkataleipsis* but prefers the word *parachoresis.* Since grace is present, in the ascetic life one may experience not so much withdrawal of grace as different levels of its manifestation. Even in the time of *parachoresis* grace is not passive, but "by ineffable assistance cooperates with the soul in order to show to her enemies that the victory over them is the achievement of the soul herself." Diadochus offers criteria for discerning whether *parachoresis* is only concealing of grace or withdrawal of grace. In the former case the sufferings inflicted upon the ascetic are fruitful in terms of their spiritual outcome. "Immediately afterward it brings into the heart the fear of God and tears of confession and great longing for the beauty of silence." The turning away of God results, on the contrary, in the soul being "left to itself and filled with despair, unbelief, pride, and anger."[88] The concept of man's freedom is equally as important for Diadochus in this context as it is for Fr Sophrony. Diadochus writes:

[84]*Brief.* 4.9.1-4, 50-51; *Hom.* 23.2, 195-96.
[85]*Hom. III* 3.1.4, 88; cf *Hom. III* 1.1.5, 75-76; cf *Hom. III* 3.2.1, 88.
[86]*Hom.* 15.29, 144; cf *Hom.* 27.11, 224; *Brief.* 6.4.1, 87.
[87]*Hom. III* 12.2.2, 169.
[88]*Chapt.* 87, 147.

... when man turns to God completely then by a certain ineffable feeling [grace] reveals its presence to the heart, and then again awaits the
soul's move, meanwhile allowing the arrows of the demons to reach to
the very depth of its senses, in order that with fervent inclination and
humble disposition it would seek God.[89]

He goes on to say that even those who reach high degrees of perfection
are given over by God to demonic attacks, so that "our self-determination is
not completely bound by the bondage of grace ... in order for man to progress
even more in spiritual skills." Here we see a parallel to Fr Sophrony's idea that
abandonment allows man to demonstrate his free hypostatic self-determination in relation to God. Like Fr Sophrony, Diadochus suggests that *parachoresis* is inevitable for ascetic progress. The element of "correcting" is relatively
diminished and the experience is seen as a spur on the way to reaching ever
greater levels of Christian perfection: "Nevertheless, at times God allows the
demons to attack even one who has reached a measure of perfection, and
leaves his mind without light ... The purpose of this is not only to overcome
sin through ascetic effort but also to help us advance still further in spiritual
experience."[90]

In Fr Sophrony we find a similarly expressed idea that godforsakenness
serves to demonstrate that "we are not ready" to receive the kingdom; he
agrees with Diadochus that the awareness of this fact becomes an impetus for
even deeper repentance. As in Diadochus, godforsakenness turns the ascetic to
the repentance, in which he realizes that the cause of the breach of union with
God lies within himself:

> Being forsaken by God indicates that all our efforts hitherto are far
> from adequate for salvation—blessed eternity is not yet ours. Bitter dis-
> satisfaction with—revulsion from—oneself is the first sign that we are
> approaching the fulness of love commanded of us by God—sur-
> mounting the terrible obstacle of self-centeredness.[91]

Finally, Diadochus draws the same threefold scheme of ascetic life as we
find it in Fr Sophrony, though in a less articulate manner. Diadochus holds that

---

[89] *Chapt.* 85, 144.
[90] Ibid., 145.
[91] *We Shall See Him as He Is*, 130.

the Holy Spirit at the outset gives the soul a full and conscious taste of God's sweetness. Later, grace works its mysteries for the most part without its knowledge. And finally, when the ascetic has acquired all the virtues, grace illumines his whole being with a deeper awareness, warming him with great love of God, so that he becomes a dwelling place of the Holy Spirit.[92]

The phenomenon of abandonment came to be well integrated into the later Byzantine ascetic tradition. In Maximus we find a fairly schematized classification of the various categories of abandonment, which recapitulates the preceding patristic ideas: there is abandonment as a test, as a purification, as an edificatory punishment, and Christ-like abandonment.[93]

In examining Fr Sophrony's teaching on godforsakenness we have seen that he is not influenced by the spirituality of John of the Cross. Having compared Fr Sophrony's teaching on godforsakenness with the notions of *parachoresis* and *enkataleipsis* in the eastern ascetic tradition, we have highlighted fundamental parallels between and have demonstrated that Lossky's statement about the absence of *enkataleipsis* in the east contradicts the evidence of many eastern ascetic writers. This analysis allows us to affirm that Fr Sophrony's teaching on godforsakenness is rooted in the eastern tradition. Yet his own contribution is not to be overlooked. He integrates the antinomies in the theology of uncreated light by stressing the hypostatic and relational dimension of the phenomenon. He thus justifies godforsakenness theologically as a normative, necessary stage of one's spiritual development. We saw that the fathers in various ways linked the event of godforsakenness with the fact of man's freedom. Fr Sophrony takes this idea further, stressing that godforsakenness assists the realization of the hypostatic principle in man. He thus restores the balance that was lost in the rationalization of the Palamite scheme in some modern Russian theologians. Reassertion of the normativeness of godforsakenness also provides a forum for exploring the relationship between the spiritual heritage of the east and that of the west.

---

[92] *Chapt.* 69, 129; *Chapt.* 82, 142; *Chapt.* 85, 145; *Chapt.* 90, 150; cf Theophan the Recluse, *The Path of Salvation: A Manual of Spiritual Transformation*, tr. S. Rose (Platina, Calif., 1996) 195-98.
[93] *Cap. car.* 2.67, 124-26.

CHAPTER EIGHT

Obedience

The idea of spiritual guidance is an indispensable element of any religious ascetic tradition. In Christian asceticism it plays a prominent role[1] and, as Kallistos Ware points out, has "retained its full significance up to the present day in Orthodox Christendom."[2] Within the Christian tradition scholars distinguish various types of ecclesiastical leadership. Neyt employs the two-fold general classification: *administrative* and *charismatic;* Ware calls them *institutional* and *prophetic.*[3] These reflect two forms of spiritual authority within the life of the church. On the one hand there is a traceable apostolic succession, which comprises the consecutive ordained clergy. On the other there is an unrecorded succession of spiritual masters (the saints), who hand down from generation to generation the tradition of life in God. Unlike the institutional principle of authority, "charismatic" guidance is based on a person-to-person relationship between the spiritual guide and his/her child in God. The Greek tradition has produced titles for the ascetic-instructor, who has a special charisma to deliver the divine will to those who ask him: most commonly he is called *abbas* (father). However, there are other terms in ascetic literature for spiritual instructors, among which the most widely used are *spiritual father* and *elder.* Russian tradition prefers the word *staretz* (elder), and the whole principle of monastic guidance and discipleship is called *starchestvo* (eldership).

However, in the eastern church these two types of leadership—institutional and charismatic—are not mutually exclusive: the administrative leader may also be a charismatic instructor. The presence of these two interpenetrating levels is reflected in the cenobitic monastic life, where institutional

---

[1]See I. Hausherr, *Direction spirituelle en Orient autrefois* (Rome, 1955).

[2]See K. Ware, "The Spiritual Father in Orthodox Christianity," in *Word out of Silence: A Symposium on World Spiritualities,* ed. J.-D. Robinson, *Cross Currents* 24:2-3 (1974) 296.

[3]F. Neyt, "A Form of Charismatic Authority," ECR 6:1 (1974) 63; Ware, "The Spiritual Father in Orthodox Christianity," 297.

obedience (i.e., compliance with the monastery's administration, its rule and *typicon*) is intertwined with obedience to the elder. We shall focus largely on the "charismatic" principle (eldership), since this point particularly attracts Fr Sophrony's theological interest.

Obedience in Eastern Monasticism

Within Christianity the image of the spiritual father had already been fore-shadowed in the New Testament in the apostolic ministry of the apostle Paul: he calls himself *paidagogos* (1 Cor 4:15) and his addressees "little children" (Gal 4:19). It is further developed in Clement of Alexandria and Origen: for them the task of spiritual guidance pertained to the function of the *teacher*. With the growth of monasticism in the fourth century the principle of eldership be-came deeply embedded in the eastern ascetic tradition. It became "the leit-motif of the religious revolution of late antiquity," to such a point that it even had political repercussions within contemporary Byzantine society.[4]

St Anthony, the father of Egyptian monasticism, valued obedience to an elder as a powerful means of ascetic growth. As an elder, he guided the her-mits who lived around him in the desert. Obedience gains its supreme status as a *basis* of ascetic life, however, in the Pachomian cenobitic institution: elder-ship became a part of the monastic rule. Pachomius discerned the manifesta-tion of Christian perfection not in miracleworking and visionary charisma but in submission to the will of God.[5] While insisting on the absoluteness of obe-dience, he was less demanding in other aspects of asceticism: his other ascetic rules were marked by "mildness." Another center of development of spiritual fatherhood was Nitria, as reflected in the *Apophthegmata Patrum*. Since then, most ascetic writers have touched on the theme of obedience. Certainly, the ascetic writers of the first millennium, who influenced Fr Sophrony, all val-ued obedience as the highest virtue.[6] We should single out John Cassian, John and Barsanuphius of Gaza, Dorotheus of Gaza, John Climacus, and Symeon the New Theologian. Obedience is seen by this tradition as one of the fastest and most fruitful means for progressing along the scale of spiritual perfection.[7]

---

[4]P. Brown, "The Rise and Function of the Holy Man in Late Antiquity," *The Journal of Roman Studies* 61 (1971) 99ff.

[5]Hausherr, *La doctrine ascétique des premiers maîtres égyptiens du quatrième siècle* (Paris, 1931) 282.

[6]Cf John Cassian, *Inst.* 4.30, 165.

[7]Cf Dorotheus, *Instr.* 1.7, 156–57; John Climacus, *Scala parad.* 4, PG 88:677C; Barsanuphius, *Repl.* 248, 153.

One point is often passed over by scholars: by the closing years of the Byzantine epoch the ascetic tradition was replete with exemplary stories of "obedience heroes," in which the virtue of obedience was singled out. These stories seem to imply that the virtue of obedience is "sufficient" for one's salvation. As examples we can cite the stories of John the Short and Abba Mucius (the second Abraham) in John Cassian, of Dositheus in Dorotheus of Gaza, and of Acacius in John Climacus. By virtue of obedience the ascetics could, for example, perform various miracles, cross crocodile-infested rivers, and stand in prayer for weeks.[8] This building up of the stereotype of the "obedience hero" is a further reminder that obedience had become deeply significant for the spirituality of the Byzantine church.

The Practice of Eldership

Eldership is guidance of the novice by the elder. The beginner renounces his own will and follows the directions of the elder. The intensity of the elder's control varies. It may be only his silent example.[9] Sometimes the beginner may approach the elder only once and receive rather general advice that he would keep throughout the course of his ascetic life. More often there is a practice of *exagoreusis*, when the elder controls every single action and all the thoughts of the beginner. Disclosure of thoughts sometimes overlaps with the sacrament of confession.[10]

The elder is a prophetic and intercessory mediator between God and the disciple. The elder's involvement in the training of the ascetic helps to form a interrelated spiritual threefold bond: elder-God-beginner, where the elder plays the role of mediator. We can subsume various characteristics of the elder's ministerial mediating functions under two highly generalized definitions: *prophetic* (downward mediation: God-*elder*-the beginner) and *intercessory* (upward mediation: beginner-*elder*-God). In his prophetic ministry the elder communicates the divine will. His whole ministry is controlled by inspiration from God. In accordance with the divine will he gives counsel (as *symboulos*, adviser) and directions, or therapeutically corrects the beginner's conduct (as *iatros*, healer). To exercise such a ministry the elder has to possess, among other

[8]*Inst.* 4.27-28, 162; Dorotheus, *Dosithée*, 87-123; *Scala parad.* 4, PG 88:720B-721A; *Inst.* 4.27-28, 162; *Verba Seniorum*, PL 73:789BC; *Hist. Mon.* 24.1-2, 132.

[9]See Ware, "The Spiritual Father in Orthodox Christianity," 30; cf *Apophth.*, PG 65:364C.

[10]See Hausherr, *Direction spirituelle en Orient autrefois*, 212ff.; K. Ware, "Introduction," in John Climacus, *The Ladder of Divine Ascent*, trs. C. Luibheid and N. Russell, 38f (Toronto, 1982).

various required virtues, the gift of spiritual discernment (*diakrisis*)—the capacity to discover the will of God through prayer, so that he maintains, according to Hausherr, the Spirit-borne nature of his replies. As a mediator of the divine will, the elder was believed to continue the work of Christ himself, and was counted among the prophets on a par with Moses (cf Ex 4:13).[11]

In his intercessory ministry the elder takes responsibility for the beginner's conduct before God (as *anadochos*, sponsor). This accountability is understood not in terms of "impersonal" judicial legalism, but as an expression of a *personal love* of the elder toward his spiritual children. The elder "presents" them to God in his continuous prayers and intercessions for them (as *mesites*, intercessor, and *presbeutes*, pleader). Thus, he bears the burden of his disciples.[12]

The novice's relation to the elder is absolute divine-like trust. The elder bears entire responsibility for the novice only if the latter fulfils everything the elder tells him.[13] The novice is to commit himself to obedience with absolute trust, which expresses itself in total and unquestioning obedience. This has been noted by Hausherr, who writes: "The doctrine of the eastern monks on obedience is characterized by absolutism."[14] Such absolutism expresses itself in the belief that the words of the elder are tantamount to the divine word, and are to be accepted as such. The injunctions of the elder may even be on a par with the commandments of God, and the elder is to be treated as Christ himself. Thus, his advice is not subject to any criticism or analysis on the part of the novice. For the fathers, as Smirnov demonstrates, criticism of the elder is a grievous sin.[15]

Eldership is a "charismatic" sacrament of the church. When requirements on the part of both sides are met, the threefold interrelationship operates in a sacramental way: God acts on the beginner through the elder. Since it is God himself who speaks through the elder, his words and actions are thus determined by God in accordance with the spiritual maturity and predisposition of the questioner.[16] Writers like Climacus, Barsanuphius, and Symeon the New

[11]Cf Anthony, *Epist.* 2.9-15, 8-9; 3.17-28, 13-15; 4.8-14, 18; 6.8-25, 38-39.
[12]K. Ware, "Foreword: The Spiritual Father in Saint John Climacus and Saint Symeon the New Theologian," in I. Hausherr, *Spiritual Direction in the Early Christian East*, tr. A.P. Gythiel, Cistercian Studies Series 116, xiiff (Kalamazoo, Mich., 1990); Ware, "The Spiritual Father in Orthodox Christianity," 303-8; cf Hausherr, *Direction spirituelle en Orient autrefois*, 124-51.
[13]Cf Barsanuphius, *Repl.* 288, 170.
[14]*Direction spirituelle en Orient autrefois*, 189.
[15]Cf John Climacus, *Scala parad.* 4, PG 88:680D, 692B, 725D-728A; Barsanuphius, *Repl.* 318, 177-78; *Repl.* 552, 261; Symeon the New Theologian, *Chap. Theol.* 1.28, 47.
[16]Cf John Cassian, *Conf.* 1.23, 107-8; Barsanuphius, *Repl.* 811, 349.

Theologian treated the practice as a sacrament of the church to such an extent that the sacramental efficacy of eldership as a "charismatic event" may even override that of the institutional system: for example, under obedience to the elder, the nonordained novice would function as a priest by blessing the monastery food.[17]

Eldership overcomes the fallen human condition and sustains the disciple's freedom. At the root of the practice of obedience lies a given anthropological doctrine: namely, that man's condition is damaged by the fall, and as such does not allow its restoration with its own resources. Vladimir Lossky summarizes: "Our free choice indicates the imperfection of fallen human nature ... It can no longer choose well, and too often yields to the impulses of a nature which has become a slave to sin."[18]

As sin distorts the right discernment of spiritual reality, the inexperienced beginner needs an instructor who has a better grasp of spiritual reality. The beginner is never to act according to his own distorted understanding and perception. This principle—mistrust of one's own judgment (as a recognition of the distortion of one's spiritual condition)—lies at the root of monastic consciousness.[19] The actions of the disciple are determined by the elder and not by the disciple's own passionate concerns: he is thus freed from them. This freedom allows him to experience *apatheia*, as the ascetic is "free for the sake of God" from various passions.[20] To do so he must renounce his own will, which is tainted by sin and which thereby reinforces his passionate condition.[21] This aspect of freedom is negative: it is a *freedom from*.

As for the positive aspect—*freedom for*—obedience liberates the novice so that he can more easily in humility concentrate upon God alone, which eventually leads him to the undistorted contemplation of divine reality, to discernment, and to right perception.[22] For that reason some fathers recommended that ascetics remain under obedience not only at the initial stage but throughout the whole ascetic life—in Barsanuphius, obedience should be practiced "until death" with "shedding of blood."[23]

[17]Cf Barsanuphius, *Repl.* 251, 154-55.

[18]Lossky, *Mystical Theology*, 125-26.

[19]Cf Climacus, *Scala parad.* 4, PG 88:680C; Dorotheus, *Instr.* 1.10, 163; *Instr.* 5.67, 260; John Cassian, *Inst.* 4.9, 132; *Conf.* 2.10-11, 120-21; Barsanuphius, *Repl.* 363, 196.

[20]Cf Climacus, *Scala parad.* 4, PG 88:709B; Barsanuphius, *Repl.* 226, 140.

[21]Cf Dorotheus, *Instr.* 5.63, 254; Climacus, *Scala parad.* 4, PG 88:680A; Barsanuphius, *Repl.* 551, 261-62.

[22]Cf Climacus, *Scala parad.* 4, PG 88:717B.

[23]Barsanuphius, *Repl.* 254, 155.

Eldership in Russia and Its Crisis

The study of the ascetic writings of medieval Russia suggests that the tradition of obedience was far from being a controlling feature of monastic life at that time. We find that in Russian practice the concept of *spiritual father* applied not to the spiritual guide as such but to the priest-confessor.[24] Early documents, such as the *Kievo-Pechersky Paterikon*, reveal little elaborated understanding of the relationship between the novice and the elder outside the sacrament of confession. The lives of Russian saints suggest that there was eldership in Russian monasteries, but as it did not play a crucial role in asceticism, the authors did not dwell on it. The scarcity of the written evidence on that theme indicates that there was no developed doctrine of eldership on the level of the Byzantine patristic tradition. More attention is paid to eldership in the life of Sergius of Radonezh. Even then, the term "elder" was applied to Sergius not without certain reservations. Russian ascetic literature of that period did not produce any significant "heroes of obedience," as we find in the ascetic writings of the first millennium.

The renewal of eldership in Russian monastic tradition is generally linked with the name of Paisy Velichkovsky (1722-1794). Having spent a few years on Mount Athos, Paisy had a good command of Greek, which allowed him to read and translate patristic writers into Russian. It is through them that he restored within Russian monasticism the centrality of obedience: "Everyone," he writes, "should have someone experienced in spiritual direction to whom he fully delivers his will and obeys, as though it were to the Lord himself."[25] He reintroduced the patristic criteria—dispassion, purity of the soul, possession of the Holy Spirit, and the capacity of spiritual discernment—for the elder.

By the nineteenth century ascetic obedience in Russia became widely accepted in monasticism, as a result of the growing interest in the patristic heritage inaugurated by Paisy Velichkovsky. Seraphim of Sarov advances the understanding of eldership as *prophetic* ministry. The replies of the elder, according to Seraphim, are based not on a purely intellectual basis or his capacity for psychoanalysis, but on the will of God. He explains how the elder comes to know the will of God:

---

[24]S. Smirnov, *The Father-Confessor in Ancient Russia* (Moscow, 1913) 8.

[25]V. Poljanomerulsky, *Life and Works of the Moldavian Staretz Paisy Velichkovsky* (Moscow, 1847) 235; cf 246-47, 262.

I count the first thought [i.e., after prayer] which comes to my soul as an indication of the will of God. I speak without knowing what my interlocutor has in his soul, but only believe that the will of God is indicated for his benefit . . . but when I spoke from my own understanding, then mistakes would occur.[26]

The growth of eldership in Russian monasticism attracted the attention of Russian intellectual circles. Thus, the center of Russian monastic spirituality of the nineteenth century—the Monastery of Optina, famous for its *startsy* (elders)—became a place of intellectual and spiritual pilgrimage for Gogol, Kireyevsky, Dostoyevsky, Tolstoy, and Soloviev. The attention of the literary world and the religious philosophers to eldership provided a significant matrix for the integration of this monastic practice into current philosophical thought.

We find an idiosyncratic example of this integration in Dostoyevsky's *The Brothers Karamazov,* where the figure of the elder Amvrosy of Optina is used as a prototype for the character of the elder Zosima. On the basis of his interest in morality and excellent capacity for psychoanalysis, Dostoyevsky contributes toward the theological justification of eldership by his stress on *love*: the elder through love "takes the novice into his own soul and will." He restates the patristic idea that obedience to the elder leads to *absolute freedom*, but he views it from the angle of psychology—it is freedom from "self."

In the Russian interpretation of the principle of ascetic obedience one may detect a certain breach of harmony between the trust of the novice on the one hand and the spiritual proficiency required of the elder on the other. The latter aspect seems to have been completely dominated, even superseded, by the former. The faith of the novice is deemed a sufficient prerequisite for profit from the answer of the elder, whatever his spiritual qualities might be.

This imbalance is manifest in A. Soloviev: "founding itself on faith in God, for the sake of whom the novice submits himself to obedience, faith in the words of the elder is effective *on its own*, irrespective of the spiritual condition of the elder."[27] This reduces obedience to a mechanical practice determined by an almost purely subjective criterion: faith of the novice is the *only* significant prerequisite for revelation of the divine will. Soloviev further supports

---

[26]V. Ilyin, *St Seraphim of Sarov* (Paris, 1930) 60.

[27]A. Soloviev, *Starchestvo according to the Teaching of the Holy Fathers and Ascetics* (Semipalatinsk, 1900) 84.

himself by referring to the words of Amvrosy of Optina, who says: "If you seek and accept my words with faith then *even through the sinner* you may gain profit, but without faith, with doubt and examining the words and the actions, this will not bring profit even if the elder is righteous."[28] A similar view is held by Theophan the Recluse, who believes that the faith of the one who asks is the guarantee of the appropriate answer. He writes: "The guide, *no matter who he might be*, will always give exact and true counsel once the guided one entrusts himself with all his soul and faith."[29]

With such emphasis on the faith of the novice, the spiritual requirements for the elder were hardly discussed by the Russian writers. This resulted in a distorted conception of the role of the elder, according to which virtually anyone could give spiritual advice. Therefore, the institution of ascetic obedience came to be misinterpreted and consequently abused. Seraphim's prophetic principle of seeking the divine will through prayer was replaced by the idea that whatever the elder says *always* works for the benefit of the novice.

Russian ascetic writings (unlike the Byzantine tradition) do not dwell on the important fact that the novice has to abide by certain criteria when choosing the elder. In the fathers, as Hausherr demonstrates, these criteria are rather strict: the elder should be a man who has all the virtues, with knowledge of the scriptures, who loves God, and is humble, without anger, vainglory, or pride. Spiritual guides should possess *the charisma of the word*; they belong to a special category of ascetics.[30]

The fathers warned that it is important to make the right choice of instructor to avoid spiritual disasters. Thus, we find in Cassian that "many of the elders have brought about harm instead of profit, bringing the one who asks into despair rather than offering consolation."[31] Climacus warns that before embarking on the way of obedience we should "discern, examine and test, so to say, our navigator, so that we should not choose a simple rower instead of a navigator, a sick man instead of a physician, a passionate man instead of a dispassionate one."[32] Monks Kallistos and Ignatius write: "It is not easy to find an instructor who would be undeluded in everything: in deed, in words, in understanding. One can discern the undeluded one by the fact that he has a

[28]G. Borisoglebsky, *The Life of Hieromonk Ambrosy the Staretz of Optina Monastery* (Moscow, 1893) 53 (my emphasis).

[29]Theophan the Recluse, *The Path of Salvation*, 214 (my emphasis).

[30]Hausherr, *Direction spirituelle en Orient autrefois*, 181–86.

[31]*Conf.* 2.12, 124.

[32]*Scala parad.* 4, PG 88:680D; cf Isaac, *Gr. Hom.* 46, 191.

testimony from scripture for both deeds and for understanding, having humble thinking about things."[33]

Climacus recommends that the choice of the elder should be determined by the spiritual condition of the novice himself: "we should choose an instructor who would fit our illness according to the types of our passions."[34] Thus, in the patristic tradition the disciple's obedience is not mechanical but has a *personal* dimension, which was forfeited in Russian spirituality and replaced by an impersonal faith.[35]

Because of the Russian stress on the faith of the questioner at the expense of the effort of the elder, the "triangular scheme" of relationship (God-elder-novice) loses its balance. The absolutism of this onesided perception was such that the unfailing involvement of God in the answers of the elder was taken as guaranteed. Kontsevich highlights such critical dangers in the understanding of eldership and points out the possibility of being misled by a *pseudo-elder*: if "the true elder communicates the will of God, the *pseudo-elder* hides God behind himself."[36] The distortion provoked doubt, fear, criticism, and even persecution of the practice throughout the nineteenth and twentieth centuries and entailed its gradual decline. Thus, Ignaty Bryanchaninov, in highlighting the distortions in contemporary Russian practice, advised abandoning the principle of eldership as a necessary element of the ascetic life. By the beginning of the twentieth century we find that among Russian intellectuals the concept of eldership became obscured; the very word itself is pronounced with a certain aversion. Thus, Berdyaev rejects the idea of obedience altogether: "As Christian spirituality was formerly understood, the greatest abuse was made of obedience and humility, especially perhaps in Orthodoxy. The way of spiritual ascent was not one of illumination and transfiguration of the will, but of exhausting and deadening it." He understands obedience as if "man should not possess his own will, but must be obedient to another will" and protests against "a perverted interpretation of humility," which "transforms man into a slave" and "debases God's image and likeness."[37] The rejection of eldership in the twentieth century even penetrated monastic circles. Thus Seraphim Rose (a convert to Russian Orthodoxy) writes: "There are no more elders like Paisius today. If we imagine there are we can do irreparable harm

---

[33]Kallistos and Ignatius, *Cap.* 14, 26.

[34]*Scala parad.* 4, PG 88:725C.

[35]G. Gould, *The Desert Fathers on Monastic Community* (Oxford, 1993) 87.

[36]I. Kontsevich, *The Acquisition of the Holy Spirit in Ancient Russia* (Paris, 1952) 35–36.

[37]N. Berdyaev, "About the New Christian Spirituality," *Sobornost* 25 (1934) 37.

to our souls."[38] The cause of this crisis, according to Smirnov, is the abuse of
the institution by people who do not meet the requirements of the elder.[39] In
Hausherr's words:"What destroyed the institution [of eldership] was ambition
and the spirit of domination."[40]

However, we still find the traditional ideal of ascetic obedience maintained
within the Russian Athonite tradition, and notably in Silouan the Athonite,
through whom it passed to Fr Sophrony. In his teaching Silouan maintains that
there is a certain guarantee of God's action through the elder in the subjective trustful predisposition of the disciples, warning thereby against dangers of
prideful self-guidance. But Silouan also points out the objective requirements
for the spiritual father: he warns of serious harm if these are not met.[41]

Fr Sophrony on Obedience

Fr Sophrony's approach reinstates eldership in Russian asceticism. He both
restores the concept of obedience and advances it to a new theological level.
This was possible, once again, through his focus on the principle of persona.
Fr Sophrony's fresh return to the patristic sources and his acquaintance with
living contemporary Athonite ascetic tradition helped to revive interest in
the practice of obedience within contemporary Russian Orthodoxy. The
centrality of persona in Fr Sophrony's approach made clearer the lack of the
personal element in much Russian interpretation of ascetic obedience. Furthermore, he thus answers the claims of the twentieth-century Russian religious thinkers that obedience destroys personal freedom.

The Principle of Operation of Eldership

In Fr Sophrony we may find various types of obedience within the monastic
community. On the one hand, there is the "administrative" obedience to the
abbot, which may or may not have charismatic significance. The abbot may
impose various tasks on the members of the monastic community in accordance with the general needs of the community and of each individual. The

[38]Quoted from D. Christensen, *Not of This World: The Life and Teaching of Fr. Seraphim Rose.
Pathfinder to the Heart of Ancient Christianity* (Forestville, 1993) 633.
[39]Smirnov, 70ff.
[40]Hausherr, *Direction spirituelle en Orient autrefois*, 228.
[41]See *St Silouan the Athonite*, 399ff.

degree of personal element may vary in this type of obedience. On the other hand, in accord with the eastern tradition, there is an obedience to the spiritual father, which rests on personal guidance. Fr Sophrony points out that the elder may be an ordained priest or a nonordained person. Referring to the experience of the history of the Russian Church in the eighteenth and nineteenth centuries, he writes: "Spiritual 'elders' need not necessarily be priests or monks."[42] His own elder—St Silouan the Athonite—was not ordained. Alongside guidance by Silouan, Fr Sophrony had his father-confessor. However, Silouan himself did connect the sacrament of confession with eldership, to the extent that he would come for confession and advice to any father-confessor at the monastery and follow the counsel obediently.

For Fr Sophrony, the elder, whether ordained or not, must necessarily meet certain requirements. Through the purity of his heart, he must have the ability to discern the voice of God and his will in his own heart. He should be a *mediator* between God and the novice. There are various levels of intensity, or depth, of one's commitment to the elder. On the one hand, one may inquire only about cardinal issues in the circumstances of the choice in life. On the other, there is a more intensive obedience, which is recommended by Fr Sophrony. In daily life the novice consults the elder about every kind of issue, and whatever the elder recommends and advises the novice will follow, or obey. It includes the practice of confession of thoughts. Monitoring thoughts includes examining initiative and intentions. Thus, before any action is undertaken on the part of the novice, it is either approved or disapproved by the elder. Fr Sophrony justifies this intensity by the conviction that in the monastic life there are no trivial issues: "Everything is important." This echoes Anthony the Great, who advises the monk "to ask the elders about every step which he takes in his own cell and about every drop of water he drinks."[43]

In accordance with tradition, Fr Sophrony gives to obedience the highest place on the scale of ascetic virtues. For him, obedience is "the basis of monasticism." As a virtue it is even higher than chastity: "Many think that the main distinction between monastic and common ways of life is celibacy. But I, following the ancient fathers and modern ascetics, attribute greater significance to obedience, since often people live their life as celibates, without becoming monks either in terms of sacrament, or in spirit."[44]

[42] *On Prayer*, tr. Rosemary Edmonds (New York, 1998) 98.
[43] *Birth into the Kingdom*, 141; cf Anthony, *Ad fil. mon.*, PG 40:1082D; Cassian, *Inst.* 4.10, 132–34; Barsanuphius, *Repl.* 344, 186–87.
[44] *Birth into the Kingdom*, 135.

Freedom From and Freedom For

Fr Sophrony echoes the fathers in his conviction that obedience overcomes the fallen human condition and sustains the novice's freedom *from* and *for*.

Fr Sophrony agrees with patristic anthropology in admitting the sinfulness of the present human condition. Obedience is a way to eschew the effects of this condition. Echoing Dorotheus, Fr Sophrony maintains that the personal attempt to discern directly the will of God is hampered by one's sinful condition: "the majority of people do not hear the voice of God in their heart, do not understand it and follow the voice of the passion living in their soul and suppressing the lowly voice of God by its noise." The spiritual father is free from partiality of judgment concerning the issue in question, and is capable of seeking the will of God with an impartial heart: "He can see [things] more clearly [than the one who poses the question], and is more easily accessible to the action of God's grace."[45] This does not presume that the spiritual father needs to possess *infallibility*, or perfection. It is God who is believed to act through the spiritual father.

Moreover, obedience provides a necessary framework for the development of *pure prayer*. If the novice is free from the responsibility of making decisions concerning issues that arise, then obedience helps him to remain impartial. This results therefore in liberation: the present reality no longer controls his existential concerns. Since he is not involved in the decision making, the novice's mind is no longer preoccupied at the level of "earthly cares." He can *entirely* give his mind over to prayer and meditation. This liberation affords him the possibility of achieving the state of pure prayer. Fr Sophrony states:

> Monasticism above all means the purity of the mind, which is unattainable without obedience. That is why there can be no monasticism without obedience. It is possible to receive great gifts of God—even the perfection of martyrdom—outside the monastic condition; but purity of mind is a special gift of monasticism, unknown on other paths, and the monk can only reach this state through obedience.[46]

Fr Sophrony observes the impact of the purity of the mind on other aspects of monastic life. Thus, via control and purity of one's mind, chastity,

[45] *St Silouan the Athonite*, 80; cf Dorotheus, *Instr.* 5.63, 252–54.
[46] *Birth into the Kingdom*, 136.

vigilance, and a humble predisposition are maintained. At this point Fr Sophrony refers to a similar idea in Climacus, who states that obedience leads to the contemplation of God.[47]

Purity of mind and heart, achieved through obedience, makes one more "sensible to the tender voice of God within us, to perception of his will." By allowing one to put aside all earthly care, obedience brings about the state of dispassion and therefore "true freedom," just as it does in Barsanuphius and Climacus.[48]

The novice's conscience is not burdened by responsibility for his actions, becoming thereby irreproachable for this action, or "inaccessible to sin." Fr Sophrony's formula encapsulating this principle is borrowed from the sayings of the Athonite fathers: "God does not judge twice." That is, God will require an answer for any action faithfully accomplished only from the elder responsible for commanding it.

Eldership as a Sacrament

The examination of Fr Sophrony's writings in relation to eldership as a "charismatic" sacrament of the church again confirms his dependence on the fathers. However, in his approach this idea becomes an explicit definition: "Obedience is a spiritual sacrament in the Church, and therefore the relationship between the elder and the novice has a sacred character." The divine action is ineffably at work: "Notwithstanding its inadequacy, the spiritual instruction, if accepted with faith and effectively heeded, will always lead to an increase of good."[49]

In the case of unbelief on the part of the novice, obedience loses its sacramental significance. This echoes the above-mentioned patristic idea: the novice's relation to the elder is absolute divine-like trust.

In Fr Sophrony the balance between the participation of the elder and the novice (which was lost within the Russian tradition) is restored. Eldership depends on the spiritual proficiency of the elder on the one hand, and the faith of the novice on the other: God acts in proportion to the novice's faith. Yet God acts *through* the elder. The elder must seek in his heart the voice of God

---

[47] *Scala parad.* 4, PG 88:681A.

[48] *Birth into the Kingdom*, 137; cf Climacus, *Scala parad.* 4, PG 88:709B; Barsanuphius, *Repl.* 226, 140.

[49] *St Silouan the Athonite*, 80.

and not say things from his own mind. Fr Sophrony expresses this perception of the will of God as "*feeling* of the divine will." In another passage, echoing Seraphim of Sarov, he refers to the *first thought* that arises in the heart of the elder after prayer as an indication of divine will. As for the questioner's predisposition, he should accept the first reply of the elder as being in accord with divine providence. However, Fr Sophrony does not go so far as to suggest that the elder is infallible in his decisions. The spiritual father always remains a vehicle of the divine action and not the source. The desire to comply with the will of God is required on his part. The spiritual father "seeks in prayer enlightenment from God." This harmony between God, the elder and the novice is expressed thus: "A spiritual confessor's reply will usually bear the imprint of imperfection, but this is not because he lacks the grace of knowledge but because perfection is beyond the strength and grasp of the one inquiring of him."[50]

In contrast to the Russian ascetic tradition of the nineteenth century, Fr Sophrony states that mistakes on the part of the elder are possible. Thus, he is aware of Seraphim's warning that when the elder speaks from his own mind, mistakes may occur. In a letter to David Balfour, Fr Sophrony discusses his own difficulty in finding an elder who would fit the requirements of spiritual guide:

> I have suffered a lot, because I did not have a faithful instructor, . . . who could satisfy in some measure my psychological and intellectual quests. I submitted [myself] to the utmost self-renunciation, despite the fact that I heard and saw from my instructor things which are too simple and elementary, which could satisfy only an illiterate and slow-thinking man . . . When I thought of the greater issues, I had to act on the basis of my own guesses.[51]

In *St Silouan the Athonite*, likewise, there is a passage where Fr Sophrony relates Silouan's experience with a certain elder and assesses the words of the latter as an error.[52]

The above comparisons demonstrates Fr Sophrony's strong dependence on the Byzantine and contemporary Athonite traditions.

[50]Ibid., 80.
[51]Letter to D. Balfour, B12 (December 14, 1932), 14–15.
[52]*St Silouan the Athonite*, 36.

Obedience and Persona

The integration of traditional elements in his teaching on persona allows Fr Sophrony to provide a deeper theology of eldership. Obedience serves as an effective means to the realization of persona in man. For Fr Sophrony, persona is the main constituent of the concept of human likeness to God, and this explains why he makes much of the dynamic dimension in human likeness to God. Man, as the image and likeness of God, is called to the fulness of immediate communion with God. Obedience as a dynamic *praxis* assists the novice in entering the current of the eternal divine will and thus in becoming a partaker of the divine life. It introduces man into divine life as the realization of his God-likeness.

Obedience and the Trinity

Fr Sophrony explores the perichoresis in the Trinity in an original fashion, to shed light on the obedience of Christ and to draw out its ascetic anthropological implications. The Byzantine tradition also sets Christ's obedience as a model for monastic obedience. However, the fathers do not link the kenotic obedience of the Christ-man with the theology of the Trinity, because there was hardly any overtly kenotic element in their teaching on the Trinity. Patristic commentaries on Philippians 2:6 link it with the incarnation. If they use the Christ-man as a human model in this passage, they stress its pastoral and moral significance. Thus, for Barsanuphius of Gaza obedience likens one to the Son of God.[53] Cassian also sees in Christ an example of obedience:

> in [my] utter submission to [my spiritual] father I could to some extent imitate the one about whom it is said, "He humbled himself, being obedient even unto death" (Phil 2:8), and I could be vouchsafed to pronounce humbly his word: "I did not come to do My will but the will of the Father Who sent Me" (Jn 6:38).[54]

Fr Sophrony goes further than this, applying the idea of Christ's example on the level of the Trinity. Fr Sophrony refers to traditional triadology, which teaches that "each hypostasis is the bearer of the absolute fulness of the divine

[53]*Repl.* 251, 154-55.
[54]*Conf.* 19.6, 46.

being." He explains that this mutual dynamic fulness is due to the kenotic self-abasement of one hypostasis in relation to the other. The Father empties himself, the fulness of his own being, to the Son and the Son "returns" it to the Father. Obedience in this context presupposes not merely fulfilment of the will of the other persona; it includes embracing the full scope of all the manifestations of the other persona. Through this ultimate kenotic obedience within the Trinity the dynamic perichoresis of the personae finds its realization. In such a kenotic trinitarian perspective, obedience is the expression of divine love. In fact, in the trinitarian model the distinction between obedience and love is somewhat erased.

The "return" of the Son to the Father is also seen in the incarnate Christ in his existential hypostatic orientation toward the Father, expressed in his "not-I-but the-Father" sayings: "I live by the Father" (Jn 6:57; cf 5:30, 7:18, 15:15). Christ, though the incarnate God, avoids any "divine action" of his own, so much so that the Father's hypostasis is manifest absolutely through the absolutely "transparent screen" of Christ's self-emptied hypostasis.[55] Through this kenosis it becomes the "express image of the Father" (Heb 1:3).

The projection of perichoresis onto the level of human relationship is assisted by Fr Sophrony's theology of image and likeness. Mankind is modeled upon the prototype of the Trinity. As such mankind is to imitate trinitarian life, and this was manifested in and by Christ.

In the life of the Trinity, which consists in love (cf 1 Jn 4:8), "love transfers the existence of the person who loves into the beloved, and thus it assimilates the life of the loved one."[56] The assimilation of the life of another presupposes assumption in one's being of that person's manifestations, and especially his or her will. The transition of this principle "love is obedience" from the Trinity onto the human plane is implicit in the gospel. In the Trinity the idea of obedience as love is found in John 14:31: "I love the Father; and as the Father gave me commandment, even so I do." On the level of humanity this principle is applied to the relationship between Christ and his followers: "If you love me, you will keep my commandments" (Jn 14:15, cf Jn 14:23).

Building on this principle, Fr Sophrony makes the same connection on the level of human relationships: "He who loves his brother, naturally wishes to fulfil his brother's will, humbling himself before him."[57]

[55] *La félicité de connaître la voie*, 44 (cf Jn 14:9).
[56] *La félicité de connaître la voie*, 21.
[57] *Birth into the Kingdom*, 173.

Obedience is viewed by Fr Sophrony as an "opening up" to the realization of hypostatic potential in man. It actualizes the principle of perichoresis between hypostases on the human level. One hypostasis takes (via obedience) into itself the other hypostasis. Fr Sophrony expresses it thus:

> Without the culture of true Christian obedience a person inevitably will remain a self-enclosed circuit ... The absence of obedience in the predisposition of a person is the genuine sign of illness of soul, which restrains that person within the confines of individualistic egoism—the opposite of the hypostatic principle of being.[58]

As was shown above, the hypostatic principle of being is linked with the idea of universality, or bearing of the fulness of the multihypostatic being. Obedience, by virtue of taking into oneself the will and ideas of another persona (will, ideas), helps one progress in the development of one's hypostatic capacities, in "the taking into oneself of other hypostases":

> Progressing in the practice of obedience, a person learns to love his own states and manifestations not only as his own but as a sort of revelation about what takes place in the human world. All pain or suffering, be it physical or moral, every success, defeat, or loss, are lived by that person not in the manner of egoistic self-enclosure, but in such a way that in his spirit he enters the suffering of other people, since at every moment thousands of people experience similar states. The natural outcome of such a movement of the human spirit is prayer for the whole world.[59]

Christ-like universality is expressed in the prayer for the whole world, which Fr Sophrony sees as the realization of the hypostatic principle. In prayer the persona unifies the whole by bearing its fulness in itself: "Compassion for the whole of mankind develops in the soul of the novice who practices obedience, and his prayer acquires cosmic character, incorporating into itself the whole Adam, that is, it becomes hypostatic, after the pattern of the prayer of Christ in Gethsemane."[60]

There are instances in the patristic tradition where obedience is related to love. For example, Gregory of Sinai, when presenting the results of obedience

[58]Ibid., 173-74.
[59]Ibid., 174.
[60]Ibid., 174-75.

in five progressive stages, ascribes "love which is God" to the highest stage.[61] Barsanuphius coins the principle: "if you do not obey it means you do not love."[62] Yet in the fathers we do not find a sufficient explanation for this connection. Fr Sophrony not only explains this connection, but views it from a new angle.

In obedience, the manifestations of one persona—its will, mentality, aspirations, experiences—are taken into oneself by another persona, imitating thereby the relationship of the divine personae in the Trinity. Such a perspective enables Fr Sophrony to explain the traditional absolutism of obedience: if the elder is obeyed (assimilated) totally, his disciple becomes his "express-image," as it were. It is not a guru's "personality cult," but the Pauline idea of imitation of one's spiritual father (1 Cor 4:16). As such, obedience is interpreted as "training in love." Fr Sophrony in a letter to Balfour calls monasticism "a special form of love." By denying himself, and giving space to the "other"—by fulfilling the will of the elder or neighbor, assimilating his thought-world—the ascetic experiences an increase of love. The greater the self-abnegation and abasement, the larger the space is, and ultimately the stronger the love. This effect becomes universal. Through obedience and love the novice comes out of his own ego and perceives other people's condition: "The practice of obedience develops in us the faculty of swift and sensitive perception of the spiritual condition of an ever-growing number of people."[63]

This shows how the practice of obedience is designed for the growth of the novice as persona. This idea is explicitly stated in the following passage:

> Progressing in obedience—to God and to neighbor—we progress in love: we broaden our being, and the limit of this broadening is the fulness which is understood as receiving by every man of the fulness of the universal human being and the fulness of the eternal being.[64]

Fr Sophrony's teaching on persona assists us in seeing why obedience is the most effective way to achieve the ultimate goal of the ascetic life, which, according to Fr Sophrony, is the realization of persona in prayer for the whole world. This is the actualization par excellence of the trinitarian prototype.

[61]Gregory of Sinai, *Chap.* 120, 54.
[62]Barsanuphius, *Repl.* 231, 143.
[63]*Birth into the Kingdom*, 173.
[64]Ibid., 138.

"Taking into": Fr Sophrony and Dostoyevsky

Dostoyevsky's idea of a person "taking into" himself of another person apparently is echoed in Fr Sophrony's trinitarian perspective of obedience. In Dostoyevsky, the elder must "take into" himself his novice—to take his will, his persona[lity]. In both Dostoyevsky and Fr Sophrony love is seen as a means of assimilation of another persona. Yet this similarity should not blind us to differences between their thinking.

Their respective backgrounds are different. Dostoyevsky writes with literary concerns. In *The Brothers Karamazov* the elder emerges as an ultimate ideal of love within the range of characters at the opposite existential pole to that of Smerdyakov. Dostoyevsky is not interested in the sacramental aspect of the instructions of the elder. Besides, the character of elder Zosima is controlled not so much by historical realism as by humanistic idealism. A discrepancy between the real saint of Optina (Amvrosy) and a literary figure becomes manifest if one thinks of other "literary relatives" to elder Zosima in world literature. Dostoyevsky's humanistic ideal of all-embracing love derives from literary stress on the moral value of love within the spectrum of human psychological interaction. As such Dostoyevsky's writings can hardly be counted as a part of the eastern ascetic tradition.

In contrast to Dostoyevsky, Fr Sophrony's principle of "all-embracing love through eldership" evolves on the basis of his dogmatic vision. It is a result of projection of the Trinity on the level of human being. This dogmatic foundation is alien to Dostoyevsky: he hardly refers to either christological or trinitarian dogmas of the church, or to the patristic heritage. In his christology (in the chapter on the "Grand Inquisitor") the stress is on humanistic and moral categories, rather than the ontological. Furthermore, Fr Sophrony is writing from his living experience both as monastic disciple and as spiritual father.

Obedience and Discipline

Fr Sophrony emphasizes the importance of obedience for Christianity, as it reflects the Christian perception of the divinity as hypostatic. Obedience manifests the immediacy of the personal relation between God and man. The concept of covenant highlights the personal character of this relationship:

> The principle of personalistic obedience is indissolubly linked with our
> theological concept of persona-hypostasis, which derives from the

Orthodox understanding of the divine revelation concerning our Creator and prototype—the Holy Trinity, where each hypostasis is the bearer of the whole absolute fulness of the divine being. The loss of, or deviation from, this theology would lead to the conscious or unconscious striving toward the "supra-personal," with the result that the "general" will prevail over the "personal." Obedience in this case will be required not in relation to the human person, but as a subjection to the "law," "rule," "function," "institution," and so forth.[65]

The same personal character of Christian obedience should also mark the life of the church. Fr Sophrony draws a sharp distinction between "gospel-type obedience" and "discipline": "Obedience is not to the rule but to a person." When discipline prevails over Christian obedience, "there is a possibility of the ultimate loss of the very aim of Christianity and the sense of life." Fr Sophrony concludes:

Deviation from the right perception of the principle of persona in the being of God will diminish the power of our striving toward the perfect personalistic obedience, which would be a loss that cannot be redeemed by any external success of an institution or the perfection of the infrastructure of any impersonal "whole."[66]

He warns against a wrong perception of monastic obedience and contrasts it to discipline:

Monastic obedience is a religious act and, as such, it should be free, otherwise it would lose its religious significance. Obedience is fruitful only when it has the character of free denial of one's own will and reasoning . . . for the sake of learning the will of God . . . If in the monastery the abbot or other spiritual guides are obliged to use 'discipline,' it is a sure sign of the decline of monasticism, and perhaps even of the entire understanding of its goal and essence.[67]

Even in its most primitive manifestations, which outwardly resemble mere discipline, obedience has a higher goal than a mere ordering of one's life.

[65]Ibid., 175.
[66]Ibid.
[67]Ibid., 141.

Freedom and Obedience

Fr Sophrony points out that obedience may appear as enslaving oneself to another person (as indeed it does to Berdyaev). In this connection Fr Sophrony refers to Climacus, who asserts that "the novice who gives himself over to voluntary slavery receives freedom in return."[68] Thus, the experience of obedience is the experience of true freedom in God. Fr Sophrony sets out to explain this paradox. The reality of the divine being transcends human categories and lies beyond the grasp of the human intellect. In such a perspective, man is seen to be the captive of his own imperfect vision of reality and is the slave of his own self: "In the act of denying the will and his own imperfect thinking for the sake of abiding within the ways of the will of God, which transcends any human wisdom, the monk in reality denies nothing else but his own passionate and egoistic self-will and his small and helpless intellect."[69] Fr Sophrony reads into 1 John 5:4 the meaning that "the way of faith, which overcomes the world" is the way of obedience. However, it is not only freedom from "imperfect thinking" that is achieved through obedience. In fallen humanity actions are controlled by existential concerns, which have their focus in the "self." Through obedience, the ascetic learns to shift his/her existential concern beyond the sphere of "self" by virtue of being conducted by "not-self," someone else's existential concern. As we saw earlier, liberation from "self" represents the negative aspect of freedom (as *freedom from*). However, Fr Sophrony's idea also implies freedom in its positive aspect: *freedom for* fulfilment of God's will. On the lowest level obedience is "a subjection of one's will to the spiritual father, for the sake of a better knowledge of the will of God." Starting from this simple form of obedience the ascetic attains to the more advanced level, which Fr Sophrony defines as "the active faculty of our spirit, which strives to follow the commandments of Christ."[70] Obedience grows from an outward monastic practice into an existential hypostatic orientation, by virtue of which the ascetic assimilates the divine will, and thus, the divine mode of being.

However these two aspects of freedom (*from* and *for*) are tightly linked: freedom "from" results in freedom "for." This ties in well with Maximus' idea of freedom. The latter sees in the possibility of choice "the sign of imperfection,

---

[68] *Scala parad.* 4, PG 88:680C.
[69] *Birth into the Kingdom*, 139.
[70] Ibid., 172.

limitation of our true freedom."[71] *Deliberation* for Maximus is precisely that: *de-liberation*. It becomes clear why obedience, voluntary denial of the choosing will, restores our perfection and natural freedom. Liberation from "self" licenses the person to follow the truly natural will (*thelema physikon*) without the hindrance of the divided preferences of *thelema gnomikon*.

In Fr Sophrony this idea is not expressed in the same terminology, but his teaching on persona does presuppose this effect of obedience. In the divine being there is one will in which, using Maximus' terminology, *thelema physikon* and *thelema gnomikon* are identical. Fr Sophrony underlines that the trinitarian dogma presupposes

> the absolute identity of the person and the essence. There is no distance (*diastasis*) between the person and the essence. The unity of personal self-awareness and of the essence is complete . . . In the unique essence of the divinity there is absolutely nothing that is not "enhypostasized," that exists beyond the self-awareness of the person.[72]

In contrast to the divine, the human being in its fallen state contains a contradiction between nature-aspect and hypostasis-aspect. Fr Sophrony writes: "We as personae find ourselves in an intense contradiction with some manifestations of our nature. We are born as persons but only potentially. When this aspect reaches within us a certain stage of development, then there take place conflicts between our persona in its self-determination on the one hand and the impulses of our fallen nature on the other." Fr Sophrony envisages the un-fallen state of human beings as free from this contradiction; these two "poles" of being—nature and hypostasis—will be in "singleness of being," "the wholeness of harmony of eternal life." In our final completion the full singleness of nature and persona should be established: "When we give up our own will . . . we surmount the 'division' that Adam's fall introduced into our nature."[73]

Obedience strikes at the heart of this contradiction between the persona and fallen nature. The ascetic practice of obedience in its negative aspect (i.e., denial of one's own will) allows the disentanglement of the connection between nature and human conduct: nature no longer controls the behavior.

---

[71]Lossky, *Mystical Theology*, 125.
[72]*La félicité de connaître la voie*, 28.
[73]*Birth into the Kingdom*, 137–38.

The existential concern moves *beyond* "self." This negation of "self" as a practice can be cultivated by conforming to any other will not one's "own" and is expressed in the Athonite formula, quoted respectfully by Fr Sophrony, "As long as it is not done the way *we* choose!" The practice of self-negation is, as we have seen, a preparation for the positive effect of obedience—the focusing of the existential concern on the "other"—ultimately on God. The connection between obedience to man and obedience to God is made in the following words of Fr Sophrony: "if we do not practice obedience in relation to our brother, how can we . . . learn to humble ourselves before God and be obedient in fulfilling his great, eternal, and divine will?"[74] Thus through *freedom from* self via obedience to the elder one gains *freedom* (or space) *for* God in one's abased self. In doing so, we do not suppress, but actually discover, our own personal freedom.

Fr Sophrony and the fathers value obedience above other virtues, and see it as a necessary stage in the progress of ascetic life. Furthermore, they agree on the results of obedience—it makes a novice "inaccessible to sin" and produces such spiritual virtues as humility and dispassion. And in both it is treated as a sacrament, in which the word coming from the elder is accepted as divine and not human. Finally, they both highlight the connection between obedience and freedom. Fr Sophrony inherits this traditional approach through the Athonite living tradition and especially through Silouan the Athonite.

However, Fr Sophrony introduces a new theological depth in the understanding of eldership. He draws significant implications from the trinitarian model, which was made manifest in Christ. The trinitarian perspective on persona allowed him to justify the practice of obedience as an imitation and reflection of the trinitarian mode of being. His theology enables him to explain how obedience leads to hypostatic growth from the state of an egoistic individual to a hypostatic center, bearing the fulness of universal being. He is aware of the concerns of the twentieth-century existentialists about freedom in the individual. As a response to the latter he integrates patristic ideas into his own theological framework to prove that obedience does not contradict freedom but leads to it. This subject distinguishes Fr Sophrony as a creative theologian, who reworks the traditional ideas about monastic obedience into the coherent framework of his own theology.

[74]Ibid., 173.

CHAPTER NINE

Mindfulness of Death

Christianity proclaims that the immortal God died on the cross and then was raised from the dead, restoring thereby the gift of everlasting life to all men. So, with the event of Golgotha, "death destroyed by death" becomes a focal point of Christian kerygma, so much so that Jaroslav Pelikan calls the New Testament "the gospel of death." In contrast to the faith of Judaism, which concentrated on the life of this world, the early church brings the victory over death to the forefront of its creed, shifting its principal aspirations beyond the confines of the visible world—into the everlasting kingdom "which is not of this world" (Jn 18:36). For Christians, the very idea of salvation came to signify the attainment of life without death, which Christ promised to all who believe in him (Jn 6:47). Death was seen as "the ultimate enemy" (*eschatos echthros*) of mankind (cf 1 Cor 15:26), so powerful that it made God himself come down from heaven to vanquish it.

In eastern Christianity the attitude to death receives articulate expression within the liturgical tradition. On the one hand, death is depicted in all its ugliness and gloominess: "I weep, and with tears lament when with understanding I think on death, and see how in the graves there sleeps the beauty which once for us was fashioned in the image of God, but now is shapeless, ignoble, and bare of all the graces."[1] Thus the fact of death shapes Christian evaluation of human existence and created things in general. In the face of death the church proclaims: "All things are weaker than shadow, all more illusive than dreams . . . Death prevails over all these vanities . . . All is dust, all is ashes, all is shadow."[2] The services thereby constitute a rich source for an otherworldly type of asceticism. On the other hand, the liturgical tradition also offers escape from this "gloominess," emphasizing the anticipation of the resurrection of the dead as re-constitution. Such a perspective is used as a

[1] *An Orthodox Prayer Book*, 109.
[2] *An Orthodox Prayer Book*, 106, 108.

theological endorsement of the monastic renunciation of the world and its
material values. In the monastic ascetic tradition the memory of death is an
ever-present leitmotif, so much so that Ilyin summarizes asceticism as a "school
of preparation for death."[3] Patristic thought on mindfulness of death (and its
reworking by the Russian ascetic tradition of the last three centuries) has three
main theses.

First, the ascetic practice of concentrating on the fact of death is designed
to provoke more effective renunciation of the world by setting the present life
into eternal perspective. The awareness of the final end of earthly existence
helps one to achieve detachment from the material world and its pleasures.[4]
Gregory of Nazianzus illustrates this in *Epist.* 31, where he advises his friend
to live the future instead of the present and to make this life a meditation and
practice of death.[5] Athanasius relates how Anthony lived among the tombs so
as to keep a physical reminder of death in front of his eyes. The whole ascetic
perspective is marked by an emphasis on the contrast between the temporal
and eternal life. From this contrast Athanasius deduces that if we live every day
as if we were to die, we will not sin.[6] Evagrius writes that "the monk should
always live as if he is to die tomorrow, but use his body as if it were to live a
long life."[7]

Second, fear of the final retribution spurs repentance and prevents sinning.
Often the remembrance of death is associated with remembrance of divine
judgment. The remembrance of eternal punishment, stimulating fear in the
ascetic, becomes "a source of almost every virtue."[8] This fear fuels one's repentance for misdeeds in the past. Thus, by reminding a fallen virgin of death Basil
calls her to repentance.[9] The fear of punishment also serves as an effective
deterrent from sin, and as such was often used by the fathers in ascetic teaching: "He who always thinks of death . . . cannot go far astray."[10] Maximus
believes that one who fears punishment refrains from passions.[11] Memory of

[3]See also Evagrius, *Prat.* 52, 618: anachoretic life is an exercise of death; cf Isaac, *Gr. Hom.*
34, 152: love of silence is a constant expectation of death.
[4]Gregory of Nyssa, *Virg.*, 258-59.
[5]*Epist.* 31, 39; *Epist.* 168, 59; cf *Carm. mor.* 1.2.5.2, PG 37:607A.
[6]*Vie.* 8.1, 156; ibid., 16.4-17.4, 178-82; ibid., 19.2, 186.
[7]*Pract.* 29, 576.
[8]Hesychius, *Epist. Theod.* 155, 165; cf Philotheos, *Chap.* 38, 286; Gregory of Nazianzus, *Or.*
32.1, 85.
[9]Basil, *Epist.* 46, 122-23.
[10]Palladius, *Laus.* 4, 6.
[11]Maximus, *Cap. car.* 1.3, 50; cf ibid., 2.81, 132.

death is sometimes recommended as a weapon against fleshly lust.[12] Clima-cus summarizes it: "Remember your last end, and you will never sin."[13] Thus, the same fear helps the ascetic to maintain vigilance (*nepsis*) and self-control, and brings about contrition of the heart.[14]

Third, anticipation of eschatological rewards stimulates aspiration after ascetic endeavor. Mindfulness of eschatological bliss serves to maintain the ascetic's inspiration.[15] It is often recommended as a means to avoid despondency.[16] Spiritual nostalgia for life after death is a vital element of monasticism. In this optimistic understanding, Christian writings echo the pagan genre of consolation literature. Theodore the Studite records a saying of an elderly monk: "Let us be vigilant . . . let us remember also the heavenly kingdom."[17] According to Dorotheus of Gaza, one reason for spiritual carelessness is that one has tasted neither the expected rest nor the eternal torment.[18]

The confrontation of the problem of death was inherent to the intellectual climate of Fr Sophrony's age, which was marked by a fundamental revision of central philosophical subjects. The theme of death figures prominently in the writings of some existentialists. Kierkegaard and Heidegger reopened investigation into death from the new existentialist perspective.[19] Both highlight a certain absolutism in the fact of death. The theme receives a fresh interpretation in psychology: in Freud it acquires central significance in the field of analysis. On the other hand, the historical reality of the beginning of the twentieth century, marked by the First World War and the Russian Revolution of 1917, made death more intensely present in the minds of Fr Sophrony's contemporaries.

Within Russian thought the question of death was raised anew and became a controlling feature of the philosophical framework of Fedorov,

---

[12]Philotheos, *Cap.* 6, 275.

[13]*Scala parad.* 6, PG 88:800A.

[14]Cf Theodore Studite, *Const.* 23, PG 99:1712B: "Let us be vigilant for we are dying"; cf Dorotheus of Gaza, *Instr.* 52, 230-32: by mindfulness of death monks maintain self-examination; *Apophth.*, PG 65:389C: memory of death helps one stay vigilant; Maximus, *Lib. ascet.* 27, PG 90:932C.

[15]Cf Isaac, *Gr. Hom.* 38, 163; ibid., 71, 277.

[16]Climacus, *Scala parad.* 13, PG 88:861A.

[17]*Const.* 23, PG 99:1712B.

[18]*Instr.* 125, 382.

[19]Kierkegaard, *Concluding Unscientific Postscript*, esp. 82; cf M. Heidegger, "Das mögliche Ganzsein des Daseins und das Sein zum Tode," in *Sein und Zeit*, ed M. Niemeyer (Tubingen, 1957).

Rozanov, and Berdyaev. In different ways they all acknowledge the supreme significance of the fact of death: it is "the most profound and significant fact of life ... [it] alone gives true depth to the question as to the meaning of life."[20]

Fr Sophrony on Mindfulness of Death

The remembrance of death was the starting point for Fr Sophrony's mystical experience. The importance of the theme for his ascetic theology is clear from the fact that he dedicated a whole chapter to it in *We Shall See Him as He Is*. It takes a high place in the scale of the ascetic virtues. Mindfulness of death is seen as one of the "negative" manifestations of divine grace, which also include kenosis and godforsakenness. All of them are seen as necessary stages in the realization of persona in man. Thereby Fr Sophrony's writing on mindfulness of death is predominantly marked by its negative implications, rather than by a positive anticipation of eschatological bliss. Though he mentions death in its positive aspect,[21] these passages are motivated by pastoral needs to console his addressees. The positive aspect—"anticipation of bliss"—has been much stressed by contemporary Orthodox writers. For Fr Sophrony, in contrast, death is recalled not so much as a transition to the eternal kingdom but as a tragic problem of the negation of life. Even in his *consolatio* passages he does not tell his readers to be reconciled, as it were, with the tragedy of death or "to grow into harmony with the ways of God," but urges them to live death's tragedy *fully as* tragedy and as God's ordinance. For him the power of this tragedy generates that force within us that would enable us to live up to Christ's calling—to "make his victory over death our own."[22]

Mindfulness of Death as an Intellectual Experience and Its Roots

Fr Sophrony speaks of his childhood fascination with the mystery of death. Later, during the First World War, when "the news of thousands of innocent victims being killed at the front placed [him] squarely before a vision of tragic reality," the problem of eternity began to predominate in his mind. This quest

[20]Berdyaev, *Destiny of Man*, 249ff; V. Rozanov, *Death and Beyond* (St Petersburg, 1910); Rozanov, *The Apocalypse of Our Time* (Sergiev Posad, 1917) 47-57; Feodorov, *Philosophy*, 163, 169, 411, 473ff, 559.

[21]*Letters to Russia*, 129-32, 136, 154-55.

[22]Cf *We Shall See Him as He Is*, 65.

is well in line with the thought of Gregory of Nazianzus, for whom the fragility of our life is a source of poetic inspiration.[23] Such a memory of death is the result of one's *intellectual* encounter with the fact of death.

To Fr Sophrony, at the heart of the matter was the question of theodicy: if life is fragile and seemingly absurd, why is it given, or even "imposed" on us?[24] This perspective on death, bringing God to "trial," is too "daring" for the patristic frame of thought, with its concern to maintain unquestionably God's goodness. Fr Sophrony's revolt against death may be more easily paralleled with that in western existentialism and in Russian philosophy. Fr Sophrony admits having read books on the subject of death,[25] which probably alludes to these authors, with whose ideas he was clearly acquainted.

However, on closer analysis it emerges that western existentialism and Russian philosophy did not play a decisive role in the formation of Fr Sophrony's concept of mindfulness of death. This becomes manifest when we compare Fr Sophrony with these thinkers.

FR SOPHRONY AND THE EXISTENTIALISTS. The word "absurd," used by Fr Sophrony, suggests a dependence on the existentialists' approach to death. For them death is the great symbol of life's finitude and absurdity.

Of all existentialists, Heidegger offers the most detailed study of the meaning of death.[26] He anticipates Fr Sophrony in regarding death as the negative abolition of *Dasein* (existence). Yet for Heidegger it is not *tragically negative*: it allows one to think of existence positively as a finite whole. As such, death serves as an integrating factor in an authentic existence. Thus, unlike Fr Sophrony, Heidegger *accepts* death by giving it a positive meaning. The same attempt to integrate death positively into human existence is found in Kierkegaard, for whom death is an intrinsic attribute of human life-existence: "The existing subject is eternal, but as existing he is temporal. Now the illusiveness of the infinite is that the possibility of death is present at every moment."[27] Thus, Heidegger and Kierkegaard make positive sense of the fact of finitude.

Much closer to Fr Sophrony's pessimism about the fact of death are Camus and Sartre, for whom death is the final proof of the absurdity of both human

[23] Cf *Carm. mor.* 2.14.17, PG37:757A; cf *Carm. hist.* 1.73.11-12, PG 37:1421A.
[24] See *We Shall See Him as He Is*, 10ff; *Letters to Russia*, 121.
[25] *Letters to Russia*, 20.
[26] See *Sein und Zeit*, 279-311.
[27] *Concluding Unscientific Postscript*, 82.

life and the universe. In Camus it produces "metaphysical rebellion."[28] This echoes Fr Sophrony, who writes:"The human spirit cannot accept the idea of death." It should not be supposed that those existentialists who place death in the center of their philosophizing are on that account nihilists. They try to find a positive philosophical solution (atheistic in Camus' case) for the problem of death within the framework of present existence, without appeal to "life after death." In respect of "this" life Fr Sophrony's attitude to death is, relatively speaking, *nihilistic*. He goes *beyond* death, and the present life is no more than a "first experience of being," which can only have any meaning if man is immortal. The absurdity of temporary life does not result in rebellion alone but in the quest for an *ontological* solution—how to become immortal.[29] This is the main difference between Fr Sophrony and the existentialists, which demonstrates that his idea of death is not simply borrowed from them.

FR SOPHRONY AND RUSSIAN PHILOSOPHERS. For Fedorov, death is also absurd: the worst and ultimate evil. Anticipating Soloviev, he criticizes the positivist theory of progress (where humanity builds its better future on the sufferings of the ancestors) as amoral. However, in contrast to Fr Sophrony, his solution is "retrospective": he is concerned to "return" life to the departed through resurrection. Fedorov's ideal was the realization of the kingdom of God in *this* world. His rather utopian reliance on science in his "resurrection-plan" rules out Fr Sophrony's dependence on him: Fr Sophrony is well aware of the limitation of scientific knowledge in the sphere of immortality.[30]

Rozanov, like Fr Sophrony, sees death as an "unacceptable" fact. Because of the "acceptance" of death in Christianity, Rozanov revolts against Christianity: for him it is a religion of death, unlike Judaism and paganism, which are religions of birth. Rozanov cannot reconcile himself with the tragedy of Christ's death. His main solution is to refocus Christian interests from death onto the fact of birth and reproduction, and seek "immortality" in human posterity.[31] Rozanov thereby deifies sexual relations. In his rejection of suffering and the tragedy of death, he verges upon the rejection of Christianity altogether. Although the question of death led Fr Sophrony also to search for a solution *outside* Christianity (during the years of his interest in non-Christian

---

[28]A. Camus, *The Rebel: An Essay on Man in Revolt*, tr. A. Bower (London, 1962) 100.
[29]*We Shall See Him as He Is*, 186; *Letters to Russia*, 19, 21-22, 129.
[30]*Letters to Russia*, 22.
[31]Rozanov, *Apocalypse of Our Time*, 47-49.

eastern mysticism), he rejects Rozanov's solution as materialistic in its core. As such it is subject to Fr Sophrony's criticism of materialism: the finality of death cannot be overcome by means of the material world.

Berdyaev, like some western existentialists, wants to "reconcile" man's existence with the fact of death, to enlarge upon a positive side of finitude. Fr Sophrony discards finitude altogether: if death is the ultimate reality then the gift of life is absurd.[32] For Berdyaev, death *gives* meaning to life: "Life in this world has meaning because there is death." The meaning is bound up with the end: "If there were no end, there would be no meaning in it . . . Life, not in its weakness but in its strength, intensity, and superabundance, is closely connected with death."[33] For Fr Sophrony, death, if it had the last word, *deprives* life of its value: it makes it meaningless.[34]

Thus, though Fr Sophrony and the Russian thinkers agree on the fact that death is an existential problem, they provide different solutions for it. Fr Sophrony rejects materialistic approaches or reconciliation with death. For him the fact of death leads to a refusal of reconciliation with present reality, and to the spiritual imperative of "breaking the barriers of finitude and temporality" so as to attain personal, eternal being.[35] This difference rules out Fr Sophrony's direct dependence on Russian philosophy. Furthermore, unlike these philosophers, Fr Sophrony employs the intellectual recalling of death within the context of monastic asceticism. Thus, in his later years, Fr Sophrony developed an ascetic technique based on the effect that the memory of death has on man's spiritual being, fixing his mind on eternal categories. This technique consists in the ascetic's refusing to lower his existential concern to the level of temporary categories. Thus he avoids engaging with negative impulses within himself and within those around him. This is a recurrent theme in Fr Sophrony's *Ascetic Discourses*. According to this technique, the ascetic must constantly control his mind and focus on the eternal.

Mindfulness of Death as a Mystical State

Fr Sophrony speaks of mindfulness of death not only as an active intellectual phenomenon but as a grace-given *mystical state*. The absence of this "mystical" dimension in the above-mentioned philosophers and psychologists provides

[32]Ibid., 21, 129.
[33]Berdyaev, *Destiny of Man*, 249, 254.
[34]*Letters to Russia*, p. 20.
[35]Ibid., 21-23.

further reasons to rule out Fr Sophrony's direct dependence on them. The prevalence of the negative dimension in Fr Sophrony's concept is due to his own mystical experience. Thus, referring to his youth, Fr Sophrony recalls mindfulness of death of a peculiar kind, which "proceeded from some superior source, independent of my will or any initiative on my part,"[36] to such an extent that he was unable to analyze the situation rationally. This goes beyond a mere intellectual awareness: it belongs to the realm of mystical experience. However, these two types of mindfulness of death are linked in that one leads to the other. As a response to human initiative, to an intellectual quest, man experiences an "ontological" change within his perception of self, characterized by the "feeling" of the "futility of any and every acquisition on earth." Fr Sophrony emphasizes that it is "an especial spiritual state, quite unlike simply knowing that one day we shall die." Thus, as a state it passes beyond mere intellectual categories. The element of transcendence is present. This *going out of oneself* can be compared with the patristic idea of *ecstasy*, yet here it takes a negative form. In connection with this Fr Sophrony compares this "negative" self-transcendence to *contemplating the bottomless abyss*. The metaphor employed suggests the "negativity" of the experience: it corresponds to transcendence in its downward, negative aspect (an unfathomable abyss), and not to the positive, upward transcendence (heaven). In *Letters to Russia*, Fr Sophrony describes the same phenomenon as "falling out" of empirical reality. This state is characterized by losing awareness of the surrounding world, even though one still sees it. The world is conceived as a sort of mirage.[37]

Second, the state is characterized by an inverse perspective in one's perception of reality. Mindfulness of death acts as a filter through which man sees objects in terms of their value in relation to eternity: "Everything subject to decay lost its value for me. When I looked at people, without thinking further I saw them in the power of death, dying ... I wanted neither fame from those 'dead mortals' nor power over them. I despised material wealth and did not think much of intellectual assets."[38]

Fr Sophrony describes this type of mindfulness of death as an "uncovering of the profound being within oneself," but "in its negative mode." Thus, mindfulness of death broadens the diapason of one's being and one's awareness in a negative, as it were downward, aspect.

---

[36] *We Shall See Him as He Is*, p. 15.
[37] Ibid., 10ff.
[38] Ibid., p. 16.

Fr Sophrony and the Fathers

Is Fr Sophrony a pioneer in distinguishing two kinds of mindfulness of death? H. Vlakhos does not mention any patristic precedent when he speaks of the two types of the mindfulness of death in Fr Sophrony.[39] Indeed, this distinction between the two types of mindfulness of death is not a common or basic theme in the fathers. Nonetheless, such a distinction is not entirely absent in the eastern tradition. We find the closest parallels to Fr Sophrony in John Climacus and Isaac the Syrian.

John Climacus on the Two Types of Mindfulness of Death

In Climacus both types of memory of death are implied. A mental awareness of death (the first type) is achieved by a personal ascetic effort to keep it in mind. Climacus offers the most developed presentation of memory of death as an intrinsic element of ascetic life. A whole chapter of his *Ladder* is dedicated to that theme.[40] He recommends that the ascetic always preserves the memory of death: at night and during the day. For Climacus it is an important ascesis, closely related to other ascetic practices.[41] It is no less important than prayer. To enhance the effectiveness of this exercise, the ascetics are recommended to abide near tombs, so as to have them constantly before their eyes as a physical reminder of death.[42] The practice of mindfulness of death incites cenobite monks to repentance and helps anchorites to lay aside earthly cares, to enhance unceasing prayer, and to guard the mind. It arrests gluttonous impulses and other passions. Its result is sanctity of life and chastity. Furthermore, Climacus makes a distinction between natural and unnatural fear of death. The former is inherent to fallen human nature (when human nature is perfect, a sense of death does not provoke fear[43]), while the unnatural fear results from the presence of some unrepented sins.

On the other hand, Climacus describes the second type, a grace-given mystical state, when mindfulness of death becomes the determining factor of the life of the ascetic, beyond his control, something "imposed" from on high.

---

[39]H. Vlakhos, *Life after Death*, tr. E. Williams (Levadia, 1996) 376.

[40]*Scala Parad.* 6, PG 88:793B–800A.

[41]Ibid., 4, PG 88:700D, 793C, 868D, 869D; ibid., 15, PG 88:889CD.

[42]Ibid., 28, PG 88:1137A; ibid., 1, PG 88:633D.

[43]Cf "natural" fear of death in Isaac, *Gr. Hom.* 38, 163; Gregory of Nyssa, *Anima et res.*, PG 46:13B; cf Maximus, *Cap. al.* 118, PG 90:1428A.

2 This second mindfulness of death is set "in the feeling of the heart" (*aisthesis kardias*). It manifests itself in a voluntary detachment from the material world and the denying of one's will. He describes this feeling as a "daily death" (*kathemerinos thanatos*). He also calls it "a gift of God." We also find a description of *ecstasis* in this state, which brings about the mystical transcendence of visible reality. Climacus describes an ascetic who, because of mindfulness of death, would be plunged into ecstasy (*existato*), and as if having passed out, was carried away, almost breathless.[44]

Isaac the Syrian on the Two Types of Mindfulness of Death

Isaac the Syrian also knows of the two types of mindfulness of death. Thus he mentions the natural thought about death that leads in its turn to a constant concern about death: "that first thought is of the material order [*somatikos*], this second one is spiritual contemplation and marvelous grace [*theoria pneumatike and thaumaste charis*]." After such a vision man abandons all worldly concerns.[45]

Thus, Fr Sophrony is not a pioneer in making the distinction between two kinds of mindfulness of death. The above-mentioned fathers anticipate Fr Sophrony in their description of the mystical state of mindfulness of death as a deep-set *feeling* (that is, a state) and spiritual contemplation. Fr Sophrony's description of the results of this mystical state resembles that of the fathers. They also agree that this state has an element of ecstasy/self-transcendence, of "falling out." Fr Sophrony and Climacus use the same term, "abyss," for the description of the state of ecstatic "falling out."

Mindfulness of Death and the Persona

Fr Sophrony's theology of persona provides a new perspective for the integration of this spiritual-mystical phenomenon within the framework of Orthodox anthropology. The above-mentioned fathers did not make a connection between mindfulness of death and the concept of hypostasis. For Fr Sophrony, the fact of death uncovers in man the hypostatic principle of being. It highlights the "micro-absoluteness," as it were, and even "microtheosity" of

---

[44]*Scala Parad.* 6, PG 88:793C–800D.
[45]*Gr. Hom.* 39, 167–68.

man, although in its "negative mode." Death makes the "micro-absoluteness" and "God-likeness" of the human persona manifest. If the persona, a God-like *centrum,* ceases to exists, then all that is held in its consciousness, the whole cosmos in the subjective perception of this persona, dies with it. "The fact that this mindfulness of death makes us see our death as the end of the entire universe confirms the revelation given to us that man is the image of God and as such able to contain in himself both God and created cosmos. And this, too, is the first step toward the concretion in us of the hypostatic principle."[46]

This phenomenon explains Fr Sophrony's idea that even the divine absolute would cease to exist with the death of persona—the subjective "micro-absolute":

> [With my death] in me, with me, all that had formed part of my consciousness would die: people close to me, their sufferings and love, the whole progress of history, the universe in general, the sun, the stars, endless space; even the Creator of the world Himself—He, too, would die in me. In short, all life would be engulfed in the darkness of oblivion.[47]

On the basis of these considerations, Fr Sophrony insists on the absolute value of every human being: "The fact that with his death the whole world, even God, dies is possible only if he himself, of himself, is in a certain sense the center of all creation. And in the eyes of God, of course, he is more precious than all other created things."[48]

That is why Fr Sophrony believes that such experiences of mindfulness of death were "contemplation of the 'absoluteness' (qua reflection of the Absolute) in our hypostatic principle, but under a minus sign."[49] This idea of the negative reflection of the persona through death was taken up by Christos Yannaras. His words well summarize Fr Sophrony's line of thought: "Death is an apophatic definition of persona." However, for Yannaras, unlike Fr Sophrony, death points to the *limitation* rather than the *infinity* of the human persona: death ultimately defines the limited character of the purely individual, atomic existence.

Death highlights man's "microtheosity," but in mindfulness of death there is as yet no awareness of any relational aspect between God and man: man's

---

[46] *We Shall See Him as He Is*, 17.
[47] Ibid., 12.
[48] Ibid., 13.
[49] Ibid., 188.

personhood becomes apparent in this experience but not that of God. Mystical awareness of death per se enables man to encounter an *impersonal* eternity, rather than a *personal* God. Fr Sophrony thus avoids speaking about the God–man relationship here and prefers to use "impersonal" terms to describe the state, such as "eternity." This apparently nonrelational character of the phenomenon is reflected in a special kind of apatheia. This dispassion is not built on the positive force of attachment to the divine reality through love, but it does effect a shift in man's existential concern away from temporal categories. Fr Sophrony expresses it thus: "Though perhaps not in a positive form it nevertheless clasps us close to the Eternal."[50] The absence of awareness of divine personeity is reflected in succinct ascetic formulas such as "eternity regenerates man," and "by mindfulness of death man's being is transferred into eternity." Thus, the state of mindfulness of death is a preparation, which on the subjective level heightens man's awareness of his being a hypostasis, of his total freedom, and of the fact of his eternity. On the objective level, due to the absence of immediate personal interaction between God and man, man feels that his self-determination in relation to God has not yet been challenged. Yet as a gift of from on high mindfulness of death singles him out of the world and builds up his self-awareness as hypostasis, before the same grace leads him further—toward a person-to-person relationship with God.

Our analysis shows that in Fr Sophrony the concept of mindfulness of death can express both a mere intellectual awareness of death and also a mystical state, as a form of divine grace. As far as the first type is concerned, there are many predecessors within the eastern ascetic tradition and also within the sphere of existentialist and Russian philosophy. However, the latter, though it heightened Fr Sophrony's awareness of the philosophical problem of death, has only partially influenced him, since his "solution" to the problem differs from theirs. As far as the grace-given mystical state of mindfulness of death is concerned, it was largely neglected by the eastern tradition, with rare exceptions such as John Climacus and Isaac the Syrian. However, in Fr Sophrony it receives a particular theological attention as it highlights the awareness in man, albeit of his existence as a hypostatic being, of his being eternal, a micro-absolute hypostatic center. Fr Sophrony's approach to mindfulness of death shows once again how Russian religious philosophy, eastern patristic tradition, and Fr Sophrony's ascetic experience are integrated into an organic synthesis through his understanding of the concept of persona.

[50]Ibid., 17.

CONCLUSION

Fr Sophrony's Theological Legacy

Though Fr Sophrony is our close contemporary (†1993), we are not entirely unjustified in raising the question of the impact of Fr Sophrony as a theologian upon modern theology. Even now one may observe certain publications that demonstrate his influence. His kerygma was heeded by various theologians in the eastern as well as western Christian worlds, opening up thereby a new possibility for dialogue between the Christian west and east.

It is the personal-hypostatic dimension of Fr Sophrony's message that has been particularly drawn upon by other theologians, who in turn have influenced whole schools of thought. Metropolitan John (Zizioulas), renowned for his ecclesiology, acknowledges his debt to Fr Sophrony.[1] Zizioulas brought the christotrinitarian perspective of Fr Sophrony's theology into interactive dialogue with western scholars. Their response to the eastern theological challenge has stirred up an ongoing trinitarian discourse, embracing a wide range of theologians. In the Greek academic world interest in Fr Sophrony's theology is increasing. His ideas are extensively explored by Mantzaridis, Vlakhos,[2] and others. His status as an epoch-making theologian was prominently featured at the Second International Colloquium on St Gregory Palamas (Athens, 1998), where his name was put side by side with that of Gregory Palamas.[3] Among Russian theologians, the same attitude to Fr Sophrony is found in the writings of Alfeyev—he often refers to Fr Sophrony as an heir of the living ascetic tradition of the eastern church and quotes him on a par with

---

[1]J. Zizioulas, "Theology is Ministry to the Church," tr. H. Alfeyev, *The Church and Time* 3:6 (Moscow, 1998) 88–89.

[2]See G. Mantzaridis, "The Ethical Significance of the Trinitarian Dogma," *Sobornost* 5:10 (1970) 720-29; "The Elder Sophrony: Theologian of the Hypostatic Principle," in Πρόσωπο καὶ θεσμοί, 19-40 (Thessaloniki, 1996); H. Vlakhos, *Saint Gregory Palamas as a Hagiorite*, tr. E. Williams (Levadia, 1997) 327f.; *Orthodox Psychotherapy: The Science of the Fathers*, tr. E. Williams (Levadia, 1994) 158, 162, 165, 175, 332-55.

[3]Vlakhos, *Saint Gregory Palamas as a Hagiorite*, 327f.

some ancient patristic writers. For Alfeyev, Fr Sophrony's example shows how even in our epoch the spiritual experience within the Orthodox monastic tradition is in the same stream as was the experience of Symeon the New Theologian.[4] In the Orthodox west his popularity is also growing. *Buisson Ardent* is a new journal dedicated to Silouan the Athonite's and Fr Sophrony's spirituality. The first four volumes highlighted the growing interest in Fr Sophrony's inheritance in the French-speaking world. They include articles by Larchet, de Andia, and others. The Association of St Silouan the Athonite, which edits this journal, has branches worldwide. Its aim is to unite and coordinate the work on Silouan's and Fr Sophrony's theological heritage. The recent colloquium on Silouan's spirituality organized by the Roman Catholic monastic brotherhood in Bose (Italy) is yet another testimony of the esteem in which Fr Sophrony's heritage is held in the non-Orthodox world. It is true that for many, initial interest in Fr Sophrony's writings is due to their quest for spiritual edification. However, the striking fact is that Fr Sophrony has provoked throughout his readership a need to unite this aspect of life to its dogmatic provenance.

This worldwide attention to his message may appear surprising. As we have seen throughout our presentation of his theology, his conceptual apparatus may appear to be not always original. For each of the constituents of his theological makeup one may find a close precedent, in every field we covered.

Why then does Fr Sophrony's message attract so much theological attention? The answer emerges while reading his books. They express his actual experience; as such they speak for themselves as a positive testimony to spiritual reality. The further one reads the more exceedingly one becomes aware that his words are not simply the fruits of the workings of his own intellect. He lived through the truths that he writes about and as such they emerge as acknowledged and sure facts. This touch of authenticity, which marks his writings, invest his words with a certain authority, which is evasive to challenges on traditionally academic grounds. It is there that his contribution to the Eastern Orthodox tradition lies—through the prism of his own ascetic experience he singles out authentic ideas from various thought-worlds into one unified *theoria*. His reassertion of the personal experiential dimension of the dogmatic heritage of the church enhanced his theological message; he was a true bearer

[4]H. Alfeyev, *St Symeon the New Theologian and Orthodox Tradition* (Oxford, 2000) 284-85; cf Alfeyev, *The Mystery of Faith* (Moscow, 1996) 206-7; *Orthodox Theology at the Turn of the Centuries* (Moscow, 1999) 333-55.

of ecclesiastical tradition. His emphasis on the personal dimension—personeity—and on existential involvement in the cognition of divine reality marks him out from contemporary theologians. He wrote as a spiritual father, as a true *staretz* of our time. Yet his books could never be classified among the multiple examples of the contemporary folklore-type "hagiographic" literature on modern *startzy-gerontas*. His dogmatically grounded vision firmly controls his perception of the ascetic life, with the result that, by enriching ascetic theory with ideas from Russian religious philosophy and theology, Fr Sophrony indeed leads the tradition to a fresh synthesis in theology.

The idea of hypostatic commensurability between God and man receives its existential confirmation in Fr Sophrony's mystical experience, which enabled him to "live" ontologically the divine dimension in human persona— I AM THAT I AM. This existential rediscovery allowed Fr Sophrony to bring ascetic life "closer" to its divine prototype, revealed in Christ. He explores existentially, through the prism of christology, the themes of humanity, the Godhead as Trinity in its economic and eternal dimensions, and the incarnation of the Logos. Such interrelation brings out a significant impact on ascetic life. Thus, the traditional aim of monastic life—communion with God—is presented with a deeper theological insight: the ascetic is to become God-like in his dynamic hypostatic manifestations. By stressing the hypostatic dimension of deification, Fr Sophrony sets forth as a goal the assimilation of the dynamic attributes of divine being: all-embracing love, the capacity for kenotic self-sacrifice in absolute measure, becoming a unifying center-principle of all that is. For the first time these divine attributes are theologically integrated to this extent into ascetic theology under the concepts of prayer for the whole Adam (prayer for the whole world), love for one's enemies, the kenosis-perfection equation, obedience, and Christ-like humility. These reflect the projection of the divine multihypostatic mode of being onto the plane of human life. In this lies Fr Sophrony's outstanding contribution toward the theological quest for the relationship between God and man.

Looking at the extent of his contribution and the boldness of his message, it may indeed seem that "Fr Sophrony lifts us up to a new theological orbit."[5] In reality, however, Fr Sophrony merely "discloses to us Christian and evangelical dimensions that we have largely forgotten,"[6] that is, "authentic dimensions" of Christ as "the way and the truth and the life" (Jn 14:6).

---

[5] Luis, "Archimandrite Sophrony," 49.
[6] Franquesa, "Archimandrite Sophrony," 131.

Selected Bibliography

Abbreviations

Archive	The Archive of the Monastery of St John the Baptist. Essex.
CCG	Corpus Christianorum, *series graeca*. Tournhout-Paris.
CCL	Corpus Christianorum, *series latina*. Tournhout-Paris.
CSCO	Corpus Scriptorum Christianorum Orientalium. Louvain.
ECQ	*Eastern Churches Quarterly*. Ramsgate.
ECR	*Eastern Churches Review*. London.
GCS	Die griechischen christlichen Schriftsteller. Leipzig-Berlin.
JTS	*Journal of Theological Studies*. London.
Messager	*Messager de l'Exarchat du Patriarchate Russe en Europe Occidentale*. Paris.
OC	Orientalia Christiana. Rome.
OCA	*Orientalia Christiana Analecta*. Rome.
PG	Patrologiae cursus completus, *series graeca*, edited by J.-P. Migne. Paris.
PL	Patrologiae cursus completus, *series latina*, edited by J.-P. Migne. Paris.
PTS	*Patristische Texte und Studien*, edited by K. Aland and E. Mühlenberg. Berlin-New York.
SC	Sources Chrétiennes. Paris.
SVTQ	*St Vladimir's Theological Quarterly*. New York.
TPMA	*Textes philosophiques du Moyen Age*. Paris.
ZAW	*Zeitschrift für die Alttestamentliche Wissenschaft*. Berlin.
Philokalia	Φιλοκαλία τῶν ἱερῶν νηπτικῶν, 5 volumes. Athens, 1957-1963.

Selected Works of Archimandrite Sophrony (Sakharov)

Translated Works

"Foreword." In *Wisdom from Mount Athos: The Writings of Staretz Silouan 1866-1938*, translated by Rosemary Edmonds, 4-18. New York, 1974.
His Life Is Mine. Translated by Rosemary Edmonds. Oxford, 1977.
La félicité de connaître la voie. Geneva, 1988.
On Prayer. Translated by Rosemary Edmonds. New York, 1998.
Principles of Orthodox Asceticism. Edited by A. Philippou. Oxford, 1964.
St Silouan the Athonite. Translated by Rosemary Edmonds. New York, 1998.
We Shall See Him as He Is. Translated by Rosemary Edmonds. Essex, 1988.
Words of Life. Essex, 1996.

In Russian

Birth into the Kingdom Which Cannot Be Moved. Edited by Nicholas Sakharov. Essex, 1999.
Letters to Russia. Edited by Nicholas Sakharov. Moscow, 1997.

239

"Liturgical Prayer." In *We Shall See Him as He Is,* Russian edition, 215-28. Essex, 1985.
"Testament." In *Birth into the Kingdom Which Cannot Be Moved,* edited by Nicholas Sakharov, 187-89. Essex, 1999.
"The Prayer of Gethsemane." In *We Shall See Him as He Is,* Russian edition, 231-38. Essex, 1985.
Letters to David Balfour from 1932 to 1987. In the Archive of the Gennadeios Library, Athens. Unpublished.

Primary Patristic Sources and Translations

Anthony of Egypt. *Admonitiones et documenta varia ad filios suos monachos.* PG 40:1079-1084 [=*Ad fil. mon.*].
_____. *Lettres de saint Antoine, version géorgienne et fragments coptes.* CSCO 149, Scriptores iberici 6. Louvain, 1955 [=*Epist.*].
Athanasius of Alexandria. *De decretis Nicaenae synodi.* In *Athanasius Werke* 2:1, edited by H.-G. Opitz, 1-45. Berlin, 1935 [=*Decr.*].
_____. *Epistula ad adelphium.* PG 26:1072-1084 [=*Adelph.*].
_____. *Orationes contra Arianos* 1-4. PG 26:12-525 (*Oratio 4–dubia*) [=*Contr. Arian.*].
_____. *Sur l'Incarnation du Verbe.* Edited by C. Kannengiesser. SC 199. 1973 [=*Incarn.*].
Augustine. *De Trinitate* 1-12. Edited by W. Mountain. CCSL 50. Turholt, 1968 [=*De Trinitate*].
Barnabas. *The Epistle of Barnabas.* In *The Apostolic Fathers,* edited by J.B. Lightfoot and J.R. Harmer, 2d ed., 274-326. Grand Rapids, Mich., 1992 [=*Epistle of Barnabas*].
Barsanuphius and John. Βίβλος ψυχωφελεστάτη Βαρσανουφίου καὶ Ἰωάννου. Volos, 1960 [=*Repl.*].
Basil the Great. *Contre Eunome* 1-2. Edited by B. Sesboüé, G.-M. de Durand, L. Doutreleau. SC 299 and 305. 1982-1983 [=*Eunom.*].
_____. *Lettres.* Edited by Y. Courtonne. Volumes 1 (1-100), 2 (101-218), 3 (219-366). Paris, 1957-1966 [=*Epist.*].
_____. *Orationes in Psalmos.* PG 29:209-493 [=*Hom.*].
_____. *Sur le Saint-Esprit.* Edited by B. Pruche. SC 17 bis. 1968 [=*De Spir.*].
Clement of Alexandria. *Stromata* 1-6, volume 2, edited by O. Stählin, L. Früchtel, and U. Treu, GCS 52 (1960); *Stromata* 7-8, volume 3, edited by O. Stählin, GCS 17 (1970) 3-102 [=*Strom.*].
Cyprian. *De dominica oratione.* Edited by C. Morechini. *Sancti Cypriani Episcopi Opera,* CCSL 3A, pars 2, 87-113. Turnholt, 1976 [=*Dom. orat.*].
Cyril of Alexandria (Ps.). *De sacrosancta trinitate.* PG 77:1120-1173 [=*Trin.*].
Cyril of Alexandria. *De recta fide ad Arcadiam marinamque.* Edited by P. Pusey, volume 7:1, 154-262. Oxford, 1872. [=*Recta Fide ad Arc.*].
_____. *In Divini Ioannis Evangelium.* Edited by P. Pusey, volume 2. Oxford, 1872 [=*Ioan. Evang.*].
Cyril of Jerusalem. *Catecheses ad illuminandos* 1-18. PG 33:369-1060 [=*Catech.*].
Diadochus of Photice. *Gnostical Chapters.* In Diadoque de Photicé, *Oeuvres spirituelles,* edited by È. des Places, SC 5 bis:84-163. 1955 [=*Chapt.*].
Dionysius the Areopagite. *De mystica theologia.* In *Corpus Dionysiacum* 2: *Pseudo-Dionysius Areopagita, De coelesti hierarchia, De ecclesiastica hierarchia, De mystica theologia, Epistulae,* edited by G. Heil and A. M. Ritter, PTS 36 (1991) 139-150 [=*Myst. theol.*]
_____. *Epistulae.* In *Corpus Dionysiacum* 2: *Pseudo-Dionysius Areopagita, De coelesti hierarchia, De ecclesiastica hierarchia, De mystica theologia, Epistulae,* edited by G. Heil and A. M. Ritter, PTS 36 (1991) 155-210 [=*Epist.*].

Dorotheus of Gaza. *Instructions diverses.* In *Oeuvres Spirituelles*, edited by L. Regnault and J. de Préville. SC 92. Paris, 1963 [=*Instr.*].

Ephrem the Syrian. *Hymnen de fide.* Edited by E. Beck. CSCO 154, Scriptores syri 73. Louvain, 1957 [=*Hymn. fid.*].

_____. *Des Heiligen Ephraem des Syrers Hymnen de paradiso* und *contra Julianum.* Edited by E. Beck. CSCO 174, Scriptores syri 78. Louvain, 1957 [=*Hymn. parad.*].

Evagrius of Pontike. *Antirrhitikos.* In W. Frankenberg, *Euagrius Pontikos*, 472-544. Berlin, 1912 [=*Antirrh.*].

_____. *Briefe.* In W. Frankenberg, *Euagrius Pontikos*, 555-635. Berlin, 1912 [=*Epist.*].

_____. *De oratione capitula.* PG 79:1165-1200 [=*Orat. cap.*].

_____. *Le Gnostique ou à celui qui est devenu digne de la science.* Edited by A. and C. Guillaumont. SC 356. Paris, 1989 [=*Gnost.*].

_____. *Scholies a l'ecclésiaste.* Edited by P. Géhin. SC 397. Paris, 1993 [=*Schol. eccl.*].

_____. *Tractatus de octo spiritibus malitiae.* PG 79:1145A-1164D [=*Tract.*].

_____. *Traité pratique ou le moine.* Edited by A. and C. Guillaumont. SC 171:2. Paris, 1971 [=*Prat.*].

Gregory of Nazianzus. *Carmina historica.* PG 37:969-1600 [=*Carm. hist.*].

_____. *Carmina moralia.* PG 37:521-968 [=*Carm. mor.*].

_____. *Discourses* 1-5, 20-43. Edited by J. Bernardi, J. Mossay, P. Gallay, and C. Moreschini. SC 247 (1-3), 309 (4-5), 270 (20-23), 284 (24-26), 250 (27-31), 318 (32-37), 358 (38-41), 384 (42-43). 1978-1992 [=*Or.*].

_____. *Orationes (Discourses 6-19, 44-45).* PG 35-36 [=*Or.*].

_____. *Lettres.* Edited by P. Gallay. Volume 1 (1-100); volume 2 (101-249). Paris, 1964 and 1969 [=*Epist.*]

_____. *Poemata Arcana.* Edited by C. Moreschini, translated by D. Sykes. Oxford, 1997 [=*Poem. Arc.*].

Gregory of Nyssa. *Commentarius in Canticum Canticorum.* In Gregorii Nysseni Opera 6, edited by H. Langerbeck. Leiden, 1960 [=*Com. cant.*].

_____. *Contra Eunomium libri.* In Gregorii Nysseni Opera 1-2, edited by W. Jaeger. Leiden, 1960 [=*Contr. Eun.*].

_____. *De anima et resurrectione.* PG 46:12-160 [=*Anima et res.*].

_____. *De beatitudinibus.* In Gregorii Nysseni Opera 7:2, *De beatitudinibus, De oratione dominica*, edited by J. F. Callahan, 77-170. Leiden-New York-Köln, 1992 [=*De beat.*].

_____. *De mortuis oratio.* In Gregorii Nysseni Opera 9:1, *Sermones*, edited by W. Jaeger and H. Langerbeck, 28-68. Leiden, 1967 [=*Mort. orat.*].

_____. *De opificio hominis.* PG 44:124-256 (Fr Sophrony, in *La félicité*, quotes from *Le Creation de l'homme*, SC 6, Paris, 1944) [=*Opif. hom.*].

_____. *De oratione dominica.* In Gregorii Nysseni Opera 7:2, *De beatitudinibus, De oratione dominica*, edited by J. F. Callahan, 5-74. Leiden-New York-Köln, 1992 [=*Orat. dom.*].

_____. *De pauperibus amandis.* Edited by A. Van Heck. Leiden, 1964 [=*De paup. amand.*].

_____. *De professione Christiana.* In Gregorii Nysseni Opera 8:1, *Opera ascetica*, edited by W. Jaeger, J. Cavarnas, and V. Callahan, 129-42. Leiden, Brill, 1952 [=*Profes. Chr.*].

_____. *De virginitate.* In Gregorii Nysseni Opera 8:1, *Opera ascetica*, edited by W. Jaeger, J. Cavarnas, and V. Callahan, 247-343. Leiden, Brill, 1952 [=*Virg.*].

_____. *In scripturae verba, Faciamus hominem ad imaginem et similitudiem nostram.* In Gregorii Nysseni Opera, *Supplementum*, edited by H. Horner. Leiden, 1972 [=*Imag.*].

_____. *The Catechetical Oration of Gregory of Nyssa.* Edited by J.H. Strawley. Cambridge, 1903 [=*Cat. Orat.*].

Gregory Palamas. Ὑπὲρ τῶν ἱερῶς ἡσυχαζόντων. In Συγγράμματα 1, edited by P. Christou, B. Bobrinsky, J. Meyendorff, and P. Papaevaggelou, 359-694. Thessaloniki, 1962 [=Triads].

――――. Ἁγιορειτικὸς τόμος. In Συγγράμματα 2, edited by P. Christou, G. Mantzaridis, N. Matsoukas, and B. Pseutogkas, 567-78. Thessaloniki, 1966 [=Ag.Tom.].

Gregory of Sinai. Λόγοι διάφοροι περὶ ἐντολῶν, δογμάτων, ἀπειλῶν καὶ ἐπαγγελιῶν, ὅτι δὲ καὶ περὶ λογισμῶν καὶ παθῶν καὶ ἀρετῶν καὶ περὶ ἡσυχίας καὶ προσευχῆς. In Philokalia 4:31-62 [=Chap.].

Hilary of Poitiers. De Trinitate 8-12. Edited by P. Smulders. CCSL 62A. Turnhout, 1980 [=De Trin.].

Hesychius of Jerusalem. Πρὸς Θεόδουλον. In Philokalia 1:141-73 [=Epist.Theod.].

Ignatius of Antioch. Epistles. In Ignace d'Antioche and Polycarpe de Smyrne, Lettres, Martyre de Polycarpe, edited by P.-Th. Camelot. SC 10, 4th ed. 1969 [=Epist.].

Irenaeus of Lyons. Contre les hérésies 1-5. Edited by A. Rousseau, L. Doutreleau, B. Hemmerdinger, and C. Mercier. SC 263-264 (1); 293-294 (2); 210-211 (3); 100 (4); 152-153 (5). 1965-1979 [=Her.].

Isaac the Syrian. De perfectione religiosa. Edited by P. Bedjan. Leipzig, 1909 [=Syr. Hom. 1].

――――. The Second Part 4-41. Edited by S. Brock. CSCO 554, Sciptores syri 224. Louvain, 1995 [=Syr. Hom. 2].

――――. Ἰσαὰκ τοῦ Σύρου εὑρεθέντα ἀσκητικά. Edited by N. Theotokis. Athens, 1871 [=Gr. Hom.].

John Cassian. Conférences 1-7, SC 42 (1955); 8-17, SC 54 (1958); 18-24, edited by E. Pichery, SC 64 (1959) [=Conf.].

――――. Institutions cénobitiques. Edited by J.-C. Guy. SC 104. 1965 [= Inst.].

John Chrysostom. Expositio in Psalmos. PG 55:35-528 [=Psalm.].

――――. Homiliae in Eutropium. PG 52:391-414 [=Eutrop.].

――――. Homiliae in Genesim 1-67. PG 53:21-54:580 [=Hom. Gen.].

――――. In Iohannem homiliae 1-88. PG 59:23-482 [=Iohan. hom.].

John Climacus. Scala paradisi (+Liber ad pastorem). PG 88:631-1210 [=Scala parad.].

John of Damascus. Expositio fidei. In Die Schriften des Johannes von Damaskos 2, edited by B. Kotter, PTS 12. 1973 [=Exp. fid.].

――――. Fragmenta in S. Matthaeum. PG 96:1408C-1413C [=Fragm. Mat.].

――――. Orationes de imaginibus tres. In Die Schriften des Johannes von Damaskos 3, edited by B. Kotter, PTS 17. 1975 [=Imag.].

John of the Cross. Ascent of Mount Carmel. Translated and edited by E.A. Peers. Exeter, 1987 [=Ascent].

――――. The Dark Night of the Soul. Translated and edited by E.A. Peers. Exeter, 1988 [=Dark Night].

Justin Martyr. Apologies. Edited by A. Wartelle. Paris, 1987 [=Apol.].

――――. Dialogue avec Tryphon 1-2. Edited by G. Archambault. Paris, 1909 [=Dialog. Tryph.].

Kallistos and Ignatius, the Monks. Μέθοδος καὶ κανὼν σὺν Θεῷ ἀκριβὴς καὶ παρὰ τῶν ἁγίων ἔχων τὰς μαρτυρίας, περὶ τῶν αἱρουμένων ἡσύχως βιῶναι καὶ μοναστικῶς, ἐν κεφαλαίοις ἑκατόν. In Philokalia 4:197-295 [=Cap.].

Macarius of Egypt. Die 50 geistlichen Homilien des Makarios Edited by H. Dörries, E. Klostermann, and M. Kroeger. PTS 4. 1964 [= Hom.].

――――. Homélies propres à la Collection III. In Pseudo-Macaire, Oeuvres spirituelles, edited by V. Desprez, SC 275. 1980 [=Hom. III].

――――. Macarii Anecdota, Seven Unpublished Homilies of Macarius. Edited by G.L. Marriott. Cambridge, Mass., 1918 [=Anecd.].

――――. Macarios/Symeon: Reden und Briefe. Die Sammlung I des Vaticanus Graecus 694 (B). 2 volumes. Edited by H. Berthold. Berlin, 1973 [=Brief.].

_____. *Two Rediscovered Works of Ancient Christian Literature: Gregory of Nyssa and Macarius.* Edited by W. Jaeger. Leiden, 1954 [=*Rediscovered Works*].

Mark the Monk. *Ad Nicolaum praecepta animae salutaria.* PG 65:1028D-1053C [=*Ad Nicol.*].

Maximus the Confessor. *Ambiguorum liber.* PG 91:1031-1418 [=*Ambigua*].

_____. *Capita alia.* PG 90:1402-1461 [=*Cap. al.*].

_____. *Capita theologica et œcumenica.* PG 90:1033-1176 [=*Cap. theol.*].

_____. *Capitoli sulla carità.* Edited by A. Ceresa-Gastaldo. *Verba seniorum* 3. Rome, 1963 [=*Cap. car.*].

_____. *Epistulae.* PG 91:362-650 [=*Epist.*].

_____. *Expositio orationis dominicae.* In *Maximi Confessoris opuscula exegetica duo,* edited by P. van Deun, CCSG 23:27-73. Turnhout, 1991 [=*Orat. dom.*].

_____. *Liber asceticus.* PG 90:912-957 [=*Lib. ascet.*].

_____. *Opuscula theologica et polemica.* PG 91:2-280 [=*Theol. pol.*].

_____. *Quaestiones ad Thalassium.* Volume 1 (questions 1-55), CCSG 7 (1980); volume 2 (questions 56-65), CCG 22 (1990) [=*Quest. Thal.*].

Methodius of Olympus. *Le banquet.* Edited by H. Musurillo. SC 95. 1963 [=*Symp.*].

Origen. *Der Johanneskommentar.* In *Origenes Werke* 4: *Der Johanneskommentar,* edited by E. Preuschen, GCS 10. 1903 [= *Com. John*].

_____. *Homélies sur le Cantique des Cantiques.* Edited by O. Rousseau. SC 37 bis. Paris, 1966 [=*Hom. Cant.*].

_____. *Traité des principes* 3. Edited by H. Crouzel and M Simonetti. SC 268. Paris, 1980 [=*Princ.*].

Pachomius the Great. *Oeuvres de S. Pachôme et de ses disciples.* Edited by L.-Th. Lefort. CSCO 159-160, Scriptores coptici 23-24, volumes 1-2. Louvain, 1956 [=*Oeuvres*].

Philotheos of Sinai. Νηπτικὰ κεφάλαια τεσσαράκοντα. In *Philokalia* 2:274-86 [=*Chap.*].

Richard of St Victor. *De Trinitate.* Edited by J. Ribaillier. TPMA 6. Paris, 1958 [=*De Trin.*].

Symeon the New Theologian. *Chapitres théologiques, gnostiques et pratiques.* Edited by J. Darrouzès. SC 51 bis. 1980 [=*Chap. theol.*].

_____. *Hymnes.* Edited by J. Koder, J. Paramelle, and L. Neyrand. Volume 1 (hymns 1-15), SC 156 (1969); volume 2 (hymns 16-40), SC 174 (1971); volume 3 (hymns 41-58), SC 196 (1973) [=*Hymns*].

Theophilus of Antioch. *Ad Autolycum.* Edited by M. Marcovich. PTS 44. 1995 [=*Ad Autol.*].

Theodore the Studite. *Descriptio constitutionis monasteri studii.* PG 99:1704-1720 [=*Const.*].

Hagiographical, Historical and Canonical Sources

Apophthegmata patrum, collectio alphabetica. PG 65:71-440 [=*Apophth.*].

Verba seniorum. PL 73:739-1062 [=*Verb. sen.*].

Historia monachorum in Aegypto: édition critique du texte grec. Edited by A.J. Festugière. Bruxelles, 1961 [=*Hist. mon.*].

Athanasius of Alexandria. *Vie d'Antoine.* Edited by G. Bartelink. SC 400. Paris, 1994 [=*Vie*].

Dorotheus of Gaza. *La vie de saint Dosithée.* Edited by P.M. Brun. OC 26 (1932) 87-123 [=*Dosithée*].

Palladius. *La storia lausiaca.* Edited by G.J.M. Bartelink. Florence, 1974 [=*Laus.*].

Liturgical Texts

An Orthodox Prayer Book. Translated by Fr John von Holzhausen and Fr Michael Gelsinger. Brookline, Mass., 1977.

The Lenten Triodion. Translated from the original Greek by Mother Mary and Archimandrite Kallistos Ware. London, 1977.

Secondary Literature

Alfeyev, H. *The Mystery of Faith.* Moscow, 1996 (in Russian).

———. *Orthodox Theology at the Turn of the Centuries.* Moscow, 1999 (in Russian).

———. *St Symeon the New Theologian and Orthodox Tradition.* Oxford, 2000.

Anderson, P. *No East or West.* Paris, 1985.

Balthasar, H. von. *Presence and Thought: Essay on the Religious Philosophy of Gregory of Nyssa.* San Francisco, 1995.

Barbour, I. *Issues in Science and Religion.* London, 1966.

Barth, K. *Church Dogmatics.* Translated by T. Parker, W. Johnston, H. Knight, and J. Haire, volume 2:1. Edinburgh, 1957.

Baumann, E. "*Iadaa* und seine Derivate. Eine sprachlichexegetische Studie." In ZAW 28 (1908) 22-41, 110-43.

Berdyaev, N. "About the New Christian Spirituality." *Sobornost* 25 (1934) 36-41.

———. *Destiny of Man.* Translated by N. Duddington. London, 1937.

———. *Dostoyevsky.* Translated by D. Attwater. London, 1934.

———. *Dream and Reality.* Translated by K. Lampert. London, 1950.

———. "Report of Student Conference." Edited by O. Clarke. *Sobornost* 3 (1935) 4-12.

———. *Spirit and Reality.* Translated by George Reavey. London, 1939.

———. *The Beginning and the End.* Translated by R. French. London, 1952.

Bockmuehl, K. *The Unreal God of Modern Theology: Bultmann, Barth and the Theology of Atheism: A Call to Rediscovering the Truth of God's Reality.* Colorado Springs, 1988.

Bori, P., and P. Bettiolo. *Movimenti religiosi in Russa prima della rivoluzione (1900-1917).* Brescia, 1978.

Borisoglebsky, G. *Life of Hieromonk Ambrosy the Staretz of Optina Monastery.* Moscow, 1893 (in Russian).

Bouyer, L. *La spiritualité orthodoxe et la spiritualité protestante et anglicane.* Paris, 1965.

Brown, P. "The Rise and Function of the Holy Man in Late Antiquity." *The Journal of Roman Studies* 61 (1971) 80-101.

Buber, M. *I and Thou.* Translated by R. Smith. Edinburgh, 1994.

Bulgakov, S. *The Lamb of God.* Paris, 1937 (in Russian).

———. "St Sergius' Testament to Russian Theology." *Put'* 5 (1926) 3-19 (in Russian).

———. "The Problem of Eternal Life." *Put'* 52 (1937) 3-23 (in Russian).

———. *Unfading Light.* Moscow, 1917 (in Russian).

———. "The Holy Chalice." *Put'* 32 (1932) 3-42 (in Russian).

———. *The Comforter.* Paris, 1936 (in Russian).

———. "The Lamb of God: Concerning the God-Man." *Theology* 28 (1934) 23-26.

Camus, A. *The Rebel: An Essay on Man in Revolt.* Translated by A. Bower. London, 1962.

Cervera, C. "Silvano del Monte Athos, il monaco che amavo teneramente la Madre di Dio." *Mater Ecclesiae* 16 (1980) 45-54.

Chetverikov, S. "The Eucharist as a Center of Christian Life." *Put'* 22 (1930) 3-45 (in Russian).

Christensen, D. *Not of This World: The Life and Teaching of Fr. Seraphim Rose. Pathfinder to the Heart of Ancient Christianity.* Forestville, 1993.

Clément, O. "Aperçu sur la théologie de la personne dans la 'diaspora' russe en France." In *Mille ans du christianisme russe (988-1988),* edited by N. Struve, 303-9. Paris, 1989.

———. *Berdiaev. Un philosophe russe en France.* Paris, 1991.

Cohen, M. *An Introduction to Logic and Scientific Method.* London, 1957.

Copleston, F. *Russian Religious Philosophy.* Tunbridge Wells, 1988.

Cremaschi, L. "La vergogna di stare ogli inferi secondo Silvano del Monte Athos." *Parola Spirito e Vita* 20 (1989) 285-303.

Daval, J.-L. *Journal de l'art moderne 1884-1914. Les années décisives.* Geneva, 1979.

Cullen, J. "The Patristic Concept of the Deification of Man Examined in the Light of Contemporary Notions of the Transcendence of Man." D.Phil. Thesis. Oxford, 1985.

Dejaifve, G. "Sobornost or Papacy." ECQ 10 (1953-1954), part 1: "The Idea of Sobornost in Contemporary Orthodoxy," 28-38, 75-85; part 2: "The Catholic Idea of Papacy," 168-76.

Egger, M. "Archimandrite Sophrony, Moine pour le Monde." *Buisson Ardent. Cahiers Saint-Silouane l'Athonite* 1 (1996) 23-41.

———. "Preface." In Archimandrite Sophrony, *Words of Life,* translated by Sr Magdalene, 1-6. Essex, 1996.

Ellverson, A. *The Dual Nature of Man: A Study in the Theological Anthropology of Gregory of Nazianzus.* Uppsala, 1981.

Emmet, D. *The Nature of Metaphysical Thinking.* 1945.

———. "Theoria and the Way of Life." JTS 17 (1966) 38-52.

Engnell, I. "'Knowledge' and 'Life' in the Creation Story." *Vetus Testamentum, Supplement* 3 (1955) 103-19.

Evdokimov, P. *La nouveauté de l'esprit: études de spiritualité.* Bégrolles-en-Mauges, 1977.

Farmer, H.H. *Towards Belief in God.* London, 1942.

Florensky, P. "The Idea of the Church in Holy Scripture." In *Collected Works* 1:318-489. Moscow, 1994 (in Russian).

———. *The Pillar and Ground of the Truth.* Translated by B. Jakim. Princeton, 1977.

Florovsky, G. "Le corps du Christ vivant. Une interprétation orthodoxe de l'église." *La sainte église universelle. Cahiers théologiques de l'actualité protestante,* hors-série 4 (Paris, 1948) 9-57.

———. "Sobornost: The Catholicity of the Church." In *The Church of God: An Anglo-Russian Symposium,* edited by E. Mascall, 51-74. London, 1934.

———. "St Gregory Palamas and the Tradition of the Fathers." *Sobornost* 4:4 (1961) 165-76.

———. "Theological Extracts." *Put'* 31 (1931) 3-29 (in Russian).

———. "The Eucharist and Sobornost." *Put'* 19 (1929) 3-22 (in Russian).

———. *The Byzantine Fathers of the Fifth to Eighth Centuries.* Paris, 1933 (in Russian).

Frank, S. *Reality and Man: An Essay in the Metaphysics of Human Nature.* Translated by N. Duddington. London, 1965.

Franquesa, A. "Archimandrite Sophrony, *Voir Dieu tel qu'il est.*" *Questions de Vida Christiana* 124 (1984) 130-31.

Garrigues, J. *Maxime le Confesseur: la charité, avenir divin de l'homme.* Paris, 1976.

Gillet, L. *Orthodox Spirituality: An Outline of the Orthodox Ascetic and Mystical Tradition.* 2d ed. London, 1978.

Gimenez, M. "*Voir Dieu tel qu'il est* by Archimandrite Sophrony." *Sobornost* 7:1 (1985) 72-73.

Gooskens, B. *L'expérience de l'Esprit Saint chez le Staretz Silouane.* Paris, 1971.

Gorodetzky, N. *The Humiliated Christ in Modern Russian Thought.* London, 1938.

Gould, G. *The Desert Fathers on Monastic Community.* Oxford, 1993.

Griffith, G. *Interpreters of Man: A Review of Secular and Religious Thought from Hegel to Barth.* London, 1943.

Hadot, P. *Exercices spirituels et philosophie antique.* Paris, 1987.

Halleux, A. de. "Archimandrite Sophrony *Voir Dieu tel qu'il est.*" *Revue théologique de Louvain* 16:3 (1985) 361–63.

Hausherr, I. *Direction spirituelle en Orient autrefois.* Rome, 1955.

———. *La doctrine ascétique des premiers maîtres égyptiens du quatrième siècle.* Paris, 1931.

———. "L'imitation de Jésus-Christ dans la spiritualité byzantine." In *Études de spiritualité orientale,* 217–46. Rome, 1969.

———. "Les Orientaux connaissent-ils les 'nuits' de saint Jean de la Croix?" In *Hésychasme et prière,* 87–128. Rome, 1966.

Heidegger, M. *Sein und Zeit.* Edited by M. Niemeyer. Tubingen, 1957.

Hick, J. "Religious Realism and Non-Realism: Defining the Issue." In *Is God Real?* edited by J. Runzo, 3–16. London, 1993.

Hussey, M. "The Palamite Trinitarian Models." SVTQ 16:2 (1972) 83–89.

Illingworth, J.R. *Personality Human and Divine: The Bapton Lectures 1894.* London, 1896.

Ilyin, V. *St Seraphim of Sarov.* Paris, 1930 (in Russian).

———. "The Nature and the Meaning of the Term 'Sobornost.'" *Sobornost* 1 (1935) 5–7.

Karambelas, C. *Contemporary Ascetics of Mount Athos.* Platina, Calif., 1992.

Kattenbusch, F. *Die Entstehung einer christlichen Theologie zur Geschichte der Ausdrücke theologia, theologein, theologos.* Darmstadt, 1962.

Khomiakov, A. "Letter to the Editor of *L'union Chrétienne* on the Meaning of the Words *Catholic* and *Conciliar.*" In *Collected Theological Works,* edited by J. Petrov, 275–280. St Petersburg, 1995 (in Russian).

———. "The Church Is One." In *Collected Theological Works,* edited by J. Petrov, 37–56. St Petersburg, 1995 (in Russian).

Khrapovitsky, A. "The Moral Idea of the Trinitarian Dogma." In *The Moral Ideas of the Most Important Christian Orthodox Dogmas,* edited by N. Rklitsky, 3–24. Montreal, 1963 (in Russian).

Kierkegaard, S. *Concluding Unscientific Postscript.* Translated by H. and E. Hong. Princeton, N.J., 1982.

———. *Der Augenblick.* 1855.

Kontsevich, I. *The Acquisition of the Holy Spirit in Ancient Russia.* Paris, 1952 (in Russian).

Kotsonis, I. *Athonikon Gerontikon.* Thessaloniki, 1992.

Larchet, J.-C. "L'amour des ennemis selon saint Silouan l'Athonite et dans la tradition patristique." *Buisson Ardent* 2 (1996) 66–95.

———. "La formule 'Tiens ton esprit en enfer et ne désespère pas' à la lumière de la tradition patristique." *Buisson Ardent* 1 (1996) 51–68.

Lossky, V. *In the Image and Likeness of God.* New York, 1985.

———. *Orthodox Theology: An Introduction.* Translated by Ian and Inhita Kesarcodi-Watson. New York, 1978.

———. *The Mystical Theology of the Eastern Church.* Translated by the Fellowship of St Albans and St Sergius. Cambridge, 1991.

———. *The Debates about Sophia.* Paris, 1936 (in Russian).

Louth, A. *Discerning the Mystery: An Essay on the Nature of Theology.* Oxford, 1989.

———. *The Origins of the Christian Mystical Tradition.* Oxford, 1981.

———. *Wilderness of God.* London, 1991.

Luis, P. de. "Archimandrite Sophrony, *Voir Dieu tel qu'il est.*" *Estudio Agustiniano* 3 (1984) 49.

Mantzaridis, G. "The Ethical Significance of the Trinitarian Dogma." *Sobornost* 5:10 (1970) 720–29.

———. *The Deification of Man.* New York, 1984.

_____. "The Elder Sophrony: Theologian of the Hypostatic Principle." In Πρόσωπο καὶ θεσμοί, 19-40. Thessaloniki, 1996 (in Greek).

Manzoni, G. "Silvano del Monta Athos." In *La spiritualità della chiesa ortodossa russa*, Storia della spiritualità 9B, 499-526. Bologna, 1993.

Mélia, É. "Le thème de la lumière dans l'hymnographie byzantine de Noël." In *Noël-Épiphanie, retour du Christ, Semaine liturgique de l'Institut Saint Serge, Lex Orandi* 40:237-56. Paris, 1967.

Meyendorff, J. *A Study of Gregory Palamas*. London, 1959.

_____. *St Gregory Palamas and Orthodox Spirituality*. New York, 1974.

Miguel, J. de. "Archimandrite Sophrony, *Voir Dieu tel qu'il est*." *Comunidades* 48 (1985) 93.

Moore, H. "Radical Redemption." *Christian Missionary Society Newsletter* 484 (1988) 1-4.

Mosley, N. "Introduction to 'Adam's Lament.'" *Prism* 5:2 (London, 1958) 38-40.

Nellas, P. *Deification in Christ*. New York, 1987.

Neyt, F. "A Form of Charismatic Authority." ECR 6:1 (1974) 52-65.

Nichols, A. "Bulgakov and Sophiology." *Sobornost* 13:2 (1992) 17-31.

_____. *Light from the East*. London, 1995.

Philaret (Drozdov), Metropolitan. "Sermon on Great Friday (1813)." In *Collected Works of Philaret the Metropolitan of Moscow and Colomna* 1:31-39. Moscow, 1873 (in Russian).

_____. "Sermon on Great Friday (1816)." In *Collected Works of Philaret the Metropolitan of Moscow and Colomna* 1:89-98. Moscow, 1873 (in Russian).

Polanyi, M. *Personal Knowledge: Towards a Post-Critical Philosophy*. Chicago, 1962.

Poljanomerulsky, V. *Life and Works of the Moldavian Staretz Paisy Velichkovsky*. Moscow, 1847 (in Russian).

Puech, H.-C. "La ténèbre mystique chez le pseudo-Denys." *Études carmélitaines* 23:2 (1938) 33-53.

Richard, L. *A Kenotic Christology*. Washington, 1982.

_____. *Christ: The Self-Emptying of God*. Mahwah, 1997.

Rozanov, V. *Death and Beyond*. St Petersburg, 1910 (in Russian).

_____. *The Apocalypse of Our Time*. Sergiev Posad, 1917 (in Russian).

Ruppert, H.-J. "Das Prinzip der Sobornost' in der russischen Orthodoxie." *Kirche im Osten* 16 (Göttingen, 1973) 22-56.

Sakharov, N. "The Uncreated Light in St Gregory Palamas and Archimandrite Sophrony." In *St Gregory Palamas in History and Today*, 307-18. Holy Mountain, 2000.

Schmemann, A. *The Eucharist: The Sacrament of the Kingdom*. Translated by P. Kachur. New York, 1988.

Smirnov, S. *The Father-Confessor in Ancient Russia*. Moscow, 1913 (in Russian).

_____. *The Spiritual Father in the Eastern Church* 1. Sergiev Posad, 1906 (in Russian).

Soloviev, A. *Starchestvo according to the Teaching of the Holy Fathers and Ascetics*. Semipalatinsk, 1900 (in Russian).

Soloviev, V. *Lectures on Godmanhood*. Translated by P. Zouboff. New York, 1944.

Soskice, J. "Theological Realism." In *The Rationality of Religious Belief*. Oxford, 1987.

Špidlík T. *L'idée russe: une autre vision de l'homme*. Rome, 1994.

Stanesby, D. *Science, Reason and Religion*. London and New York, 1985.

Staniloae, D. "Orthodoxy, Life in the Resurrection." ECR 2:4 (1969) 371-75.

_____. "The Cross in Orthodox Theology and Worship." *Sobornost* 7:4 (1977) 233-43.

Stylianopoulos, Th. "Staretz Silouan: A Modern Orthodox Saint." In *God and Charity: Images of Eastern Orthodox Theology, Spirituality and Practice*, edited by T. Hopko, 33-54. Brookline, Mass., 1979.

Sullivan, J. *The Image of God: The Doctrine of St Augustine and Its Influence*. Dubuque, Iowa, 1963.

Swinburne, R. *The Christian God.* Oxford, 1994.
_____. *The Existence of God.* Oxford, 1979.
Theophan the Recluse. *The Path of Salvation: A Manual of Spiritual Transformation.* Translated by
    S. Rose. Platina, Calif., 1996.
Vlakhos, H. *Life after Death.* Translated by E. Williams. Levadia, 1996.
_____. *Orthodox Psychotherapy: The Science of the Fathers.* Translated by E. Williams. Levadia,
    1994.
_____. *Saint Gregory Palamas as a Hagiorite.* Translated by E. Williams. Levadia, 1997.
Ware, K. "Foreword." In G. Mantzaridis, *The Deification of Man.* New York, 1984.
_____. "Foreword: The Spiritual Father in Saint John Climacus and Saint Symeon the New
    Theologian." In I. Hausherr, *Spiritual Direction in the Early Christian East,* translated by A.P.
    Gythiel, Cistercian Studies Series 116, vii–xxxiii. Kalamazoo, Mich., 1990.
_____. "Introduction." In John Climacus, *The Ladder of Divine Ascent,* translated by C. Luib-
    heid and N. Russell, 1–70. Toronto, 1982.
_____. *Kenosis and Christ-like Humility according to Saint Silouan.* 1998.
_____. " 'One Body in Christ': Death and the Communion of Saints." *Sobornost* 3:2 (1981)
    179–91.
_____. *Spirituality: Eastern and Western Perspectives.* Cambridge, 1995.
_____. "The Debate about Palamism." ECR 9:1–2 (1977) 45–63.
_____. "The Human Person as an Icon of the Trinity." *Sobornost* 8:2 (1986) 6–23.
_____. "The Unity of the Human Person according to the Greek Fathers." In *Person and
    Personality,* edited by A. Peacocke and G. Gillett, 197–206. Oxford, 1987.
_____. "The Letter to Archimandrite Sophrony" (July 13, 1984). In *Archive,* 1984.
_____. "The Mystery of the Human Person." *Sobornost* 3:1 (1981) 62–69.
_____. "The Spiritual Father in Orthodox Christianity." In *Word out of Silence: A Symposium
    on World Spiritualities,* edited by J.-D. Robinson. *Cross Currents* 24:2–3 (1974) 296–313.
_____. "The Transfiguration of the Body." *Sobornost* 4:8 (1963) 420–34.
_____. " 'We Must Pray For All': Salvation according to St Silouan." *Sobornost* 19:1 (1997)
    34–55.
Wickham, L. "Soul and Body: Christ's Omnipresence." In *The Easter Sermons of Gregory of Nyssa,*
    edited by S. Klock, 279–92. Philadelphia, 1981.
Williams, R. "The Theology of Vladimir Nikolaevich Lossky: An Exposition and Critique."
    D.Phil. Thesis. Oxford, 1975.
Winslow, D. "The Concept of Salvation in the Writings of Gregory of Nazianzus." Thesis. Cam-
    bridge, Mass., 1967.
Wunderle, G. "La technique psychologique de l'Hésychasme byzantin." *Études Carmélitaines*
    23:2 (1938) 61–67.
Yannaras, C. *The Freedom of Morality.* Translated by E. Briere. New York, 1984.
Zernov, N. *Russian Religious Renaissance of the Twentieth Century.* London, 1963.
Zizioulas, J. *Being as Communion: Studies in Personhood and the Church.* London, 1985.
_____. "On Being a Person: Towards an Ontology of Personhood." In *Persons, Divine and
    Human,* edited by C. Gunton and C. Schwöbel, 33–46. Edinburgh, 1991.
_____. "Theology is Ministry to the Church." Translated by H. Alfeyev. *The Church and Time*
    3:6 (Moscow, 1998), 87–97 (in Russian).
Zouboff, P. "Introduction." In V. Soloviev, *Lectures on Godmanhood,* translated by P. Zouboff,
    9–66. New York, 1944.

Index of Names

Works by Archimandrite Sophrony published by
St Vladimir's Seminary Press

WISDOM FROM MOUNT ATHOS
The Writings of Staretz Silouan 1866–1938

HIS LIFE IS MINE

ST SILOUAN THE ATHONITE

THE MONK OF MOUNT ATHOS
Staretz Silouan 1866–1938

ON PRAYER